The experience of suburban modernity

MANCHESTER
1824

Manchester University Press

STUDIES IN
POPULAR
CULTURE

General editor: Professor Jeffrey Richards
Already published

The experience of suburban modernity

How private transport changed interwar London

MICHAEL JOHN LAW

Manchester University Press

The right of Michael John Law to be identified as the author of this work has been asserted by him in accordance with the Copyright, Designs and Patents Act 1988.

Published by Manchester University Press
Altrincham Street, Manchester M1 7JA, UK
and Room 400, 175 Fifth Avenue, New York, NY 10010, USA
www.manchesteruniversitypress.co.uk

Distributed in the United States exclusively by
Palgrave Macmillan, 175 Fifth Avenue, New York,
NY 10010, USA

Distributed in Canada exclusively by
UBC Press, University of British Columbia, 2029 West Mall,
Vancouver, BC, Canada V6T 1Z2

British Library Cataloguing-in-Publication Data
A catalogue record for this book is available from the British Library

Library of Congress Cataloging-in-Publication Data applied for

ISBN 978 0 7190 8919 0 hardback

First published 2014

Typeset in Adobe Garamond by
Servis Filmsetting Ltd, Stockport, Cheshire
Printed in Great Britain by
TJ International Ltd, Padstow

STUDIES IN
POPULAR
CULTURE

There has in recent years been an explosion of interest in culture and cultural studies.
The impetus has come from two directions and out of two different traditions. On
the one hand, cultural history has grown out of social history to become a distinct
and identifiable school of historical investigation. On the other hand, cultural studies
has grown out of English literature and has concerned itself to a large extent with
contemporary issues. Nevertheless, there is a shared project, its aim, to elucidate the
meanings and values implicit and explicit in the art, literature, learning, institutions and
everyday behaviour within a given society. Both the cultural historian and the cultural
studies scholar seek to explore the ways in which a culture is imagined, represented
and received, how it interacts with social processes, how it contributes to individual
and collective identities and world views, to stability and change, to social, political
and economic activities and programmes. This series aims to provide an arena for
the cross-fertilisation of the discipline, so that the work of the cultural historian can
take advantage of the most useful and illuminating of the theoretical developments
and the cultural studies scholars can extend the purely historical underpinnings of
their investigations. The ultimate objective of the series is to provide a range of books
which will explain in a readable and accessible way where we are now socially and
culturally and how we got to where we are. This should enable people to be better
informed, promote an interdisciplinary approach to cultural issues and encourage
deeper thought about the issues, attitudes and institutions of popular culture.

Jeffrey Richards

Contents

List of tables

List of figures

General editor's introduction

Michael John Law is a man with a mission – to rescue interwar suburbia from the 'enormous condescension' of contemporary intellectuals who made the term 'suburban' a byword for dullness, narrowness and emptiness. Drawing on a rich and varied range of evidence, including statistics, reports, newspaper and magazine journalism, popular fiction, newsreels, documentaries and feature films, he advances the proposition that the London suburbs were in the vanguard of modernity, particularly when it came to travel, transport and technology.

The car is the principal focus of his analysis. Endorsing the verdict of *Autocar* magazine from 1938 that a car was 'an indispensable adjunct of middle class life', he charts the growth and pattern of car ownership as suburbanites increasingly used cars for commuting to work and gaining access to leisure. He traces the development of new arterial roads, exploring the debate about the transformative effect this had on the landscape. He examines the culture of speed that grew up with the car and the debate over the introduction of restrictions on motoring as car accidents hit the headlines. He discusses the 'motorisation of consumption', as the arterial roads attracted the construction of shopping parades, garages and car showrooms, public houses, cinemas and that distinctive interwar phenomenon, the roadhouse, a glamorous combination of restaurant, dance hall, swimming pool and nightclub, which could be reached only by car.

For those unable to afford a car, the bicycle and the motorcycle provided means of mobility and the opportunity to participate in such characteristic interwar pursuits as 'health and fitness' and rural rambles. The suburbanites were 'air-minded' as well as 'car-minded', with many aircraft manufacturers based in suburban London, where those icons of the airways, Croydon Airport and the annual Hendon air display, were also located. By linking modernity with mobility and demonstrating its centrality to suburban life, Law enables us to view the whole suburban experience with fresh insight.

Jeffrey Richards

Acknowledgements

I have had a great deal of help in producing this book. From a scholarly standpoint, I am very grateful for the encouragement I received during my time studying at Royal Holloway, particularly from David Gilbert and the Landscape Surgery group. At Royal Holloway, I met Phil and Madeleine Hatfield on my first day there and they have provided me with well-informed advice ever since. A little earlier, at Birkbeck, I met Geoff Levett who has patiently listened to me talking about the various incarnations of this book for the best part of ten years. More recently, Mark Clapson and David Gutzke have both helped me with sound advice informed by their many years' experience of writing academic books.

Closer to home, my wife Katie and my daughters, Lizzie, Charlie and Pippa have been amazingly tolerant of my change of career direction (from writing consulting proposals to writing for myself and the academy). Of course, Katie has borne the brunt of my preoccupation and has been constantly supportive and patient.

List of abbreviations

AA	Automobile Association
ABC	Associated British Cinemas
BBC	British Broadcasting Company/Corporation
CPRE	Council for the Preservation of Rural England
CTC	Cyclists' Touring Club
DVLA	Driving and Vehicle Licensing Agency
GPO	General Post Office
LCC	London County Council
MoT	Ministry of Transport
RAC	Royal Automobile Club
RAF	Royal Air Force
RBA	Roads Beautifying Association
RRA	Roads of Remembrance Association
SMMT	Society of Motor Manufacturers and Traders
TNA	The National Archives

Part I

Introduction

1

Driving on the Kingston Bypass

This book came about through my looking out of a car window. I have lived in suburban south-west London for the last thirty-five years and getting around this part of the world obliges you, if you are a car driver, to use the Kingston Bypass. This is a worrying road, its lanes are too narrow and it carries a lot of traffic heading to and from town. It is mostly ribboned by semi-detached houses that seem far too close to the road for comfort of driver or resident. Speed limits and the occasional traffic camera have reduced its propensity for accidents, but you have to concentrate hard when driving.

My over-familiarity with this route was such that driving on it, ten years ago, my mind wandered and wondered and I found myself imagining what the road was like when it was first built in the 1920s. I did some research and looked at early photographs of the road and discovered that they were, for me, strangely affective. There was something about the high-contrast black-and-white images of the empty new road that I found both intriguing and aesthetically appealing. I get the same feeling when I look at modernist buildings from the same period; there is something so optimistic about them, they are both surprising and poignant. I think that this is because we know how the story ends; those in the photographs could not then guess what was in store for them at the conclusion of the 1930s.

The independent mobility of driving a car, something we take for granted, is an important starting point for me, both in my research and in this book. It moves my observations away from that static cliché of suburbia, the house, to the car, motorcycle, bicycle and, in a more distanced sense, the aeroplane. The purpose of this book is to study these mobilities to improve the understanding of London's interwar suburbia. It intends to add to research that has increased our knowledge of suburban life by paying greater attention to this unusual time and space. This work finds unexpected interest and modernity in lives that had been considered, by some, as meaningless and dull. Looking for modernity in suburbia is an unconventional idea as its expected locus is the city. As Alan O'Shea puts it, 'Many accounts of "modern times" both intellectual and popular, lay a central emphasis on the experience of city life'.[1] This book investigates the modernity of suburbia by concentrating its attention on the nature of independent mobility in outer London, that is the mobility free from the constraints of public transport. London's train, tram and bus services helped form new suburbs as early as the 1850s. By the 1930s, these arrangements were already eighty years old and their repetition did not amount to anything genuinely modern. What was new and exciting was the opportunity to travel at the drop of a hat.

Known suburbia

This book aims to reveal previously hidden aspects of life in London's interwar suburbia that show it to be surprisingly varied and, at times, exciting. This contradicts the received view of the period, an idea of suburbia that was pre-eminent throughout the twentieth century. Where does this restricted understanding of interwar suburban life come from? Why was this type of life thought to be so boring, so static, with its mobility dominated by the train timetable?

The answer partly lies from within the period itself, in the intellectual discourse of the time on suburbia. One important theme of that discourse was incursion, and many commentators of the 1930s responded to it. In their thinking, there were two sorts of suburbia: the old sort, where they lived, large Victorian villas with extensive gardens, and the new sort, cheap repetitive housing built not on wooded hills but on fields of former market gardens and scruffy farmland. Here, the ladder was being pulled up pretty sharply. The scions of wealthy families established in the nineteenth century resented the blurring of class lines brought about by this new wave of suburbanisation. John Carey has written the definitive account of this mindset in *The Intellectual and the Masses* in which he shows how writers such as H. G. Wells and Evelyn Waugh responded to the supposed dangers of the new suburbs.[2] John Betjeman can also be included in this group, and his poem 'The Metropolitan Railway – Baker Street Station Buffet', identifies the theme of a suburban idyll ruined by incomers.

Cancer has killed him. Heart is killing her.
The Trees are down. An Odeon flashes fire
Where stood their villa by the murmuring fir.[3]

This poem demonstrates the passing of one type of suburbia for another and announces, with the arrival of the neon-signed cinema, that this period was witnessing a signal change in British society that was both important and permanent, a new and Americanised form of suburban life. It is also significant that Betjeman's nostalgia for Edwardian suburban life reinforced the relationship between the suburban home and the railway commuter.

Incursion was also at the heart of worries about this new suburbia in a group of activists whose concern was to preserve the countryside. In particular, they worried about the way that the binary of town/countryside was upset by suburbanisation, producing places that didn't fit efficiently into either category. Planners and architects such as Patrick Abercrombie and Clough Williams-Ellis tried to save the British countryside from suburban growth. To these figures could be added C. E. M. Joad, a populist thinker of the interwar period, and others who rode this particular bandwagon. One of their preoccupations was the new arterial roads, such as the Kingston Bypass. They saw these roads as the means by which suburbia and the road combined together to produce ribbon development that pushed suburbia into the countryside. They thought it ugly and a betrayal of the efficient planning proposed by modernist road building. Joad questioned the arrival of new suburban housing:

> Why are they there? Again I can only answer, because if some obscure impulse which causes them to feel dissatisfaction with life in towns without fitting them for life in the country ... they spread like locusts over the land.[4]

Other interwar writers criticised suburbanites for how they thought and how they spent their lives. To the fore were J. B. Priestley, George Orwell and T. S. Eliot, who characterised suburban life as meaningless, consumerist, secular and tied to an empty fascination with American cultural sources with, as Orwell put it, more knowledge of the workings of a magneto than the Bible.[5] In reality, their criticism was highly superficial and based, in Priestley's case, largely on observations made from a chauffeur-driven car. Some of it was fair comment; the success of Hollywood in suburban cinemas and American music in suburban dance halls was very evident in interwar life. Suburbia was, indeed, consumerist, where high levels of disposable income allowed for the purchase of domestic appliances, radios and eventually cars. Secularism was a worry too, with both the Church of England and the Catholic Church concerned with the need to build missionary churches in suburbia. What all these commentators missed was the variety of interests and activities that filled suburban lives outside work, for example cycling, motoring and other leisure pursuits.

Finally, Britain's new suburbia was criticised for its impoverished aesthetics. Much suburban housing was built at the lowest possible cost in a very competitive housing market. The result was a need to maximise housing density whilst still providing enough garden and trees to deliver on the promise of a *rus in urbe* life where, if you were not actually in the country, you could imagine that you were. The most efficient way of building houses with gardens and a side door where the butcher's boy could call was the semi-detached house, laid out on parallel streets. Cost-saving required that any variation in house-design could be possible only in small details like porches and windows. It was a small step to connect the lack of variation and repetitiveness of suburban houses to similar concerns about their occupants. The semi-detached house was, in effect, a form of anti-modernism. Interest in new modernist architecture was at its height in the early 1930s, just at the point when these new housing estates were being laid out in a gauche mock-Tudor form. As a consequence, they were criticised and ridiculed as tawdry and sham. To choose one example, the critic and cartoonist Osbert Lancaster considered that suburban semi-detached houses 'will inevitability become the slums of the future'.[6] He was, of course, wrong.

By paying too much attention to the musings of these well-educated and privileged commentators, we miss the reality of interwar suburban life. This newly formed lower middle class did not have a powerful voice, so we were left for much of the twentieth century with the results of intellectual prejudice, a negative view of suburbia that was very evident in literature, popular music, radio and television. *Hancock's Half Hour, The Fall and Rise of Reginald Perrin* and many others of lesser merit portrayed suburbia in the same light as the critics of the 1930s.[7] It was mediocre, boring and/or pretentious. Later, J. G. Ballard took this formula and added to it danger and transgression.

In the fifty years that followed the intellectual criticisms of the 1930s, there was little academic study of suburbia. Where it was studied it was to explain the nature of its housing and public transport links. H. J. Dyos led this genre in his study of the development and history of Camberwell, a south London suburb.[8] Alan Jackson, a transport historian, produced the still definitive work on interwar suburban London, *Semi-detached London*, in 1973.[9] This was, at the time, such an unusual enterprise that his publisher described his interest in this topic as 'perverse'.[10] This important book concentrated its attention on the new lower middle classes and their houses and emphasised the way that railway development helped form suburbs. Later in this book, I take Jackson to task for his failure to notice car usage in suburban London, but I am a great admirer of the depth and quality of his research. His emphasis on the built environment does, however, obscure the reality of suburban life, its practices and stories. This presentation of suburbia as just the sum of its architecture can be seen in many otherwise excellent later works on London suburbia such as *Dunroamin* and *London Suburbs*.[11]

Reconfiguring interwar suburbia

Some academic writers have found the exercise of studying suburban life problematic; even those who wish to cast new light on suburbia cannot liberate themselves from a century of intellectual prejudice. The lower middle classes can be shown as modern and surprisingly variegated but their aspirations are nevertheless gently despised. This is a consequence of suburban class positioning. Neither oppressed by capitalism nor a dominating force within it, neither worthy nor powerful, their humble lives and empty culture are ripe for disdain. Some writers have succeeded in discarding these prejudices and, in doing so, reveal far more. Mark Clapson's work comes to mind here; he has produced a history of suburbia in the twentieth century in a passionate and supportive manner.[12] David Gilbert, as a geographer, takes a wider view, but in a similarly unprejudiced way.[13] Both realise that suburban culture can be passive and reductive, but can also provide enormous insight into how we all live our lives today. I mention these two writers, both of whom I have worked with closely. Each, in his own way, has provided me with the direction for this book.

This book proposes that the received view of suburbia does not present a full or appropriate picture of outer London between the wars. It argues that new mobilities were fundamental to this life, which for many was nuanced, exciting, fast, fluid, dangerous and fun. In short, the newly mobile suburbanite experienced modernity. It is useful to state here what I mean when I use the term 'modernity'; it is a contentious term and is hard to define.

Miles Ogborn wisely considered that 'its periodisation, geographies, characteristics and promise all remain elusive'.[14] I use the term to signal the social experience of technological change. These experiences can be seen in the time-space compression brought about by new transport technologies and in the simultaneous encounter with order/chaos or possibility/peril brought about by new technology.[15] It is significant for this book, that the most influential writer on modernity, Marshall Berman, used a suburban road-building project in Queens, New York, to exemplify a profound experience of modernity in his own life.[16]

Orwell's observation on the suburban knowledge of the magneto is suggestive of the wider relationship between new suburbia and the adoption of technology. Another, better, example he might have chosen would be the effect of the radio on suburban life. It was in the suburbs that a more passive, domesticated life developed, fuelled, in the south-east of England, by disposable income that allowed for the adoption of new technologies. Using the early crystal set required a practical engagement with new technology to gain access to radio broadcasts. Here, the unsung suburb rather than the metropolis became a locus for modernity. This is an example of a rather static modernity; independent mobility provided even greater possibilities. I distinguish here between self-actuated movement and the type of mobility provided and restricted by public transport systems. Wider independent mobility was a defining modernity of interwar suburbia in its contribution to time-space compression and in the disturbances of new road-building to the suburban landscape which provided order through modernist engineering and chaos in its many road accidents. My thinking here is, of course, informed by the mobility turn in humanities in recent years. I use the work of John Urry and Tim Cresswell, amongst other leading names, to provide support to the way that I have linked mobility and modernity in this book. Cresswell has, for example, explained the ancient relationship between mobility and the resultant concerns of the establishment.[17] As far as interwar suburban life was concerned, this theme evidenced itself in worries about sprawl and the inappropriate behaviour of some new motorists when they toured the countryside; ideas that have been dealt with by David Matless and others.[18] I, for my part, emphasise the uplifting and liberating aspects of new suburban mobility rather than concentrate on its critics.

The suburbs were founded through mobility. Without the carriage, or the horse-tram or the train, suburban living could not make sense within a metropolitan economy. For London, the tram and, especially, the train drove suburban development in the nineteenth century. The Victorian house in which I am writing this book was built because of the arrival of a railway branch line to Hampton Court. It surprised me to learn that this dramatic new technology arrived here as early as 1849. Eighty years later, new interwar railway development was encouraging further suburban development around London. For public transport historians this provided a fascinating topic that cemented a train/house/commuter/suburb set of relationships that is still highly resonant.

Railways and the Underground were, of course, very important to inter-war suburban development in London. They prompted and responded to, in a powerful recursive relationship, the building of hundreds of new housing estates across the capital. For the newly formed lower-middle classes, the train became their most important form of public transport; it allowed them to make a living and provided opportunities for leisure at the weekends. First the Metropolitan line and then extensions to the Northern and Piccadilly Underground lines powered the spread of London between the wars.

I have not written about trains, or for that matter trams and buses, in this book, and, so, have not presented a comprehensive picture of suburban transport. Alan Jackson has dealt with this aspect of the suburban story comprehensively, so there is little to be gained by repeating it here. The interactions between car and train were very limited, so I have not ignored any significant network connections.[19] As I have pointed out, trains were not new. It is easy, for example, to misunderstand the modernism of Charles Holden's designs for new Piccadilly Line stations, to imagine that they demonstrated modernity. I suggest that, in reality, this was a re-presentation of, by then, a very old technology. Electrification was just a change in the fuel, not a change in the way suburbia was experienced.

Suburban life may have appeared to be dominated by the railway time-table and radial movement from the centre to the suburb; the daily com-mute from Bexleyheath to London Bridge or from Northolt to Piccadilly Circus defining the direction and timing of travel. In reality, suburban mobility, even before the wider adoption of the car, was much more complex. Private, autonomous movement was already available in the new suburbs through walking, cycling and motorcycling. Little has been written about the contribution of these forms of mobility to the development of suburban life.

Walking was a much more common activity in the interwar period than today. Children walked, unaccompanied, to and from school. Housewives walked to the high street and shopping parade for daily purchases before the arrival of the refrigerator allowed for less regular outings. Walking was also seen in the more organised form of rambling and hiking clubs. Suburbia, positioned near to open countryside, was well placed for this enthusiasm.

Cycling became the numerically dominant form of independent vehicular mobility in the interwar period, providing the opportunity for journeys in non-radial directions. The bicycle was used for short journeys that would today be made by car, for pleasure trips out of the suburbs into the countryside, for cycling club outings and even for quite long-distance commuting. The motorcycle provided a similar autonomous mobility, but at a much higher speed and, when coupled with a sidecar, the possibility of carrying as many as three people together on a single journey. Motorcycles were not, though, suitable for those suburbanites who valued their respectability and appearance. The increasing adoption of the cycle and motorcycle each in its way fuelled modernity in the lives of working-class and lower-middle-class Londoners.

Air-mindedness was a key theme in interwar life. A governmental campaign to promote flight and flying emphasised the futuristic aspects of air travel and proposed that they were central to Britain's economic, political and military plans. This formal campaign was supported by a wide variety of sources ranging from detective stories and air displays to boys' books of wonder. Aeroplanes provided a surprising addition to London's interwar suburban mobility. Outer London was ringed by military, public and private airfields, and flight and flying were more of an everyday experience here than anywhere else in the country. Cheap pleasure flights provided access to the air for suburbanites, and large-scale air displays and regular visits to airports fuelled a strong sense of air-mindedness. In this way, a general sense of the modernity of air travel was heightened, for suburban Londoners, by direct local experience and a more widely felt association with air travel.

The single biggest change to suburban independent mobility was the widespread adoption of the car. The south-east of England and, particularly, the London suburbs and Home Counties were early adopters, taking advantage of a new method of travel which could include the whole family, which was fast and protected its occupants from the effects of the British weather. The car, driven on newly built arterial roads, transformed the lives of many Londoners, making leisure, shopping and commuting to work easier and more enjoyable.

This book sets out the transition between the suburb as part of a radial network based on railway tracks to something more modern and complicated where the suburb was at the centre of a network of autonomous and non-radial movement. I concentrate my attention in this book on the car, the most transformative technology, and its associated road system, and to a lesser extent on the motorcycle, bicycle and aeroplane.

Research: time, place, class and gender

The approach I took to researching and writing this book was to use an iterative assembly of material that demonstrated unusual connections to time, place and class. I drew this material from a wide selection of sources over a period of about eight years. I have relied on documentary material from governmental and private sources varying in size from The National Archives to a one-room local history centre. I have connected this to information gleaned from memoirs, oral histories, and interwar literature describing the suburban scene. As I write this introduction, I am planning a visit to the British Library to look at some obscure traffic surveys. Perhaps I will learn to stop, but the archive draws you in further than any normal person would call sensible.

Later in this book, I criticise *Semi-detached London* for the way it unconsciously periodises the interwar years and, in the same manner, proposes that one type of suburbia can metonymically stand for all of it. This is a danger for all historians and one that I will try, for this book, to address here. The interwar period is particularly prone to periodisation, because it sits between two of the most important events in world history. The danger here is that these action-packed twenty-one years can be inadvertently compressed into one lump. Historians are often preoccupied with studying discontinuity or unexpected continuities of the period between the wars and those peacetime years that preceded and followed them, and may, consequently, ignore the hidden stratifications within the period itself. For example, on the topic of suburban mobility the wide use of the car by 1938 has been forgotten, because it was followed by fifteen years of restrictions on the use of private vehicles due to war, rationing and austerity. It has been subsumed in the 'streets were empty of cars' type of memoir, which in reality is a memory more appropriate to the 1920s and was not at all representative of the period as a whole.

In the chapters that follow, I set out a history of the increasingly independent mobility found in the London suburbs. To avoid the problems I have just described, I will be specific about time, place and class. I concentrate on the period from about 1928 to 1938. The starting point was determined by the introduction of the closed car, which prompted car prices to come tumbling down, the establishment of the arterial road network in London and the introduction of roadside leisure destinations. The year 1938 serves as a good finishing point as it was the last when life was carried out normally before the war.

Place is harder to pin down, and is often connected to class. Generally, independent mobility is a privilege afforded to the wealthy and, as is seen in Chapter 2, this wealth was mostly confined to the western side of the capital. Many of the examples drawn from archival sources and contemporary literature feature life lived around three main western arterial roads: the Great West Road, Western Avenue and the Kingston Bypass. I found this a surprising aspect of my research, and consequently examples of the experiences of car drivers and motorcyclists in wealthy north-eastern or south-eastern suburbs such as Chingford or Chislehurst have not been, generally, included in this book. I would expect their experience to have been similar to their western compatriots. As far as the closely related subject of class is concerned, I have concentrated on the most mobile of all groups, the middle of the middle classes. This was the group who had the disposable income to buy cars, fly in aeroplanes and visit roadhouses. In describing the histories of suburban cycling and motorcycling, I also cover what can be loosely thought of as the lower middle or prospering working classes. It would be fair to say that I largely ignore the least wealthy part of suburban society, ordinary working people including those living on the new suburban council estates. This is partly because they were particularly bound to public transport, and also because there is less in the archive describing their specifically suburban experiences. There is no doubt that for working-class Londoners their move to suburbia presents, through their use of public transport for long-distance commuting, a distinct modernity, but this would not fit into the themes of this book. A study of interwar cycling by politically active groups such as the Clarion Cycling Club would be of inherent interest, but would not say much about new suburbia. I also pay less attention to the very wealthy, the original early adopters of both the car and aeroplane. Their story has been told elsewhere and would also tell us little about suburbia.

It would be fair to say that most of the journeys examined in this book were taken for reasons of leisure or consumption. This was a consequence of studying modernity from a suburban and domestic point of view. There was a parallel urban experience of modernity in play in the interwar period, which was the introduction of, mostly, working-class men to driving commercial vehicles for a living, extending skills they had gained in the Great War. This potentially fascinating area of interwar history would not say much about suburbia. I do, however, show how suburbanites started using their cars for commuting to work by the end of the 1930s.

Independent mobility was highly gendered between the wars. In particular, driving and motorcycling were dominated by male ownership and control over the vehicle, leaving the bicycle as the most important means of independent transport for women. The history related in this book is, consequently, often masculine. I have tried not to fall into the trap of overstating the importance of the small numbers of, generally, very wealthy women who were famous drivers and flyers between the wars. This too was not a suburban story.[20]

The structure of the book

This book has three main sections: *Technologies*, *Roads* and *Journeys*.

The first section, *Technologies*, sets out the rise of independent transport in London's new interwar suburbia based on the key forms of relatively new technology that presented itself in this time and place. Chapter 2 describes the rise of the car into London's suburban life. This most important technology transformed suburban life in the 1930s and presented a vivid precursor to the life we live today. Chapter 3 shows how, for those who could not get access to a car, the bicycle and the motorcycle became a vital means of independent transport in suburbia, and provided a more directly kinaesthetic appreciation of suburban modernity. Chapter 4 demonstrates how suburban Londoners took to the air for the first time and experienced the spirit of air-mindedness of the period through joyrides and visiting suburban airports and air displays.

The second section, *Roads*, considers the practical and cultural aspects of the new suburban arterial road-building programme of the interwar period. This was the equivalent of the nineteenth-century railway-building programme and its construction generated suburban growth in the same way as the railway. Chapter 5 explains how a modern arterial road network was built in London's outer suburbs and describes its characteristics. It shows how cycle paths were used by some cyclists, but were rejected by others. The chapter then considers the impact of ribbon development and 'road-mindedness' on suburban life. Chapter 6 looks at the way that the arterial road challenged public conceptions of what suburbia should look like. It demonstrates how nostalgia was a powerful force in interwar life and how resistant many were to the idea of modernisation. The contestation over the roads' appearance also demonstrates some unexpected insights into memorialisation and teenage suburban vandalism.

The third section, *Journeys*, shows how mobility generated suburban modernity in a variety of ways.[21]

Chapter 7 looks at the unusual case of the roadhouse, an Americanised country club located on the suburban arterial road that was the epitome of an exciting and highly fashionable destination for the wealthy and motorised. As such, it provides an example of how elite driving gradually changed into an activity for middle-class drivers. In addition to providing swimming, music, dancing and dining, the roadhouse also presented possibilities for transgressive behaviour.

Chapter 8 describes how the changing form of the car in the interwar period promoted a domestication and suburbanisation of the experience of driving, moving it away from the exploration of the countryside and the open road to a more modern experience. This context is explored through an examination of how the changing form of the cars affected the way that drivers and passengers saw the landscape they passed through. In particular, it looks at driving on the Great West Road and considers the possibility that the Californian-styled white factories of this road's 'Golden Mile' presented a form of transplanted American technological sublimity for drivers. It also shows how other more cynical observers found the road vulgar and tawdry.

Chapter 9 is an examination of the more negative aspects of independent mobility. The chapter looks at the culture of speed and accidents in both literature and in real life to illustrate a potentially dangerous suburban world. It proposes, using the work of Virilio and Berman, that car and plane crashes and their impact on cyclists, pedestrians and suburban residents revealed the chaos and peril associated with new mobilities and demonstrated a condition of suburban modernity.

Chapter 10 looks at how the cycle of suburban modernity unwound towards the end of the 1930s and motoring became normalised and closely associated with ordinary journeys, everyday life and the worlds of consumption and work. It considers the role of the car in suburban consumption, both in traditional centres and in newly motorised locations of consumption on the suburban arterial road such as cinemas, garages, and petrol stations. Finally, it shows how cars began to be used for the ultimate everyday journey: commuting.

Notes

1 M. Nava and A. O'Shea, *Modern Times: Reflections on a Century of English Modernity*, London 1996, p. 14.

2 J. Carey, *The Intellectuals and the Masses: Pride and Prejudice Among the Literary Intelligentsia, 1880–1939*, London 1992.

3 J. Betjeman, 'The Metropolitan Railway Baker Street Station Buffet', *A Few Late Chrysanthemums*, London 1954.

4 C. E. M. Joad, *The Horrors of the Countryside*, London, 1931.

5 G. Orwell, *The Lion and the Unicorn: Socialism and the English Genius*, London 1941.

6 O. Lancaster, *Pillar to Post: English Architecture Without Tears*, London 1938.

7 D. Nobbs, *The Fall and Rise of Reginald Perrin*, Harmondsworth 1978.

8 H. J. Dyos, *Victorian Suburb: A Study of the Growth of Camberwell*, Leicester 1961.

9 A. A. Jackson, *Semi-detached London: Suburban Development, Life and Transport, 1900–39*, London 1973.

10 A. A. Jackson, *Semi-detached London*, Endpapers.

11 P. Oliver, I. Davis, I. Bentley, *Dunroamin: The Suburban Semi and Its Enemies*, London 1981; J. Honer and English Heritage (eds), *London Suburbs*, London 1999.

12 M. Clapson, *Suburban Century: Social Change and Urban Growth in England and the United States*, Oxford 2003.

13 D. Gilbert and R. Preston, 'Suburban Modernity and National Identity' in D. Gilbert, D. Matless, B. Short (eds), *Geographies of British Modernity: Space and Society in the Twentieth Century*, Oxford 2003, pp. 187–203.

14 M. Ogborn, *Spaces of Modernity: London's Geographies, 1680–1780*, London 1998, p. 2.

15 I have, of course, borrowed my title for this book from M. Berman, *All That Is Solid Melts Into Air: The Experience of Modernity*, London 1983.

16 M. Berman, *All That Is Solid Melts Into Air: The Experience of Modernity*, p. 295.

17 T. Cresswell, *On the Move: Mobility in the Modern Western World*, London 2006.

18 D. Matless, *Landscape and Englishness*, London 1998.

19 These connections were limited to the construction of station car parks for commuters and the building of Tube stations on the line of some arterial roads.

20 S. O'Connell, *The Car and British Society: Class, Gender and Motoring 1896–1939*, Manchester 1998, is an excellent source on the topic of women motorists.

21 See I. Borden, *Drive: Journeys Through Film, Cities, and Landscapes*, London, 2013, for an interesting account of automobility and cinema, which takes a particular note of kinaesthetic and embodied driving encounters.

Part II

Technologies

2

The car indispensable

In 1954, as the privations of austerity in post war Britain were beginning to lift, Austin Motors presented a film that portrayed life centred on the car.[1]

> I am a car; I am more than a machine on four wheels. I share your working days and your leisure hours. I am your home on wheels; I am your good companion. I am your business partner, I belong to the third of your life that you spend at your job … The carefree days I share with you too, as I am your getaway to the quiet places … I am your escape to happiness.[2]

In this manner, Austin showed the buyers of its modest vehicles that its car was a natural accompaniment to a modern way of life that provided an autonomous mobility. The film illustrated the possibility of a spontaneous trip to the countryside, a complex journey to several business contacts and, in an emergency, driving a pregnant woman to the hospital. Although it may seem that this post war development was the dawn of an era of wider access to the car, an investigation into motoring in the period immediately before the Second World War contests the view that Britain's interwar suburban roads were empty of cars and that suburbia was under the thrall of the train and bus timetable.

By 1939, there were some two million cars on Britain's roads. The car had become an important status symbol and means of independent transport for many wealthier Britons and was a key ingredient in what has become known as 'the new consumerism' of this time.[3] The south-east of England was the most prosperous part of Britain in the 1930s and suburban London was central to this economic development.[4] Where better to look for signs of continuity between this time and place and a more general change in mobility that was encouraged by wider prosperity in the 1950s?

In the well-known works on interwar suburban London, the car is either excluded or is damned with faint praise. A prominent example of exclusion can be found in Alan Jackson's still-dominant work on interwar suburban growth, *Semi-detached London*. Jackson makes two important claims about the role of the car in suburbia. First, he uses his personal memories to dismiss the importance of cars, claiming that they 'were few and far between in suburban London'.[5] This is reinforced by an unreferenced assertion that 'At Tolworth in 1937, the only car owner in a quarter mile road of new homes was a civil service clerical officer'.[6] This is an odd piece of evidence; one small street in the poorer section of Surbiton is expected to provide support for a conclusion covering several million people. As will be shown, the reality was different and more complex.

Jackson's second claim is evident in its absence, a dog that did not bark; in a book of three hundred pages devoted to 'suburban development, life and transport' he mentions the car only four times, concentrating his attention on the railway, Underground, bus and tram.[7] Of course, these forms of public transport were fundamental to suburban development in the interwar period, but this concentration on public mobilities has occluded our understanding of the role of flexible, independent private transport brought about by the use of the car. Jackson's generalisations about the car are not unusual in the history of this period, and such is the authority of his work that he may well have been inadvertently responsible for the continuing absence of any serious interrogation of the role of the car in interwar suburbia.

By contrast with American scholarship on interwar suburbia, studies of British suburbia tend to marginalise the role of the automobile.[8] For example, Mark Clapson remarks that 'cars were not yet fundamental to suburban life in the 1920s and 1930s'.[9] This ignores the growing importance of the car to many wealthy and not so wealthy drivers in the years prior to the Second World War. Another important work on London's suburbia, *Dunroamin*, recognised that there were two million cars in Britain by 1939, yet argued that the car was used primarily for family outings.[10] The co-author, Paul Oliver, states, baldly but without any supporting data, that 'the car was not used for going to work'.[11]

Weightman and Humphries, in their history of interwar London, briefly acknowledge the rise of the car, and reach an accurate conclusion, when taking London as a whole, that 'mass ownership had not really quite begun when the Second World War broke out'.[12] In more general works on the history of London in the twentieth century, however, little time is spent discussing the car, either before or after the war, which is surprising considering its impact on the city.[13] Outside of suburban studies, Sean O'Connell's work on the social history of interwar motoring provides important insights into the penetration of car ownership into wider social groups. He does not, though, go further to examine the strongly regional and suburban aspect of this development.[14]

By the end of the 1930s, the car was able to provide an increasing number of suburbanites with a means of transport that was clean, dry, warm and highly convenient. Separated from the constraints and restrictions of the radially organised train, car owners could choose from a new selection of potential destinations. In the 1920s, suburban motorists tended to use their cars for special outings to the seaside and countryside on summer Sundays. One man, remembering a 1926 childhood outing, recalled that 'my parents and I had spent the day at Bognor and now in our Chrysler 70 we had joined the migration of lobster coloured, ice cream–gorged humanity heading back to the suburbs'.[15] As early as 1928, Dorothy L. Sayers commentated on this herd instinct. 'It is not known why motorists, who sing the joys of the open road, spend so much petrol every week-end grinding their way to Southend, Brighton and Margate.'[16]

Car use in the 1930s brought about a wider autonomous mobility that presaged the casual use of the car that we associate with the 1950s and beyond. By 1938, the leading motoring magazine, *The Autocar*, announced the car as 'indispensable' in its role in daily life.[17] This was accompanied with illustrations of cars arriving at a wide variety of places. Some were 'traditional' destinations – touring the countryside, camping and picnicking. Significantly, though, *The Autocar* also included more everyday destinations such as the cinema, the railway station, the golf club, a suburban house and for shopping.

The widespread adoption and apparent ubiquity of the car

British motoring literature published just before the Second World War suggests two emergent themes: the widespread adoption of the car by new motorists and the apparent (to our modern-day eyes) ubiquity of cars in everyday life. These ideas can be seen in the reportage of popular motoring magazines. Expanding on its theme of the indispensability of the car, *The Autocar* announced that:

> Nowadays everyone is a motorist … lucky then the new motorist who is experiencing the pride of ownership for the first time and who has at his service one of the finest man-made servants. No longer is a car a luxury. It is the reliable servant for all manner of people, and as time goes on, will become available to every class of owner.[18]

A few months later, in an article also aimed at new motorists, *The Motor* described the type of motoring that could be obtained for £150. This, a fairly modest sum for the period, would allow for the running of a small new car, or a larger second-hand car.[19] The implication was that motoring was becoming much more widely available than a few years earlier.

These themes were also seen in satirical writing on suburbia.[20] The humorous *How to Be a Motorist*, by W. Heath Robinson and K. R. G. Browne, published in 1939, intersperses teasing with insights into the life of the suburban motorist at the very end of the 1930s.[21] Ostensibly a handbook for the new motorist, *How to Be a Motorist* was more likely aimed at the knowing, experienced driver which, in itself, acknowledged the rise of new drivers drawn from the low to middle section of the middle classes whose milieu was the suburb not the city. The authors explain that 'This modest but quite attractive little book … is designed to assist, soothe and instruct the motorist-in-embryo who longs to join the procession on the Kingston By-Pass but is uncertain how to set about it'.[22]

How to Be a Motorist portrays car ownership as the norm in middle-class suburban life, claiming that 'cars are more numerous than kids in many English households' and that 'people who have never owned or driven [a car] are considered slightly odd'.[23] An *Anthropological Report on a London Suburb*, a satirical inspection of an imagined London suburb, similarly observes 'standardised' cars outside every suburban house and suggests that motoring is second only to the weather as a topic of conversation.[24] The car also played a leading role in Osbert Lancaster's caustic satires on suburbanisation as a contrast to mock-Tudor modernity or as the cause of arterial road ugliness.[25] The themes of new motorists and the ubiquity of the car were neatly captured by Heath Robinson in one of the illustrations for *How to Be a Motorist*, titled 'Uncertain How to Set About It' which showed a new motorist staring apprehensively at a road completely filled with cars.[26]

Moving towards ubiquity in interwar suburban driving

In the mid-1920s, a number of conditions produced the possibility for a rapid advance in suburban motoring. First, many of the new residents of London's suburbia were employed in new light industrial jobs and in the governmental and service sectors. These well-paid jobs were resilient to the impact of world depression, which meant that London and the Home Counties had far lower rates of unemployment and poverty than Britain as a whole.[27] Second, when the period is taken as a whole, real incomes rose considerably over the twenty years between the wars. By 1938, real income was 32 per cent higher than in 1920.[28] This new surplus income was used for the purchase of cars and consumer durables and provided the impetus to buy on widely available hire-purchase terms. Third, the price of new and second-hand cars fell dramatically over the interwar period, making them accessible to a much larger number of buyers. The acquisition of cars by the lower and middle sections of the middle classes had to wait until their rising incomes met the rapidly falling cost of car ownership brought about by simpler, smaller designs and mass-production.[29] This began in the late 1920s and accelerated through the 1930s. The real cost of car ownership fell by over 40 per cent in the twelve-year period between 1924 and 1935.[30]

The introduction of many low-powered small cars also reduced the average cost of buying a car. Austin started the trend towards smaller cars with the release of their ground-breaking Seven in 1922. This tiny, light car produced seven horse-power and was, as a consequence, taxed favourably. This small low-powered format was copied and adapted by other manu-facturers and by the mid-1930s dominated car production. The leading manufacturers in the interwar period were Austin, Morris, Singer and, after production started in Dagenham, Ford. The Morris Eight, for example, had a production run of 272,000 cars and was priced at between £95 and £140. By 1936, this small car was twice as popular as the second and third most purchased cars, which were the Ford Y and the Austin Seven.[31]

Small cars were attractive to the new suburbans for reasons other than price; their narrow wheelbases allowed them to be parked in the restricted driveways at the side of semi-detached houses. The proportion of small cars bought in Britain rose from 23 per cent in 1927 to 70 per cent in 1936.[32] *How to Be a Motorist* satirised this development as it suggested that the small car was the most likely choice of new motorists. Heath Robinson's illustration shows a Ford-type car, but it is the depiction of its occupants that is most interesting. This newcomer to driving, having only recently passed the driving test, and his wife, are clearly lower middle class in their dress. This is not the portrayal of a bank manager or solicitor, but a clerk or shopkeeper tentatively entering the world of motoring for the first time.[33]

Sean O'Connell identified two important elements in the acquisition of cars by the less well-off middle classes: the purchase of new cars by instalment credit and the use of second-hand cars. O'Connell showed that to publically admit to buying a car on hire purchase was embarrassing, but that this could be avoided by acquiring the car in the anonymous surroundings of Central London.[34]

There was a highly active second-hand market in cars in the interwar period, which K. R. G. Browne described in an earlier humorous account of suburban life: *Suburban Days*.[35] The impact of cheap second-hand cars on the increasingly crowded suburban roads was also seen in *Roadways*, a 1937 film that came out of the documentary movement. It made the point that second-hand cars were available from under £10, and showed how this was promoting mass motoring.[36] For the mechanically minded, second-hand cars provided access to motoring at a cost much below that indicated by the price of new cars.

Suburban car demographics

In the 1930s, car ownership in Britain was highly regionalised. This was, of course, a reflection of the regional nature of the interwar depression that laid waste to much of the north of the country, while at the same time much, but not all, of the south was experiencing a boom in the production and acquisition of consumer goods made in new light-industrial factories. An analysis of car ownership per household by region in 1931 reveals a southern bias with the western Home Counties such as Middlesex and Surrey to the fore. Table 1 shows some of the more significant findings.

Car usage in the Home Counties grew far more rapidly than in the rest of England (almost fourfold in twelve years), with only a slight deceleration in the troubled years of 1930 to 1932. This suggests that the 86 per cent of the south-east workforce who were in work in 1932 were becoming increasingly affluent and able to spend their disposable income on cars.[37] The figures for the County of London show a much lower rate of growth which is a reflection of two factors, firstly the early adoption of cars at the centre, which did not support much further growth in the 1920s and 1930s, and the relative

Table I Car ownership patterns in England 1931 (suburban Home Counties in bold)

County	Percentage of households with cars 1931
Surrey	**19.6**
Oxford	16.7
Bucks	16.6
Berkshire	16.0
Herts	15.9
Middlesex	**12.9**
Kent	**12.2**
Essex	**8.2**
London	8.2
Northumberland	7.2
Lancs	6.5
Durham	3.9

Derived from *The Motor Industry of Great Britain 1939* and www. visionofbritain. org.uk for official census data.

Table 2 Percentage of cars per household for each Home County in 1938

	1931	*1938*	*Growth 1931 to 1938(%)*
Surrey	19.6	31.6	61
Middlesex	12.9	21.4	66
Kent	12.2	17.7	45
Essex	8.2	13.5	64

The Motor Industry of Great Britain 1939 and www.visionofbritain.org.uk for official census data. The figures assume that average household size remained constant from 1931 to 1938.

poverty of the inner, Victorian, suburbs of the County of London in comparison to the newer and wealthier suburbs and Home Counties.

Table 2 shows that Surrey and Middlesex led the other suburban Home Counties in the adoption of the car. By 1938, one household in three in Surrey had use of a car compared to one household in five in Middlesex, which was more suburbanised but poorer than Surrey. This provides high-level information about possible suburban car usage, but must be used cautiously as a Home County like Surrey consisted, as it still does, of large areas of open rural land, individual towns, and wide areas of suburbia. The householders of the eastern Home Counties and the County of London

Table 3   Categorisation of houses in Surrey by class

	'A' Class	'B' Class	'C' Class
Number of houses	24,400	86,100	189,800
Percentage of total	8.1	28.7	63.2

Associated Newspapers Ltd, *Sell to Britain Through the Daily Mail*, London 1935.

were much less likely to be car owners than their western neighbours. Essex was particularly slow to adopt the car.

The level of car use in Surrey is particularly striking and is suggestive of very high levels of adoption by the middle classes. In 1935, Associated Newspapers undertook an exercise that divided Surrey's homes into three categories (see Table 3). 'A' Class houses were described as being owned by 'people of means' and as the 'exclusive market for higher-priced cars' and were illustrated by a picture of a detached house with a large garden.[38] 'B' Class houses were owned by 'people with moderate means' and their occupants were described as 'families graded between the better classes and the working classes'. The houses pictured typify the simpler form of suburban semi. Significantly, 'much of the new property occupied by this class' was said to be 'equipped with garage accommodation' because its owners 'often call for the purchase of cars'.[39]

In contrast, 'C' Class houses were of the poorest type, a large proportion of their occupants having incomes that were 'below or only on a par with a normal subsistence level and there is little balance left out of the weekly budget for expenditure upon goods classified outside of bare necessities'.[40]

This categorisation intended to show *The Daily Mail's* advertisers that the paper reached further into the wealthy and professional classes than generally thought.[41] Similar information was provided for other counties in Britain. In 1935, 27 per cent of Surrey families had cars, but, using the information in Table 3, it can be estimated that some 50 per cent to 60 per cent of Surrey households in the 'B' Class owned a car, which is a very surprising outcome. The low overall adoption rate in Essex can be explained by its low numbers of 'B' Class houses in 1935.[42]

Historical statistics are not available at a borough-by-borough level for car usage in London's suburbia, but SMMT (Society of Motor Manufacturers and Traders) statistics for new car purchases reveal detailed information on the variations in suburban motoring. The SMMT recorded details of cars sold in each borough in Greater London in 1934. By com-

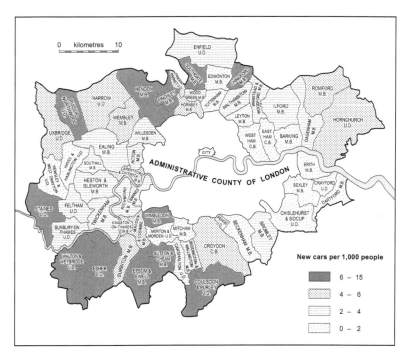

Car acquisition in Outer London in 1934
Author's illustration

paring these figures to an inter-census estimate of population by borough, a relative measure of new car acquisition for each suburb can be established.[43]

There were substantial variations in new car purchases in the suburbs. Figure 1, which shows higher levels of car purchases in darker tones, reveals a predominately western outer ring with high proportions of suburban motorists.[44] But fifteen times as many new cars were purchased per capita in Esher than in Mitcham, Surrey, suburbs only a few miles apart but completely different in their consumption patterns.

Some outer suburbs experienced very high levels of population growth. Hendon, an exemplar of the generally received view of new suburbia, had relatively high levels of new car purchases, a trend also seen in neighbouring Harrow, Wembley and Ruislip. Hendon had approximately one car for every three households in 1934 and almost one car for every two households by 1938.[45] This was a reflection of Hendon's very low unemployment rate (4.7 per cent in 1931) and having 50 per cent more managers and professional people living there than Middlesex as a whole.[46]

Another outer suburb, Kingston, home to Alan Jackson's Tolworth example, was a mixture of expensive Victorian and much cheaper new suburban homes. This borough was, counter to Jackson's view, in the second quartile of car purchasing, buying 5.1 new cars per 1000 capita in 1934. This equates approximately to 1 car for every 5.5 households by 1938. These unexpected results in Hendon and Kingston are, perhaps, a reflection of another wider suburban trope that emphasises consumption and display and keeping up with the Joneses. Buying a car, new or second-hand, with cash or on hire purchase was a key status symbol in the 1930s, and this was nowhere more true than in the newest suburbs.

In the east, the new suburbs of Hornchurch and Romford attracted many residents from the East End who were also relatively likely to buy new cars. Other eastern boroughs had fewer cars. Ford did not appear to be selling many of its new cars to its workers in Dagenham who were buying one new car for every six bought in Hendon. In the west, Hayes and Harlington, a western suburb with access to two good arterial roads and strong local employment, bought fewer new cars per household than Dagenham. This was a suburb with many large estates of cheaper semi-detached houses priced at the very low end of London possibilities at £450. This attracted new residents who were clinging on at the lowest levels of the middle classes, typified in suburban accounts as buying furniture on hire purchase and furnishing rooms one-by-one when they could afford to.

It is a tenet of *Semi-detached London* that the new outer suburbs, with their streets of cheap housing, were particularly dependent on public transport, because their occupants could not afford or did not need to buy a car. An examination of those boroughs that saw both high levels of suburbanisation and relatively high levels of car usage produces some unexpected results.[47] Wealthy south-western suburbs led the way in car ownership while experiencing high population growth, but surprisingly the north-western suburbs, with cheaper semi-detached housing typical of new suburbia, also had more car buyers than average. The SMMT records suggest that, by 1938, there were approximately 200,000 cars in the outer ring of suburbia to add to the 144,000 registered in the County of London.[48]

Accommodating the car in suburbia

During the interwar period, suburban housing changed to accommodate the car. The manner in which this happened provides some detailed clues to how far the car reached into the lower reaches of the suburban middle classes. The cars of the period were costly to their owners, highly prized and temperamental when left out in the open. To own a car almost always meant having a garage. Studying the development of the garage through the interwar period tells us a lot about the where and when of car use.

Suburban homes can be categorised into terraced, semi-detached and detached houses. Terraced housing does not allow room for a garage at the front of the house. Jackson points out in *The Middle Classes 1900–1950* that garages developed haphazardly along the service roads that ran around the back of many terraces.[49] This observation sits awkwardly with his earlier thoughts on the absence of cars in the less-wealthy parts of suburbia. Accommodating the car in detached houses was straightforward. Detached houses priced at £1000 and upwards were the first to include garages. Jackson places this development as early as 1912.[50] Certainly, by the late 1920s most new suburban detached houses came with either an integrated or a separate garage. The latter form was optional and was often priced separately from the house and would cost between £30 and £50 extra.[51]

Semi-detached houses are the most interesting for discovering how houses reflected the adoption of the car. The semi changed greatly over the interwar years. In the 1920s, builders of semi-detached dwellings ignored the car, then began to provide a space for the new light cars of the period before integrating the garage into the design of the house by the end of the 1930s.[52]

Washing the car, 1930 **2**
Herbert Felton/Hulton Archive/Getty Images

A review of the leading London house sales advertising magazine of the period, *Homefinder*, shows this developing trend. In the 1931 editions, garages are mentioned only in relation to detached properties. By 1933, one developer presented a pair of semis, at the higher end of the price bracket at £875 each, one with a porch and the other with an integrated garage. At a slightly lower price, Ideal Homes of Surbiton offered semis at £675, but noted that 'all the sites have room for a garage'.[53] By 1936, integral garages, with a box room over the top were becoming more common, with one developer in South Harrow advertising such houses at £790.[54] By 1939, house builders were offering more and more semis with garages; at Hayes in Kent a semi in a modernist style was offered with a separate garage at £725.[55]

The provision of garages for lower-middle-class semi-detached house buyers might well have been as much about aspiration and future expectations as about car ownership. Nevertheless, slightly lower down the house price rankings, where streets of semis had been built in the late 1920s and early 1930s without garages, but with room for a common access, some homeowners bought garages in kit form, constructed from asbestos and concrete panels with corrugated iron roofs. As Jackson pointed out, the space between pairs of semis was increased to provide room for garages to be built at the rear, sharing the same driveway.[56]

Each new garage required planning permission, and their acquisition can be seen in cheaper streets of semis during the 1930s, for example, in Pembroke Avenue, Tolworth, the area Jackson thought devoid of cars. If one mentally erases loft conversions, paved front gardens and satellite dishes, what remains are examples of modest interwar London semis. They are typical of Associated Newspapers' 'B' type houses. In the common area between some of the houses stand pairs of garages constructed after the house builder had departed to (literally) pastures new.

Planning records show that six householders out of fifty-four in the street built garages behind their houses between 1936 and 1939 and eleven more between 1947 and 1952.[57] The records show a modest street where, by 1939, 11 per cent of the residents had or, were planning to have cars. There is a possibility that people might have built a garage without owning a car, or, as likely, that some rash souls might have bought a car without building a garage, perhaps covering it with a tarpaulin.

The implications of the arrival of suburban car ownership

The pre-automobile twentieth-century suburb was defined by its rela-tionship with the metropolis. Radial transport lines led out from central London to its outlying suburbs. This was no coincidence; these very lines were the network that, in conjunction with speculative builders, formed the vast estates of suburban housing in the late Victorian and Edwardian periods and then again further out from town between the wars. Travel at speed was controlled by the timetable. For commuters, the railway timetable dominated their journeys for six days a week. Trams provided for cheaper, slower but largely radial journeys; local buses made more eccentric cross-suburban travel available, but still in thrall to the timetable.

Other mobilities were found in the suburb. Cycling provided inde-pendent transport for some. Walking was far more commonplace and over much longer distances that we might manage today. The organisa-tion of the suburb was focused on either the railway station or the local high street. Walking to the station extended the reach of the train, so that each house was tied to the metropolis in a combination of journeys. This version of suburbia was a place created by movements, a place to sleep between journeys, a suburban example of de Certeau's proposal that pedestrian mobility produced a place 'composed of the intersection of mobile elements'.[58] For those men and increasing numbers of single women who worked in the West End and the City of London, the suburb was accurately described as a dormitory, It did not take long, as I have already noted, for this actual sleep to be converted into a literary trope. The whole suburb was condemned by intellectuals to be metaphorically asleep; no prince was expected to wake up its citizens, but change eventually came in the form of the car.

As the analysis in this chapter has shown, a number of London's sub-urbs adopted the car with such enthusiasm in the 1930s that by the end of that decade, in places, the car had begun to dominate life in a way that would not be seen more widely until the late 1950s. The effect of this was to change how journeys were made in the suburb. First, journeys became more spontaneous and randomised in their direction; radial journeys were complemented by short intra- and inter-suburban routes. Second, subur-ban journeys became dramatically faster and not tied to a slow timetable. Third, journeys became a joint rather than an individual undertaking, where families travelled together. Fourth, the car allowed for a direct and immediate connection with destinations outside the suburb, loosening connections with the centre.

This changed relationship between the suburb and the city and the increase in speed of each journey amount to a remaking of time and space, a symptom of a developing suburban modernity.[59] The changed social practices associated with car use changed the nature of the suburb to produce a different version of place from its predecessor. As Lefebvre describes it:

> Formal boundaries are gone between town and country, between centre and periphery, between suburbs and city centres, between the domain of automobiles and the domain of people.[60]

The move from the high street and railway station to the arterial road and the bypass promoted a stronger sense of anonymity and alienation, both features of life traditionally associated with urban modernity. Families travelling together in a shared car became more nuclear and consumerist and separated from their neighbours, weakening suburban community links. Driving on arterial roads disconnected central London drivers from the suburbs to increase the sense of separation for the suburb.

The introduction of the car into suburban life changed the suburbs for ever. Life speeded up, became more family-centric, more consumerist, more distanced from community life, less in thrall to the domination of the public transport timetable. In short, these new drivers both experienced and generated suburban modernity.

Conclusion

In many interwar memoirs, the writer looking back to his or her childhood might remember streets empty of cars, where it was possible to play all day without danger or interruption. Of course, it may well have been true in their streets when they were little, but it shows the problems involved in generalising from a personal experience. There were two million cars in Britain by 1938, so they must have driven down somebody's streets. This contradiction is explained in two ways. The first is in the periodisation in some historical accounts and in personal memory that, effectively, narrows interwar experience into a single event, albeit one that lasted twenty years. As has been shown, the increase in car ownership was very pronounced in the latter part of the 1930s. The second is in the strong regionalisation of this growth. It was mostly a southern phenomenon, and, within that, concentrated in the western Home Counties and outer London suburbs.

It is the suburban aspect of this acquisition that is the focus of much of this book. Within the London suburbs, there were local hotspots where car ownership was highly prevalent. These were mostly in the west, although some areas of western London bought few cars. There were two types of suburb where cars were most likely to be found. The first was the older, Victorian, outer suburb that already had an established middle class. A good example of this would be Esher, with many wealthy residents with high-paying jobs in the professions who lived in large houses. These families had large amounts of capital and high disposable incomes that allowed for a luxurious lifestyle: some would have been car owners since before the First World War. After the war, as prices of cars came down, they increasingly bought new cars. The second and more surprising type of suburb to get the car habit was what would have been called at the time the 'better class' of new suburb. Here, brand new suburbanites with good incomes and secure jobs could use instalment credit to buy a car to show to their new neighbours that they were modern and successful.

By the late 1930s, for these two groups the car had truly become indispensable. Consumption of cars provided them with at least three aspects of cultural capital simultaneously. First, it gave them an autonomous mobility that allowed them to travel to the countryside or the seaside on a pleasant day, or to go quickly to the shops if they had forgotten something. They no longer needed to use the train for outings, constrained by the timetable and forced to share a compartment. Second, this new mobility could be converted into social prestige when dropped into conversation with neighbours and colleagues. Car ownership suggested wealth, sophistication and a forward-thinking view of the world. Finally, once all your peers owned a car, it could be used to provide social distinction through the very wide choice of different models available at that time.

To propose, as I have done, that the wealthy middle class enjoyed driving cars is not a particularly startling idea. What is intriguing is just how far down into the strata of the middle classes and into the higher reaches of the working classes car acquisition had spread by the end of the 1930s. The high ratio of cars per household in suburbs with a majority of working-class and lower-middle-class citizens can be explained only by concluding that the middle sections of the middle class were also very likely to own a car. As has been shown, this idea is further evidenced by changes in house design and in home improvements made to accommodate the car. This revolutionary development was a key enabler of suburban modernity, and this idea is developed in the following chapters.

Notes

1 Much of the material in this chapter first appeared in M. J. Law, '"The car indispensable": the hidden influence of the car in inter-war suburban London', *Journal of Historical Geography*, 38:4, 2012, pp. 424–433, published by Elsevier.

2 British Pathé, *I Am a Car*, reel: 2721.02, 1954, www.britishpathe.com [accessed 1 December 2011]. Austin was, by 1954, part of the British Motor Corporation.

3 S. O'Connell, *The Car and British Society: Class, Gender and Motoring 1896–1939*, Manchester 1998; S. Bowden, 'The New Consumerism' in P. Johnson (ed.), *Twentieth-century Britain: Economic, Social and Cultural Change*, London 1994.

4 G. Weightman and S. Humphries, *The Making of Modern London 1914–1939*, London 1984.

5 A. A. Jackson, *Semi-detached London: Suburban Development, Life and Transport, 1900–39*, London 1973, p. 183.

6 A. A Jackson, *Semi-detached London*, p. 183.

7 A. A Jackson, *Semi-detached London*, index.

8 See K. T. Jackson, *Crabgrass Frontier: The Suburbanization of the United States*, Oxford 1985, and A. Brilliant, *The Great Car Craze: How Southern California Collided with the Automobile in the 1920's*, Santa Barbara 1989, J. R. Stilgoe, *Borderland: Origins of the American Suburb, 1820–1939*, New Haven 1988.

9 M. Clapson, *Suburban Century: Social Change and Urban Growth in England and the United States*, Oxford 2003, p. 27.

10 P. Oliver, I. Davis and I. Bentley, *Dunroamin: The Suburban Semi and Its Enemies*, London 1981, p. 200.

11 P. Oliver, 'Great Expectations – Suburban Values and the Role of the Media' in P. Oliver, I. Davis and I. Bentley, *Dunroamin: The Suburban Semi and Its Enemies*, London 1981, p. 123.

12 G. Weightman and S. Humphries, *The Making of Modern London 1914–1939*, London 1984, p. 97.

13 For example, J. White, *London in the Twentieth Century: A City and Its People*, London 2001; S. Inwood, *A History of London*, London 1998.

14 S. O'Connell, *The Car and British Society*, p. 11.

15 Reminiscences of M. S. Hughes, Sutton Local History Service, Oral History, undated, SBAR 629.

16 D. L. Sayers, *Lord Peter Views the Body*, London 1928, p. 63.

17 *The Autocar*, 4 March 1938.

18 *The Autocar*, 4 March 1938.

19 *The Motor*, 3 January 1939.

20 John Tosh warns that 'satire is a potent but difficult source for historians' owing to the fleeting nature of humorous allusions. Satirical sources are used cautiously here to point the way for further empirical analysis. See J. Tosh, *The Pursuit of History: Aims, Methods and New Directions in the Study of Modern History*, Harlow 2010, p. 115.

21 W. H. Robinson and K. R. G. Browne, *How to Be a Motorist*, London 1939.

22 W. H. Robinson and K. R. G. Browne, *How to Be a Motorist*, p. 114.

23 W. H. Robinson and K. R. G. Browne, *How to Be a Motorist*, pp. 7–8.

24 C. S. L. Duff, *Anthropological Report on a London Suburb*, London 1935, p. 43 and p. 31.

25 O. Lancaster, *Progress at Pelvis Bay*, London 1936; *Pillar to Post: English Architecture Without Tears*, London 1938.

26 W. H. Robinson and K. R. G. Browne, *How to Be a Motorist*, p. 115.

27 M. E. F. Jones, 'The Economic History of the Regional Problem in Britain, 1920–38', *Journal of Historical Geography*, 10:4, 1984, pp. 385–395.

28 See D. K. Benjamin and L. A. Kochin, 'Searching for an Explanation of Unemployment in Inter-war Britain', *The Journal of Political Economy*, 87:3, 1979, pp. 441–478.

29 P. Nieuwenhuis and P. Wells, 'The All-steel Body as a Cornerstone to the Foundations of the Mass Production Car Industry', *Industrial and Corporate Change*, 16:2, 2007, pp. 183–211.

30 Society of Motor Manufacturers and Traders, *The Motor Industry of Great Britain 1937*, London 1937, cost of cars after adjusting for inflation.

31 M. Sedgwick, *A–Z of Cars of the 1930s*, London 1989.

32 That is cars producing less than ten horse power, Society of Motor Manufacturers and Traders, *The Motor Industry of Great Britain 1937*.

33 W. H. Robinson and K. R. G. Browne, *How to Be a Motorist*.

34 S. O'Connell, *The Car and British Society*, p. 24.

35 K. R. G. Browne, *Suburban Days*, London 1928.

36 *Roadways*, Directors, A. Cavalcanti, S. Legg and W. Coldstream, GPO Film Unit, 1937.

37 M. E. F. Jones, 'The Economic History of the Regional Problem in Britain'.

38 Associated Newspapers Ltd, *Sell to Britain Through the Daily Mail*, London 1935, p. 33.

39 Associated Newspapers Ltd, *Sell to Britain Through the Daily Mail*, p. 35.

40 Associated Newspapers Ltd, *Sell to Britain Through the Daily Mail*, p. 36.

41 It was stated that County estimates have been arrived at as the results of grading most of the large cities, going through each city and town street by street.

42 A formula that assumes 80% ownership in 'A' Class, 57% ownership in 'B' Class and 5% in 'C' Class produces an accurate prediction for each of the Home Counties in 1935 (Correlation = 0.93). The result is not sensitive to changes in ownership in 'A'. This percentage for 'A' needs to be set at a level that produces a lower result for 'B' but does not assume every wealthy house had a car. It could

be set between 70% to 90% without much change to the result of 'B'. Although the ownership in 'C' could go as high as 10% before producing illogical results (i.e. too many cars), this does not seem likely on the basis of the definition of 'C' Class. The result is also not sensitive to a possible miscategorisation of houses between classes by Associated Newspapers.

43   As a proxy for total car use these statistics have a number of limitations. First, the SMMT records ignore car purchases made in the many car showrooms in Central London by those who lived in the inner Home Counties. This may understate new car purchases in the suburban Home Counties by as much as 20%. Second, the ratio between new cars and total cars is likely to vary between richer and poorer boroughs. At a county level this is generally about 1:6, but very poor boroughs would have a much lower ratio of new cars than average, and rich boroughs a higher ratio, see 1936 survey of age of cars in Middlesex, Society of Motor Manufacturers and Traders, *The Motor Industry of Great Britain 1937.*

44   Society of Motor Manufacturers and Traders, *Home Counties Registrations*, London 1934.

45   P. Oliver et al., *Dunroamin*, p. 12. See Appendix for the calculation of this figure.

46   1931 Census, Employment Tables.

47   A measure for the level of suburbanisation can be found in the national census, by calculating the relative increase in the number of households in each London borough between 1921 and 1938. A partial census taken in 1938 for the issue of identity cards provides overall population numbers, but not the number of households. This figure can be derived by assuming that average household size (which would be fairly stable over an eight-year period) had not changed since 1931.

48   See calculation in Appendix.

49   A. A. Jackson, *The Middle Classes, 1900–1950*, Nairn 1991, p. 108.

50   A. A. Jackson, *Semi-detached London*, p. 150.

51   See, for example, *The Homefinder Small Property Guide*, January 1933.

52   K. A. Morrison and J. Minnis, *Carscapes*, London 2012, p. 90.

53   *The Homefinder Small Property Guide*, January 1933.

54   *The Homefinder Small Property Guide*, January 1936.

55   *The Homefinder Small Property Guide*, January 1939.

56   A. A. Jackson, *Semi-detached London*, p. 151.

57   Royal Borough of Kingston-upon-Thames planning records from maps.king ston.gov.uk [accessed 1 November 2011].

58   M. de Certeau, *The Practice of Everyday Life*, London 1984, p. 117.

59   H. Lefebvre, *The Production of Space*, London 1991, p. 96.

60   H. Lefebvre, *The Production of Space*, p. 97.

3

'In the joyous rush' – Bicycles and motorcycles

The car had engrained itself into the sensibilities of suburban London by the mid-1930s, but, in parallel, two other stories were in play. The bicycle, a late Victorian and Edwardian craze, began a journey, after the First World War, towards a ubiquitous involvement in suburban life by the 1930s. In a similar way to the car, it benefited from mass-production and lowered prices resulting in a rapid growth in ownership as the 1930s progressed.

The motorcycle had a different story. Adopted by male riders who had used it in the Great War, the motorcycle became the dominant form of independent powered mobility in the early 1920s. By 1925, it had been overtaken by the car, and became increasingly déclassé in the nuanced world of London's suburbs. By the end of the interwar period, the motor-cycle had become confined to being a form of independent motor transport for those who could not afford a car, but was also an object of enthusiasm for members of suburban motorcycling clubs.

In contrast to the car, neither the bicycle nor the motorcycle was seen as an object of middle-class desire. As a consequence, it is harder to recover archive material on the way people felt about cycling and motorcycling, compared to cars, because the experience was either so quotidian that it was unremarkable or because it was a working-class preoccupation that did not generate much literary interest. Nevertheless, this chapter considers the world of bicycles and motorcycles in suburban London using a wide variety of sources, to show how significant they were in everyday life.

Cycling in interwar suburbia

In 1929, there were somewhere between six and eight million bicycles in the United Kingdom, meaning that roughly two out of three households owned a bicycle.[1] This accords with one memory of life in Middlesex between the wars that 'most families seemed to own some sort of bicycle'.[2] It was difficult, even then, to calculate exactly how many bicycles there were in Britain. They were not licensed in the manner of cars and motor-cycles; it was known how many bicycles were manufactured, exported and imported, but it was difficult to calculate how many had been scrapped. As a consequence, it is impossible to analyse with any accuracy the distribution of bicycles in London's suburbia.

The bicycle entered the interwar period as a mass-produced product of, mostly, Midlands factories and was sturdy, heavy and un-geared. During the later 1920s and 1930s, bicycles became cheaper, lighter and more sophisticated with the introduction of Sturmey-Archer three-speed gears and Derailleur five-speed gears.[3] Price reductions met with the rising incomes of suburban London to encourage cycle adoption. An analysis of bicycle prices shows that both cheap and mid-range bicycles experienced a 20–25 per cent reduction in price between 1928 and 1934, just when the economic conditions in suburban London were beginning to improve.[4] At the same time, annual production of bicycles for the domestic market dramatically increased from 400,000 in 1927 to 1.6 million by 1936.[5]

These increases are reflected in the information on London's suburban cycling available from the Ministry of Transport (MoT)'s traffic surveys, which collected statistics on the number of bicycles passing survey points on many of London's roads for August 1931, 1935 and 1938. These surveys demonstrate the extent of cycling practices and the large increase in the use of bicycles between 1931 and 1935. Summing 44 survey points in suburban London shows that a daily average for August of 71,500 bicycles was observed in 1931 and an average of 151,000 at exactly the same points in 1935. This indicates that suburban cycling more than doubled in this five-year period. Some roads in suburban London experienced an intense change in the number of cyclists. The A412 near Watford showed a three-fold increase. This may have had to do with an improvement in the road surfaces, or because this was a good route to the countryside, a preoccupation with suburban cyclists at this time. For example, *Cycling* magazine reported that cyclists extensively used the A111 road from Palmers Green to Potters Bar.[6]

Cycling can be divided into two distinct types of activity, first to satisfy quotidian needs, going to work, to school or to the shops and second, for sport, leisure and fun. Recovery of quotidian cycling is generally confined to oral history exercises rather than through written sources, for example, cycling to the shops was such a universal and commonplace activity that recording it for posterity would have seemed pointless. The Mass Observation archive, for example, holds only one instance on cycling and that is about the connection between cycling and anti-fascism in the Clarion Cycling Club. Significantly, in his teaching, the historian E. H. Carr used the topic of his students' journey by bicycle to his lecture to provide an example of something that would not be recorded for later historical analysis.[7]

Cycling to work

For the working and lower middle classes, cycling to work was one of the most common everyday uses of a bicycle. One cycling evangelist, who was rather apologetic about the bicycle in an era of fast transport, advanced its benefits:

> it is ideal for travelling to and from work, for business journeys involving calls from house to house or shop to shop, for all kinds of public servants and for everyone who in the first place, has not the means or inclination to drive a motor, or who in the second place, requires something that can be picked up and be always ready under all conditions, and something that the user can step from on a second's inspiration, make a call … be off again without trouble.[8]

Working-class men were prepared to cycle long distances in search for a job. Weightman and Humphries, using oral history sources, record long-distance commuting from Bow to the new Hoover Factory in Perivale, a return journey of some forty miles each day.[9] Juliet Gardiner records Bill Waghorn, who commuted from Becontree in the Essex suburbs to the Isle of Dogs. He recalled that he 'ended up cycling the fourteen-mile round trip to and from work … Lots of people travelled to work along the A13 and in the winter it was bitter cold … when a lorry came along all the cyclists would crowd behind it, jockeying for position as it gave us protection from the wind.'[10] My father-in law recalled that when he was a builder's clerk in Sydenham in the mid-1930s he would take the wages, on his bicycle, to building sites as far away as Tottenham, a round trip of thirty-two miles.

Pooley and Turnbull have shown that, in London, only 6 per cent of commuting was done by bicycle in the 1920s and 1930s, but for the poorer occupants of London's suburbs the bicycle provided a far cheaper and flexible means of commuting than public transport.[11]

Cycling clubs in suburbia

Club cycling was a popular activity in the interwar period. Martin Pugh has described how cycling epitomised the connection between the 'vogue for healthy athleticism and love of the countryside'.[12] John Stevenson considered cycling to be 'one of the most popular mass recreations of the inter-war years'.[13] London cycling clubs organised rides out from the suburbs into the countryside and also took part in track events at Herne Hill in South London. *Cycling* magazine regularly reported the activities of suburban cycle clubs such as Ealing, Crouch Hill, Southgate, Harrow and Malden Paragon.[14]

Recovering the history of suburban cycling clubs is dependent on them either depositing their records with a public archive or, alternatively, publishing a formal history. An example of the former is the Surrey Bicycle Club, based in South London. This was a small-scale, closed, invitation-only club, attempting to provide a more personal experience than the popular open membership clubs. It attracted its original members by the circulation of a letter that stated:

> A proposal has been made that a private cycling club should be formed amongst certain members of the CTC [Cyclists' Touring Club, the dominant national cycling club with many local federated clubs] who, while fully in sympathy with the District Association movement, do not care for the large crowds which are normally inseparable from these institutions. The club would be concerned with the purely social aspects of cycling and membership would be strictly limited.[15]

Suburban cycling clubs either had their meeting place at a local pub or hall or alternatively, nominated an attractive country pub in the Home Counties as their headquarters. The Surrey Bicycle Club chose the White Hart at Bletchingly near Redhill in Surrey for their first meeting and annual, as they described it, 'saturnalia'.

The club's objects were clear, albeit with a Pickwickian flavour:

> To promote the principles of good fellowship and the cause of cycling, and to encourage the social, convivial and cultural interests of the members. It shall be the aim and obligation of every member, without undue self-assertion or strain, to make his contribution to the atmosphere of good fellowship at the meetings of the club and in particular at the annual dinner.

Its membership was set at 25 in number and was 'restricted to men only of good address. The term men in this context shall not include women.'[16]

The club's minute book gives the names and addresses of its members in its early years and thus provides useful information on the wealth and status of its members based on the type of houses they occupied. The members were almost all based in the outer ring of suburbia, just at the point where new housing was expanding London's borders. The members lived in suburban Surrey in Norbury, Croydon, Wallington, Colliers Wood, Mitcham and Kingston. Invariably they lived modestly in streets of Victorian and Edwardian terraced houses and, in one case, in North Cheam, in a smaller mock-Tudor semi-detached house that must have been very new, in 1933.[17]

The types of houses lived in by these cycling enthusiasts positions them as members of the suburban lower middle class. The objects of the club were pretentious, proposing members of 'good address', suggesting that cyclists from working-class backgrounds would be excluded. The themes of *Diary of a Nobody* are unconsciously repeated here.[18] Civil service and bank clerks, teachers and salesmen joined together in the fellowship of a bicycle club that excluded the class immediately below them, but with aspirations to ape the mentality of their social superiors. A photograph from the club's archive shows club members stopping for a smoke on a country outing with a member of the club flicking a 'V' sign to the photographer indicating an informality that would not have been approved of in a larger club and a suggestion that their aspirations for a certain type of member had not been met.[19]

In contrast with the Surrey Bicycle Club, the Catford Cycling Club was a much older and larger organisation formed at the height of the first cycling boom of the 1880s. It is likely that its wider membership included working-class cyclists, just the sort of people that the Surrey Bicycle Club was seeking to exclude. The club was committed to the 'promotion of sport, road riding, racing, touring and good fellowship'.[20]

This set of objects was an accurate description of the activities of the many cycling clubs that grew with the expanding suburbs before and after the First World War. A good example of the club's activities was the Annual Hill-Climbing Championship of England. In 1931, this event was run for the thirty-seventh time.[21] This climb was undertaken on Brasted Hill near Sevenoaks and was a major public event with 'between six to seven thousand spectators' present lining the narrow country road.[22] Pathé filmed the event for a newsreel, and showed an excited crowd who shouted encouragement to the riders in working-class London accents, suggesting they had followed the competitors out from the suburbs into the Kent countryside.[23]

3   Southern section of the Cyclists' Touring Club at Mitcham, 1931
J. A. Hampton/Topical Press Agency/Getty Images

Another important activity of this and other clubs was the club run, a mapped long-distance route cycled in groups into the countryside of Sussex and Kent at weekends. In 1933, the club captain reported on a run to Alfriston in Sussex. It is clear that good fellowship was in strong supply with the team of cyclists getting up to a regular 30 mph, exhausting themselves on the long journey and one of their number getting involved in an accident. The riders would look up occasionally from their drop handlebars to admire the beautiful countryside.[24]

The role of cycling clubs in providing a regular and organised link between suburbia and the countryside is intriguing. Of course, cycling, like motoring, was something that could be undertaken in an informal manner, but the club formalised the connection between suburbia and the country.

Cycling as suburban modernity

Suburban cycling was not a new practice of the interwar period; it had been popular in suburban London long before the First World War. What was new was the sheer ubiquity and widespread use of the bicycle in suburban homes and the inter-operation of cyclists with cars and the new arterial roads. This conjunction can be clearly seen in an advertisement for Currys, one of the leading bicycle retailers of the 1930s. In an advertisement from 1936, prospective buyers are shown as smartly dressed and middle-class in appearance and their cycling is presented as modern and embracing the technologies of the arterial road. Currys' head office on the Great West Road is shown as up to date and sophisticated, the road outside dominated by cyclists coming home to the mother store, in a world independent of cars, who are in this picture shown as marginal and faint elements.[25]

This engagement with the road was also exemplified by the life of a keen, perhaps even obsessive, suburban cyclist, John Sowerby, who, unusually, recorded his everyday suburban cycling. One reviewer of Sowerby's published diaries noted this unusual subject matter:

> If Mr. Sowerby had not kept a diary this book could hardly have been written, for it is a record of events and observations so little out of the ordinary that the unaided memory would have not retained them. Indeed on a cursory and inconsiderate view they may not seem worth printing.[26]

John Sowerby, now an obscure and forgotten figure, was the *nom de plume* of Percival Bennett, an eccentric man and enthusiastic cyclist. His diary was published to some acclaim, firstly in the literary magazine *The London Mercury* in 1938 and then in book form in *I Got on My Bicycle*, which was published in 1939.[27] Sowerby's diary of his daily cycling in London's suburbia and surrounding countryside had been first shown to *The London Mercury* by his psychiatrist.[28] Sowerby was a very small and slight man, who had suffered from TB during the First World War and then, contrary to medical advice, had continued his habit of daily long-distance cycling. He lodged with his sister in Tolworth near Surbiton, spending much of his time living in her garden shed. It is a nice thought for this book that Alan Jackson, who lived in the same suburb as Sowerby, might have regularly seen this strange man cycling down the arterial road.

Sowerby made daily excursions of two types: first, a series of local errands to visit nearby Kingston for food, pipe tobacco and spare parts for his bicycle from a cycle dealer, and, second, exploration of the new arterial roads that took him through the suburbs into the Home Counties' countryside. He kept his diary on a daily basis, initially without any thought about the possibility of publication. After he became known on the literary scene, he was aware that his thoughts would reach a wider audience, but it does not seem to have occasioned any moderation or change in the tone of his writing. He committed to public inspection his thoughts on his loneliness and shared a simple sense of humour with his readers.[29]

Sowerby cut a lonely figure on his solitary cycle rides. He was always looking for someone to share his journeys with, but was not a member of a cycle club. He explained that this was a result of his low speed; younger more modern cyclists raced past him. His eccentric and unstylish appearance may also have put off other cyclists: 'My kind of weather, so out came the "shorts" and the green eyeshade … small pullover and beret in case it turned cold'.[30]

He was not afraid to describe the loneliness of his cycle rides in his diaries. His solitary world is evident in his personification of his bicycle to show that it suffered as much as he did on their long cycle rides over the Surrey Hills: 'The poor bike suffers the most: it is the dearest friend I have, but I show it no mercy on the hills'.[31]

Unlike most cyclists, Sowerby did not look backwards to the halcyon days of cycling before the arrival of large-scale car ownership. He viewed the new arterial roads as exciting and believed that cars were there to be enjoyed as fellow travellers on the modern road. As he put it: 'The more poetically minded will rave about quiet lanes and byways … but give me the main roads and great highways to really enjoy cycling'.[32]

As Sowerby travelled round the network of London's arterial roads he described his feelings for each one he visited. As he was perched precariously on a bicycle he was particularly attuned to the kinaesthetic quality of this experience. He was probably much more aware of speed and danger than the occupants of the cars. For example, on the A4:

> Espy the Bath Road in the distance, looking like some toy track with many toy motors and lorries rushing up and down it (and its ribbon development). Got on out to it to join in the joyous rush with the traffic (needs much care too in emerging on this any rate you like road). They all think they are on Brooklands track.[33]

Further north, he showed his appreciation for the newly built environment: 'I gained the North Circular … What a road! Full of interest, circles or roundabouts, signals, the home of well known wares and commodities. Square bridges, arched bridges. Many great arteries intersecting here and there.'[34]

His relationship with cars provides an insight into how an elderly cyclist could appreciate the modern world of cars and driving. He imbued cars with a sense of personality embracing their modernity but simultaneously humanising them. For example he recalls:

Passing a badly smashed up car which had been pulled off the road and abandoned … it always hurts me to see a thing that is a marvel of mechanical ingenuity … all smashed up and made useless … Many cars take my side of the road and drive me into the gutter and over the gratings there and I'm horrified and shocked at their lack of manners … but when I see them broken up I forget all that and only feel sorry for them.[35]

In his love for and obsession with the arterial road, Sowerby embraced on a direct and daily basis the suburban modernity of an assembly of road, car, bicycle and cyclist. Perhaps most cyclists didn't notice or care about the arterial road in this way, but some would have identified with this connection between cycling and the modern world.

The nature of cycling is such that it could never fully encompass the increasingly domesticated qualities of modern life. In a 1930s saloon car, the driver was isolated from the elements and was located in a comfy, suburbanised world where the sensations of speed and danger were attenuated; this is discussed in more detail in Chapter 8. This is never the case for cyclists, who are always aware of the elements and seasons and whose appreciation for the landscape they pass through is amplified through their direct engagement. One cyclist recalled, 'we coped with wind and rain, frost and fog, sun and snow. I remember leading a car one foggy night whose driver could not see anything beyond me and my bike.'[36] Even Sowerby could be separated from his beloved roads by the forces of nature. 'A howling raging gale today … after setting out this afternoon down the bypass and getting quite out of breath battling against the wind and driving rain, I threw in the towel.'[37]

Cycling networks

Cyclists may have felt, like Sowerby, that cycling was an independent and rather lonely pursuit, but in reality it involved a modern complex network of roads, cycle paths, cycling clubs, shops and cafés. Chapter 5 describes in detail the nature of arterial roads and their associated cycle paths that provided a direct connection for cyclists to ride from the suburbs into the countryside on a smooth and well-engineered surface. This new technological development also made for a more efficient connection between points on a new network of cycling infrastructure.

Sowerby was dependent on his local cycling shop to provide the spare parts necessary to keep his bicycle on the road. His diary features regular trips to Kingston, often to face the disappointing news that spares had not arrived. As with other types of shops in the 1930s, bicycles had begun to fall under the domination of the multiple store. Sainsbury's and International Stores were dominant multiple grocers in the suburban high street, and similarly, Halfords and Currys ruled the roost in bicycles and cycle accessories. Both shops had signalled how modern they were by dropping their old-fashioned apostrophes. Currys had, for example, a network of over two hundred cycle shops in Britain. In the 1930s, Currys was, solely, a retail organisation, having ceased bicycle production in the previous decade.

Currys and Halfords did not have it all their own way, as each small town in the London suburbs still had a good number of independent cycle stores. Sowerby had his unnamed favoured store, but could have chosen from fourteen competing shops within a short ride. This phenomenon was noted in an oral history of Middlesex before the war: 'in 1939 cycle shops were as commonplace as petrol stations are today'.[38]

Sowerby and his fellow cyclists met, socialised and rested in a network of cyclists' cafés on trunk roads where suburbia merged with Home Counties countryside. These rest stops allowed cyclists to make long journeys, and acted as a meeting point for club runs. Sowerby was always a solitary cyclist, but took a vicarious pleasure from sitting near other groups of cyclists. For example, he enjoyed a 'Super tea hut at Hooley. Cycles all over the show outside … sit with a crowd of London boy cyclists who like thousands more are making their way home from the coast.'[39] Back in suburbia he visited Ben's Tea House: 'The usual mob of cyclists in and out at Ben's. Mostly the speed merchants of the Bath Road use Ben's Tea House. It has a proper cycling atmosphere.'[40]

Gender and class in suburban cycling

'My husband got a car very soon for his business, which was a great excitement, but *bicycles* were the means of locomotion for me and the children.'[41] This record from an oral history project was taken from a memory of 1950, but is also probably representative of most men's attitude towards women drivers in the 1930s. There is little in the way of comprehensive statistics on the number of women driving, but Sean O'Connell tells us that, in 1933, women held 12 per cent of all driving licences.[42] This disparity was even more pronounced for motorcycles; Steve Koerner concludes that only 3.5 per cent of motorcyclists were women.[43] During the week, from Monday to Friday when her husband was at work, the average woman had little access to a motor vehicle and was reliant on either public transport or a bicycle.

This challenges the ungendered conclusion arrived at in Chapter 2 that demonstrated the availability of motoring to the suburban middle classes in Greater London. In reality, the use of this new independent mobility was highly gendered and reinforced the male domination of suburban technology just at the point when women were taking advantage of a more liberal and modern view of their role. As is often pointed out, there were many famous women drivers in both life and literature in the 1930s, but their fame was derived from how unusual they were. The norm for female independent mobility was, in reality, the bicycle.

For children, the bicycle also played a vital part in providing them with speedy independent mobility. I have emphasised how many cars the wealthier suburbs had access to in the 1930s, but cars would have driven far less frequently down the streets of the poorer suburbs, providing a safe place for children to cycle. One interwar suburban cyclist recalls his experience in Ruislip Manor:

> It was a time when schoolboys exhibited a prowess in controlling and riding their machines which would be impossible on our roads today. A whistling paperboy riding 'no-handed' but in complete command of his bicycle was a frequent sight. Also not unusual was the 'three boy bike' with one on the handlebars, one in a standing position and pedalling, with the third lad sitting on the saddle and urging the 'engine room' to pedal faster.[44]

Chapter 9 shows though that, when encountering fast motor traffic, young cyclists were particularly vulnerable in their encounters with cars.

Bicycle usage in London's suburbia the early 1930s increased twofold. It might have been expected that the poorer eastern suburbs would have had a greater proportional increase in cycling use, but this was not the case. Evidence of the importance of the bicycle in poorer areas can be seen from an analysis of the location of London's suburban cycling clubs. As has been shown, these clubs provided a focal point for the more gregarious type of cyclist. London was a centre of cycling club activity; David Patton records that 'nearly a third of all the cycling clubs in the country were within a ten mile radius of *Cycling*'s [London] printing plant'.[45] Mapping the addresses of the secretaries of London's cycling clubs reveals a wide distribution across London's suburbs. Superimposing this on to the map shown in

Figure 1, which sets out the areas with the highest car use, is revealing.[46] It can be seen that areas with low car usage were most likely to be the sites of cycling clubs. This is not altogether surprising. As the fashion for cars and their associated status arrived in the wealthier suburbs, attention turned away from cycling clubs.

Cycling was the most important form of independent mobility for the suburban working and lower middle classes. For poorer Londoners, bicycles provided a colder but more flexible and cheaper option than the train, Tube or the tram. For lower-middle-class cyclists, the motivation for cycling may have differed – a trip to the shops or a pleasant trip to the countryside – but the vehicle was the same.

Motorcycling in suburbia

As has been shown, cycling enjoyed a boom in the 1930s encouraged by lower prices and its association with the preoccupation with fitness and outdoor life of the period. This was not generally the case with motorcycles. In the period from 1924 to 1936 there was an overall 12.4 per cent decline in the number of motorcycle licences issued in England.[47] The reasons behind this decline were quite complex, but had two main components that worked in opposite directions. These were first, and most important, the replacement of motorcycles with new small cars and, second, the acquisition of motorcycles by working-class buyers using the new spending power brought about by the economic recovery of the 1930s.

There is little statistical information on motorcycle use in interwar suburbia, but there is a proxy available, which is motorcycle use in the County of London and in its surrounding Home Counties: Essex, Kent, Middlesex and Surrey. These counties were, save for Essex, at the forefront of car adoption and even Essex had more cars than motorcycles by 1927. There were 120,000 motorcycles in use in London and these four inner Home Counties in 1934, compared to 350,000 cars and perhaps as many as one million bicycles. By the end of the decade, the car and bicycle would become even more dominant.

Statistics are available that allow us to compare the Home Counties' use of motorcycles in a way that can show at a crude level how each county was responding to the changing patterns of motorcycle use brought about by the increasing dominance of the car and increasing wealth. It is possible, for example, to compare the rate of growth of motorcycle use for each county and also the changing adoption rate for motorcycles per household.

In 1934, in England, there was one motorcycle for every eighteen households and an 18 per cent decline in motorcycle use in the previous eight years. It would be fair to say that the motorcycle was not central to interwar life, and interest in it, as a primary means of transport, was already past. There was some variation to that general state of affairs in each of the suburbanised Home Counties. As might be expected from its role in the early adoption of cars, Surrey was an outlier. The number of motorcycles had declined by 23 per cent over the eight-year period, but this county was still in the second quartile for usage. This is a reflection of early lower-middle-class wealth in Surrey, where the motorcycle was a cheap and effective means of transport for those who could not afford expensive hand-made cars. As cars became cheaper, motorcyclists switched from two wheels to four. With rising incomes, those just below them could afford to buy a motorcycle, but not a car, so continued to fill some of the decline with their purchases. At the other extreme, Kent saw an unusual net growth in motorcycle use of some 2 per cent and quite high adoption rates. This is a reflection, perhaps, of the slower uptake in cars in this county and a strong motorcycle culture resulting from motorcycle manufacturers such as Matchless and AJS who were based in suburban Kent in Plumstead.[48] Essex saw both a strong decline in motorcycle use and low adoption rates. Essex was the slowest county to adopt the car, and these statistics may suggest that the division in income in this county was such that the small propor-tion of wealthy citizens bought motorcycles early in the period and many of them swapped to cars, but the group immediately below them did not have the income to support a motorcycle purchase.

Motorcycles, light cars and suburban disdain

The choice of switching from motorcycle to car became more straightfor-ward after the development of the cheap light car that was described in Chapter 2. Car firms, such as Austin, deliberately took on the motorcycle market:

> In 1922 Herbert Austin gave the first indication that the equation was going to change. Significantly and with more than a little audacity, he announced his plans for a light car at the annual dinner of the Birmingham motor cycle club. Austin Motors was, he declared, in the process of designing a

small-sized low-powered automobile, which would later become known as the Austin Seven and was scheduled to go into production. Austin was supremely confident of its future and predicted his new car would 'knock the sidecar combination into a cocked hat'.[49]

This was particularly true for the suburban areas of the Home Counties. It was here that a widely held disdain for the dirty motorcycle was at its highest. For example, one trade writer thought that it was 'the suburbanite, not too sure of his social standing, who is a bit doubtful about what the neighbours are thinking if he is seen going about by motor cycle instead of a small car'.[50] V. Addenbrooke, a reporter of the motorcycling scene of the late 1920s, suggested that travelling salesmen who rode motorcycles attracted disdain because they were not using a car.

Car owners also looked on motorcyclists with disdain: one writer remembered that:

> Nobody loved the motorcyclist with or without a sidecar, … leather-helmeted, goggled, gauntleted, crouched demoniacally over his handlebars, noisy oily, smelly, dirty, he was a figure of scorn to his financial superiors, who imagined that his sole purpose in life was to terrify them.[51]

Addenbrooke suggested that the motorcycle's reputation for dirt was misplaced, 'A portion of the lay press has done much to paint the motor cycle as a smelly and dirty machine, only capable of making a noise and covering its owner with oil and mud'.[52] A more honest appreciation of these characteristics is found in an advertisement in a motorcycle magazine: 'Where there's a bike there's dirt – use Chemico Hand Soap'.[53]

Steve Koerner has shown how pricing as well as disdain drove the move away from motorcycles. This is well represented in his table (Table 4). As can be seen from the first column, the price of new motorcycles increased

Table 4   Comparison of prices between motorcycles and second-hand cars

Sales season	New 350cc motorcycle and sidecar	Price of a two-year old 8hp car
1929/30	£63.30	£81.20
1932/33	£64.70	£73.10
1934/35	£66.00	£66.10
1935/36	£68.10	£66.60

S. Koerner, 'Four Wheels Good, Two Wheels Bad' in D. Thoms, L. Holden, T. Claydon (eds), *The Car and Popular Culture in the 20th Century*, p. 169.

gradually in the 1930s, just at the time when mass production and new welding and painting techniques were rapidly reducing the price of cars (see Chapter 2). This was a reflection of the small-scale manufacturing and diffuse ownership of motorcycle production.

Christopher Potter has described how interwar motorcyclists could be categorised as racers, tourists or bike-to-work types.[54] As the 1930s progressed, middle-class motorists exchanged the motorcycle for the car, leaving it to the working-class and lower-middle-class rider who could not yet make the move upwards. One notable exception to this general trend was the people who owned a motorcycle for the high levels of excitement and fun that it provided. T. E. Lawrence, one of the most famous motorcyclists of the interwar period recorded in 1927:

> The greatest pleasure of my recent life has been speed on the road. The bike would do 100 mph but I'm not a racing man. It was my satisfaction to purr along gently between 60 and 70 mph ... that's a thing that the slow coach will never feel. It is the reward of speed. I could write for hours on the lustfulness of moving swiftly.[55]

Lawrence also enjoyed the fast speeds available by riding on arterial roads:

> The Great North Road (what a dream, what a drunkenness of delight of a name!) is as you know very wide smooth and straight ... traffic this morning was mainly Morris Oxfords doing their thirty up or down. Boa [his bike] and myself were pioneers of the new order, which will do seventy or more between point and point. Like all pioneers we incurred odium. Boa leapt past them, a rattle and roar and glitter of polished nickel with a blue button on top.[56]

Class and motorcycle clubs

As with cycling, the employment of the motorcycle for racing and touring was organised through clubs, and these were seen throughout suburban London. A female writer on the pleasures of motorcycling described how:

> Motorcycle clubs are to be found in practically every district of the kingdom now and they are a tremendous boon to all motorcyclists. The motorcycle club fills the great need of the social side. The subscription varies from 7/6d to 1 guinea.[57]

An analysis of the distribution of motorcycle clubs in suburban London in the 1930s shows that, in Kent and Surrey, clubs were located nearer the inner ring of suburbia. In Middlesex, home to new cheaper suburbs, the clubs were located within the outer ring of suburbia built in the 1920s and 1930s. This would suggest that lower-middle-class and respectable working-class motorcyclists formed these clubs. As was seen in the example of the Surrey Bicycle Club, it is possible to assess this by looking at the type of houses their club secretaries lived in.[58] The addresses of the secretaries to suburban clubs demonstrate their lower-middle-class orientation; they typically lived in small terraced houses or in new semi-detached houses on housing estates.

Some motorcycle clubs had originated from a special interest section of an older cycling club and they shared the cyclists' interests in what they called ride outs and social outings. *The Motor Cycle* magazine regularly recorded the activities of suburban clubs, and those of the Carshalton Motorcycle Club provide a good example of how they were not welcomed by respectable new suburban residents:

> A classic pillion event, starting at Rose Hill filling station to Sunningdale Avenue. In theory, a brake and acceleration test were to have been held here, but there was a spot of disagreement with local inhabitants, who attempted to bar an open and apparently public road. Finish at the Greyhound Hotel Carshalton, where a little tea was taken by riders.[59]

A more ambitious programme, 'The London Rally of Motorists', was organised by the North London Motorcycle Club at Alexandra Park, 'a pleasure resort' in North London which every year drew large bank holiday crowds. It featured:

> Gymkhana events [which] were well supported, over 560 rides for one competition. With the exception of a motor cycle football match practically every kind of gymkhana event was staged. The event of the day was undoubtedly the motor cycle steeplechase confined to solo machines. Riders started singly and had to proceed round the cinder and grass enclosure, circle a tree, and complete the circuit after climbing a grass bank. The riders' antics on the corners and grass bank caused much excitement and amusement, whilst 'Southport' cornering brought forward gasps of amazement.[60]

In this way, the private activities of motorcycle club members were transformed into a public display of modern technology, comparable to air displays or motor shows.

Conclusion

The bicycle was a fundamental element of suburban mobility between the wars; almost every home had access to one, as prices came down steeply in real terms over the period. They were used for everyday trips to the shops and to school, and also formed the basis for one of the most popular forms of outdoor activity, informally with friends or as part of one of the many cycling clubs of the day. These clubs provided association and fun for largely lower-middle-class cyclists, just the sort of people who might have been thought by intellectuals to live lives as undifferentiated as their suburban housing. For women and for working-class men, both of whom, for different reasons, had less opportunity to drive a car, the humble bicycle transformed suburban life. Here was an unexpected modernity. The car dominates our thoughts on what it was to be modern in the 1920s and 1930s, but the bicycle was important to more people. Working-class men would use their bicycles to allow them to work at long distances from their suburban homes, either in the centre of London or, perhaps, in the new light industrial factories of the western suburbs, which provided many new job opportunities in the 1930s. Bicycles provided both working-class and middle-class women with mobility. Middle-class women may have lived in households with a car, but were far less likely to hold a licence or to be the main driver than their husbands. The bicycle was Victorian in origin, but changes in its mass production and distribution enabled suburban mobilities in this period.

John Sowerby was a strange, sad and lonely man whose legacy was a diary that defied the idea that suburban cycling was an activity that was so dull that to record it was pointless. In his strangely affective manner he was able to convey the deep connections between the cyclist, the bicycle and the new arterial roads of suburban London. Cycling in all weathers, he revelled in its modernity, in his appreciation of the road surface, his excitement at motorisation or the sense of wonder that he conveyed in seeing new arterial road factories. Sowerby was an unusual person, and it would be foolish to generalise from his very individual experiences, but others will have shared his sense of wonder in this most mundane of transport technologies.

T. E. Lawrence, before his death in a motorcycling accident, provided a vision of how this form of high-speed transport could be seen as independent, manly and dashing. The suburban experience was rather different. Use of motorcycles declined in suburban London throughout the period and had been overtaken in popularity by the car by the late 1920s. As soon as a family could afford one of the new small cars, they bought one, abandoning the motorcycle and sidecar for ever. Club members continued their use of motorcycles for runs to the countryside, which, as an enthusiasm, was socially permissible, but everyday use was met with increasing disdain in suburbia.

Moving in the opposite direction to this general middle-class trend, working-class riders bought motorcycles in the 1920s and 1930s when they could afford to. Motorcycles provided working men with the possibilities of fast travel that allowed them to work at some distance from their home, provided the thrill of speed and produced a specific modernity in their lives.

Notes

1 British Cycle and Motor Cycle Manufacturers' and Traders' Union, *Review of the British Cycle and Motor Cycle Industry*, Coventry 1929.

2 Middlesex Federation of Women's Institutes, *Middlesex Within Living Memory*, Newbury 1996, p. 46.

3 P. Dodge, *The Bicycle*, London 1996.

4 British Cycle and Motor Cycle Manufacturers' and Traders' Union, *Review of the British Cycle and Motor Cycle Industry*.

5 A. Miliward, *Factors Contributing to the Sustained Success of the UK Cycle Industry 1870–1939*, unpublished thesis, University of Birmingham, 1999, p. 335.

6 TNA MT/44/16; *Cycling*, 20 May 1936.

7 E. H. Carr, *What Is History?*, Basingstoke, 2001, p. 6.

8 Anonymous, *Cycling Manual*, London 1937, p. 1.

9 G. Weightman and S. Humphries, *The Making of Modern London 1914–1939*, London 1984, p. 75.

10 J. Gardiner, *The Thirties: An Intimate History of Britain*, London 2011, p. 276.

11 Data provided by Colin Pooley and derived from a national sample of 12,439 journeys to work taken from 1,834 individual life histories. For more details of the source see C. Pooley and J. Turnbull, 'The Journey to Work: a Century of Change', *Area*, 31, 1999, pp. 282–292; C. Pooley and J. Turnbull, 'Modal Choice and Modal Change: the Journey to Work in Britain Since 1890', *Journal of Transport Geography*, 8:1, 2000, pp. 11–24.

12 M. Pugh, *'We Danced All Night': A Social History of Britain Between the Wars*, London 2008, p. 237.

13 J. Stevenson, *British Society, 1914–45*, Harmondsworth 1984, p. 392.

14 *Cycling*, 25 March 1936.

15 Letter from F. Stevenson, 8 November, 1933, Surrey Bicycle Club Minute Book, Modern Records Centre, MSS 328/N9/1/1.

16 Surrey Bicycle Club Minute Book, Modern Records Centre, MSS 328/N9/1/1.
17 Based on an inspection of typical housing stock for each road shown on Google Maps, maps.google.com [accessed 2 July 2012].
18 G. Grossmith and W. Grossmith, *The Diary of a Nobody*, London 1892.
19 Surrey Bicycle Club Photograph Album, courtesy of Modern Records Centre, MSS 328/N9/12/1. The 'V' sign in English culture at this time was an unambiguous invitation to f**k off.
20 E. J. Southcott (ed.), *The History of the Catford Cycling Club*, London 1937.
21 This is still being run as of 2012, the 117th occasion.
22 E. J. Southcott (ed.), *The History of the Catford Cycling Club*, p. 413.
23 British Pathé newsreel, *37th Annual Hill Climb Championship 1931*, 1931, Film ID: 871.30.
24 E. J. Southcott (ed.), *The History of the Catford Cycling Club*, p. 432.
25 *The Cyclist*, 20 May 1936.
26 *The Manchester Guardian*, 11 Aug 1939, p. 5.
27 J. Sowerby, *I Got on My Bicycle*, London 1939.
28 I will use 'Sowerby' throughout this book to describe Bennett.
29 J. Sowerby, *I Got on My Bicycle*, p. 98.
30 J. Sowerby, *I Got on My Bicycle*, p. 67.
31 P. Bennett, 'A Cyclist's Diary', *The London Mercury*, May 1938.
32 P. Bennett, 'A Cyclist's Diary', *The London Mercury*, May 1938, p. 25.
33 J. Sowerby, *I Got on My Bicycle*, p. 156.
34 J. Sowerby, *I Got on My Bicycle*, p. 244.
35 J. Sowerby, *I Got on My Bicycle*, p. 106.
36 Middlesex Federation of Women's Institutes, *Middlesex Within Living Memory*, p. 174.
37 J. Sowerby, *I Got on My Bicycle*, p. 250.
38 Middlesex Federation of Women's Institutes, *Middlesex Within Living Memory*, p. 46.
39 J. Sowerby, *I Got on My Bicycle*, p. 64.
40 J. Sowerby, *I Got on My Bicycle*, p. 57.
41 Middlesex Federation of Women's Institutes, *Middlesex Within Living Memory*, p. 42. Author's emphasis.
42 S. O'Connell, *The Car and British Society: Class, Gender and Motoring 1896–1939*, Manchester 1998, p. 52.
43 S. Koerner, 'Whatever Happened to the Girl on the Motorbike? British Women and Motorcycling, 1919 to 1939', *International Journal of Motorcycle Studies*, March 2007.
44 Middlesex Federation of Women's Institutes, *Middlesex Within Living Memory*, p. 46.
45 D. L. Patton, 'Aspects of a Historical Geography of Technology: a Study of Cycling, 1919–1939', *Cycle History – Proceedings of the 5th International Cycle History Conference*, San Francisco, 1995.
46 A. Miliward, *Factors Contributing to the Sustained Success of the UK Cycle Industry*

1870–1939, for cycling club locations, and Society of Motor Manufacturers and Traders, *Home Counties Registrations*, London 1934, for car purchase data.

47 British Cycle and Motor Cycle Manufacturers' and Traders' Union, *Review of the British Cycle and Motor Cycle Industry*, Coventry 1927 and 1937.

48 Motor Cycle Association, *22nd International Bicycle and Motor-cycle Show, Earls Court, Catalogue*, London 1937.

49 S. Koerner, 'Four Wheels Good, Two Wheels Bad' in D. Thoms, L. Holden, T. Claydon (eds), *The Car and Popular Culture in the 20th Century*, Aldershot 1998, p. 155. The 'sidecar' or 'sidecar combination' was a motorcycle with an outriding capsule capable of holding one adult and provided transport for up to three people.

50 Francis Jones, *The Motor Cycle and Cycle Trader*, 7 June 1939.

51 B. T. Cleeve, *1938, A World Vanishing*, London 1982, p. 48.

52 V. Addenbrooke, *Motor-Cycling*, 1928, p. 8.

53 *The Motor Cycle*, 1 May 1930.

54 C. Potter, 'Motorcycle Clubs in Britain During the Inter-war Period, 1919–1939: Their Social and Cultural Importance', *International Journal of Motorcycle Studies*, March 2005.

55 R. Knowles, *Two Superiors: The Motor-cycling Friendship of George Brough & T. E. Lawrence*, Upper Denby 2005, p. 23.

56 R. Knowles, *Two Superiors: The Motor-cycling Friendship of George Brough & T. E. Lawrence*, p. 57.

57 B. Debenham, *Motor-Cycling for Women, etc*, London 1928, p. 71.

58 C. Potter, *An Exploration of Social and Cultural Aspects of Motorcycling During the Inter-war Period*, Unpublished Thesis, University of Northumbria at Newcastle, 2007; Auto-Cycle Union, *Official Pocket Handbook, 1937 [etc.]. Supplementary edition. Guide to Affiliated Clubs and Important Fixtures*, London 1937.

59 *The Motor Cycle*, 1 May 1930.

60 *The Motor Cycle*, 4 June 1925. Southport cornering is likely to be a reference to taking corners at a precarious angle, with a leg extended to balance the bike.

4

Suburban air-mindedness

In comparison to the bicycle, motorcycle and car, the aeroplane might seem to have been a remote and exotic technology in London life, used only by the wealthiest traveller. In fact, flying was much more significant to London's suburban life during the interwar period than it is today. London's suburbs boasted a wide variety of airfields that were home to scheduled services to the continent, the Royal Air Force, famous air pioneers, private flyers and visiting flying circuses.[1] At these airfields, local suburbanites took to the air in five-shilling flights over their homes, or in sightseeing trips over London. They also witnessed air displays and the celebration of Charles Lindbergh's and Amy Johnson's record feats of exploratory air travel. In these ways, suburban Londoners directly and indirectly experienced the modernity of flying.

London's suburban airfields

In London's new suburbs of the 1920s and 1930s, airfields competed for space with housebuilders. They raced each other in moving out from the centre of town, with airfields eventually moving beyond the housing in order to find space for safe flying. The most important London airfields of the period are shown in Table 5.

There were a good number of aircraft manufacturers based in suburban London, and they are some of the most famous names in Britain's aviation history. They provided employment to thousands and gave, through the families of their workers and local residents, a widespread familiarity with aeroplanes and flying that was unusual and particular to western London. The number of workers employed at these factories varied depending on defence considerations. For example, Hawker employed some three

Table 5 London's interwar airfields

Name	Type	Manufacturing base
Brooklands	Private aerodrome	Vickers
Cricklewood	Private aerodrome	Handley-Page
Croydon	Commercial airport	Desoutter
Great West	Private aerodrome	Fairey
Hanworth	Private aerodrome	
Hendon	RAF station	
Heston	Commercial airport	
Hornchurch	RAF station	
Kenley	RAF station	
Northolt	RAF Station	
Stag Lane	Private aerodrome	De Havilland

thousand workers at their Kingston and Brooklands factories in 1919 and the same number again by 1938, but with far fewer during the years of disarmament.[2] Fairey had a large factory in Hayes and at the Great West aerodrome.[3] These factories also evidenced the competition between flying and the development of suburban housing. Handley-Page had a factory and flying field at Cricklewood, but, by 1930, had moved out to Radlett in Hertfordshire.[4] De Havilland moved from its pioneering site at Stag Lane to Hatfield in the mid-1930s.[5] Of the commercial airfields, the two that attracted the most attention and visits from nearby suburban residents were Croydon and Hendon, and this chapter concentrates its attention on them.

Croydon Airport, which began life as a Royal Flying Corps airfield in 1915, grew into one of the world's premier international airports within the next twenty years. From Croydon, London's airport, one could take a scheduled flight to many European cities, but its most famous and glamorous route was the Imperial Airways service that operated between London and Paris. Croydon airport boasted an arrival and departure terminal, an airport hotel and viewing facilities for visitors. Passengers were bussed to and from central London, a quicker journey in the 1930s than we would expect today.[6]

Croydon Airport was located in suburban Surrey, a few miles from the town that shares its name. As the interwar period progressed, the nearby farmland was gradually built over with modest houses, until the airport was surrounded. For example, the borough of Beddington and Wallington, which was nearest to the airport, increased in population from 16,300 in 1921 to 30,900 by mid-1938.[7]

London's first airport was a landmark of interwar modernity and was recorded in gushing tones in many of the books on popular science aimed at older children that are so typical of the period: 'The busyness of [such] an aerodrome comes as an astonishing revelation when first observed, with aircraft arriving and departing, each with its appointed "platform" with the regularity of railway trains. More than sixty machines a day pass in and out of Croydon.'[8]

Hendon, on the suburban fringes of north-west London, had been a destination for aviators and sightseers since before the First World War, when it attracted upmarket motorised customers to its dramatic air displays. A vintage poster shows an example from Hendon from as early as 1912. It is entitled 'Night Flying at Hendon' and advertises 'Races every Saturday at 3.30, Exhibition flights every Sunday and Thursday afternoon, Motors 2/6d (includes chauffeur)'.[9] After the First World War, Hendon became an RAF station and the site of regular, large-scale air displays that attracted huge audiences. This is described in detail later in the chapter.

Five-bob flips and cheap air-mindedness

A direct experience of flight in the 1920s and 1930s was easier for ordinary suburban residents than might be first thought. The opportunity to fly came from visiting 'flying circuses' or by going to the local aerodrome for a short flight. Flying circuses provided cheap, short flights basing themselves in a local field for a few days and then moving on. They were often formed by ex-RAF pilots looking for a way to keep flying and earn money after their war service had ended. In the 1920s these organisations provided many people with their first flight; by the 1930s they had developed more sophisticated flying displays that featured aerobatic flying, unusual aircraft and comedy routines.[10]

One example of this type of suburban flying is seen in a 1927 advertisement for the Cornwall Aviation Company flying circus that was active across Britain in the late 1920s.[11] The advertisement promised 'flying daily ... over 50,000 passengers carried without a single case of dissatisfaction'.[12] The notice makes clear that flights were available from five shillings, which would have bought a quick trip round the airfield. In this particular case, the field was a narrow strip of land alongside the new Kingston Bypass, which was, at this time, partially completed. It is interesting to note that the advertisement felt the need to distinguish Cornwall's machines from a rival company operating from nearby fields, suggesting that this novelty was a competitive, if not yet common, new form of entertainment. Interest in this type of introduction to flight persisted well into the 1930s. For example, the Ace of Spades roadhouse (see Chapter 7), had a flying field for its wealthier patrons and this was used by C.W.A. Scott's Flying Displays as late as 1936.[13] Sir Alan Cobham, a British pioneer aviator, knighted for his long-distance record attempts, was by 1932 a one-man spokesman for air-mindedness in Britain. He took a particular interest in a campaign for building municipal airports around the country. Air-mindedness was a government-led initiative that aimed to raise the profile of flight in Britain, to show it as central to both its military and everyday future.[14] Cobham used his flying circus as a means of fund-raising for his work and was often found in small airfields in the London area. He was seen by cinemagoers, in 1932, in a newsreel shot at Hanworth airfield, showing the capabilities of the autogiro, a predecessor to the helicopter.[15] In 1933, he visited the Ditton Hill aerodrome in Surbiton, which was, in reality, an open field temporarily adapted for the purpose. The programme offered twenty thrilling events with fifteen aircraft and bombing exhibitions, parachute descents, pylon racing and flying lessons. Flights were available from four shillings.[16] Cobham visited many other airfields in the London area from 1932 to 1935.[17]

Joyriding continued to be popular throughout the 1930s and was at Croydon Airport combined with another interwar obsession, outdoor swimming. *Flight* magazine reported: 'Last week-end Surrey Flying Services … had a record week for joyriding, something like 500 short flights being made. Fine weather and the proximity of the big swimming pool opposite to the airport have much to do with the increased business.'[18]

These first flights, not unreasonably, stuck in the minds of those who experienced them. Seymour Johnson looked back over fifty years to a difficult, if cheap, visit to Croydon in about 1928:

> 5/- was charged at weekends for a flight around the drome. The last seat was not often taken and one day I found out why. The gatekeeper taking the money said 'There you are, last seat for free, off you go'. As I climbed the steps to the cabin I was handed a piece of wood about 2 feet by 1 with two hooks at each end. "Slot it in there when the door shuts' they said. The door shut, the plane started and I fell over. As I scrambled up the plane took off at a steep angle and so I fell again. We levelled off and at last I got the seat in place, as I turned to sit down the engine was cut and we came down to land with me once more on the floor.[19]

One woman recalled her trip with her older brother for a joyride in 1936:

> It was months, I suppose, before my brother saved enough for the fares, tram
> and bus for two to Croydon. The year was 1936 and I was 10, my brother
> Jack was 14. I remember taking a train to Croydon [which] seemed like a
> strange country, nothing like the South London area I called home … It
> was a de Havilland Puss Moth. Our pace quickened. A 'five bob' flight. The
> thrill of it![20]

It is hard to imagine two youngsters being allowed to make such a
journey on the bus on their own today, never mind taking their first flight.
This memory reflects the wide independent mobility available to children
in London's suburbs of the 1930s.

Other more sophisticated trips were available from suburban airfields.
Airlines based at Croydon offered flights to view London from the air.
Seymour Johnson remembered 'My next flight in 1929 was from the
Purley Way site – it was now 'Croydon'. 'Tea over London' it was called
and I think cost £1 and lasted about half an hour'.[21] By 1931 the price
of these sightseeing trips had fallen further to 12s 6d. Imperial Airways
suggested on Pathé News that at this price 'poor and rich alike' would be
able to see their home city from the air. This rather optimistic suggestion
was backed by Pathé's title for the newsreel, 'Get airminded cheaply!'[22]
Venturing even further afield, a Mrs Newbold recalled a trip to Le Touquet
in France taking off from Croydon: 'The trip, for the sum of only £3 15s,
included tea at the Casino, plus dinner on the plane coming back! I cycled
to the aerodrome … I love flying. It gives me a feeling of excitement and
pleasure.'[23]

Joyrides and sightseeing trips provided ordinary suburbanites with
the chance to directly engage in the excitement and liberation of flight
that were otherwise available only through scheduled air services, a
preserve of the very wealthy. It is clear from personal accounts that
flying in this way often for the first time provided a thrilling and potentially dangerous experience that stayed with people for the rest of their
lives.

For those lucky enough to get the opportunity, these flights provided
an unusual totalising view of London and its outlying suburbs. From the
ground, the suburbs might seem repetitive and dull, but from the air their
intricate morphology and sheer scale would be discernible, resulting in a
very modern experience and way of seeing the world.

Suburban observation of flight

The proximity of new homes to suburban airfields meant that the residents of London's outer suburbs were more familiar with the world of interwar flying than those anywhere else in the United Kingdom and, perhaps at the time, the world. This relationship is clearly expressed in oral histories of the period, where a number of respondents recall the excitement of seeing aeroplanes from their suburban gardens as children. For example, one Croydon resident recalled this striking example: 'I remember when the great airships used to fly over here in the 1920s. The whole surrounding area used to be enveloped in a vast ear-numbing drone. We lived at Wallington when I was a small child and I used to rush into our back yard so as not to miss anything'.[24]

This recollection provokes an evocative image of a small child in a suburban garden, looking up at an enormous grey airship, dominating the skyline by its sheer scale and, surprisingly, by the noise of its engines. These airship visits must have had a strong effect on suburban memories as another resident recalled 'the R34 [airship] passing low over our house, with a large roundel on its nose'.[25]

The sighting of giant airships over suburban London rooftops was an exciting, but not unique occasion. British airships like the R34 and its German rival the Graf Zeppelin made trips to London aerodromes. The Graf Zeppelin attracted the attention of the newsreels, with Pathé reporting its arrival at Hanworth Aerodrome, showing very large crowds against a background of new suburban semi-detached houses.[26] Rather touchingly, the massive airship was secured, after landing, by 'Two hundred or so Middlesex Eagle Scouts'.[27] Three of these scouts were offered the chance to fly in the airship; one was brave enough to take the chance of a return flight to Berlin.

Spotting planes and, less frequently, airships from suburban back gardens was a common pursuit for teenage boys. Certainly numerous 'modern wonder' annuals featuring chapters on flying and planes were aimed at them.[28] Their sisters might also get the enthusiasm for flight. A Mrs Wood remembered 'We'd talked aeroplanes it seemed for many happy months'.[29] The impact of the airport was also visible on nearby suburban streets. One newspaper reader recalled: 'A familiar sight in the 1930s was the aerodrome coach which took the passengers from Piccadilly to the aerodrome in time to catch the airliner'.[30]

The giant airship R101, 1929   **4**
Photo by Puttnam /Topical Press Agency/Getty Images

Plane-spotting and visiting the airport

As Croydon Airport became more developed, the Air Ministry recognised that it was a very attractive day out for visitors.[31] They could be divided into two sorts. The first were the more sophisticated, who were described as 'those who desire to be given an insight into the administration of the air port and to be shewn, so far as is admissible, installations and equipment there, which are of technical interest'. These typically consisted of 'parties of technical and social organisations'. Each visitor was charged sixpence, which included a guide to the airport. The second were the much larger number of people who 'merely desire to watch the flying and visit the public enclosure at the aerodrome for this purpose'.[32]

Each plane-spotter was charged one penny, or a little more if they came on two wheels. In the spirit of the prevailing air-mindedness of the period, the Air Ministry considered that 'the main object of the provision of the enclosure is to encourage public interest in flying'.[33] It was also possible to gain a good view of the airfield from the balcony roof of the adjacent, commercially operated, Aerodrome Hotel. For special occasions, this could accommodate as many as a thousand visitors who would pay 6d for the balcony and 1s for the garden enclosure.[34]

Local resident John Stroud recalled his visits to the enclosure: 'I lived at Streatham Common. On 1 July 1931, I paid my first "real" visit to the airport and spent most of my time on the hotel roof. There I had a fine view of an aeroplane in flight at close quarters as a blue Desoutter skimmed past the hotel on its landing approach with joyriders'.[35] Visitor attendances at Croydon grew steadily as the 1930s progressed. In the early years the preference was for the enclosure, which provided a cheap and close-up view of the planes. For many, simply watching the planes take off and land was enough entertainment and interest. Geoff Perrott recalled that 'My father took me on many occasions riding on the top deck of a Croydon Corporation tram... Contact with aircraft using the field was most inti-mate, they were only a few feet away and would cover one with dust and grass as they taxied away.'[36]

From 1934 onwards, the majority of visitors opted for the air terminal itself with its panoramic balcony view and more direct contact with the hustle and bustle of international travel. This is suggestive of a change in the relationship between the visitor and the airport. At first, viewing the actuality of flight itself was an end in itself. Later, when flying had become a more workaday experience and increased disposable income had made visiting the terminal affordable, visitors wanted to engage with the sophistication of international flight. Douglas Cluett, a local historian, describes the action in the enthusiastic and evocative style of a true fan:

> The highlight of every day at Croydon was the departure of the '12.30 to Paris', the Imperial Airways Silver Wing service which left every day with great punctuality … The pilot would arrive and inspect his machine with the air of a naval captain inspecting his ship. Invariably it was shining, the crew ready, and the stewards in their smart uniforms poised for action.[37]

Suburban cyclist John Sowerby noted in his diary:

> I resume my way to Purley and the 'drome – otherwise Air Port of Croydon. What with 'liners' coming and going, tennis courts, swimming baths, recreation grounds, groups of coaches all ready to whisk the air-minded to London, the signal tower, the crowd on the hotel roof (3d admission) tractors dragging planes into position, gangways being made ready etc., well it's pretty busy there.[38]

By 1936, over 170,000 visitors a year were welcomed by the airport; most of them came in the warmer months from April to September. Plane-spotting in the enclosure in December and January would really appeal only to the hardy few, typically about 150 a day.[39] The visitors' enclosure did not have a car park, but the airport did keep statistics for the number of people arriving on bicycles. About 13 per cent of the total made there way to Croydon on two wheels, which demonstrates the suburban nature of the audience and the normality of making journeys by cycle at that time.[40]

Peter Adey has described how the new municipal airport at Speke on the suburban outskirts of Liverpool provided visitors with a 'new and modern experience' and how the airport balcony provided a kind of 'optical apparatus' where 'spectator enclosures were positioned close to the aircraft so the public could get up close to the machines'. Adey showed that, at Speke, the authorities were keen to admit school tour parties only after the new terminal building had been completed. This was in order to promote a combination of observation and technological modernity that would stimulate an appropriate sense of awe in the mind of the visitor.[41]

The spectacle of air travel was less stage-managed at Croydon. The brochure that was sold to visitors to the airport building was dull and functional, describing the facilities in the most matter-of-fact terms.[42] It suggested that the real purpose of visiting the airport was to admire and understand its technology, rather than positioning it as a glamorous attraction. The enclosure was an even more functional space, a fenced-off area with a gatekeeper and some public toilets. Croydon's minimalist approach compares poorly to what Speke would achieve only a few years later. Croydon, as the world's first airport, suffered from the problems of what more cynical business writers call 'first-mover disadvantage'. That is, by being the first it eventually came to lag behind more forward-looking businesses who had learned from Croydon's mistakes. By 1938, *Popular Flying* was able to condemn Croydon as 'an airport fit for a second rate Balkan state'.[43] Moving beyond London's suburban circle, Gatwick, with its modern circular terminal, provided a glimpse of the postwar future.[44]

Suburban spectacle – air displays

In addition to their increasingly popular role as a place of entertainment and education, London's suburban airports also provided the location for a large-scale celebration of air-mindedness through the Empire Air Day and RAF Display Day.

After the First World War, Hendon's location and the unprecedented growth of London's suburban population into a new ring of housing coupled with a wider interest in flight and flying presented the possibility for very large-scale air displays embracing a much broader and more suburban audience than before. Hendon was a relatively wealthy area of this new outer London (see Chapter 2 for Hendon's car usage) and one that experienced a very high rate of suburbanisation. In 1921, Hendon's population was 57,500. Seventeen years later, it was 145,100.[45]

The RAF Display Day was established at the end of the First World War as a way of raising money for the RAF Benevolent Fund. This display of aeroplanes and flying skills was held each year at Hendon Aerodrome. It grew in popularity during the interwar years, reaching a peak in the 1930s when vast crowds attended. From 1936 onwards, the increased speed of the aeroplanes and the need to concentrate on defence matters made Hendon less attractive for the RAF and the last prewar display was held in 1937.[46]

In 1935, *The Times* recorded that 150,000 people attended the RAF Display Day, with many more watching from the surrounding fields and hills.[47] The RAF accounts for the day indicate that 87,000 tickets were paid for, the difference accounted for by service personnel.[48] This is an astonishing figure and demonstrates the centrality of air-mindedness in the public's consciousness at this time. As *The Aeroplane* remarked about the 1935 display, 'As air-mindedness grows ... people go to Hendon'. This message was accompanied by the striking image of an Aircraftman holding up two small children 'helping to bring British children up in the way they should go, for the good of our race and our people'.[49] Schoolchildren were invited to watch the display's rehearsal day, and this attracted parties from schools all over North London.[50]

The display catered for a wide range of visitors, ranging from the society elite, through the wealthy and motorised middle classes to the ordinary Londoner who would travel to this outpost in suburban North London via Colindale Tube station on the Northern Line.

Flight magazine published a map of the forthcoming 1935 display that shows the arrangements for the various classes of visitors.[51] In the south enclosure, there were boxes for the Royal Family, the House of Lords, the House of Commons and public schools. This area, visited by the Prince of Wales in 1934, was, in effect, as much part of the London season as the Eton v. Harrow cricket match at Lords. The exclusivity of this part of the display is suggested by the price of boxes for six spectators at between £4 and £7.[52] The middle classes could station themselves in the ten shilling and five shilling enclosures, close by their cars. It is a striking feature of this event that so many visitors came by car, observing the show from the roofs of their vehicles, giving them a much better view than could be obtained in the stands.[53] Peter Adey notes how this combination of spectator and car 'cemented the modernity and inequality of flight'.[54] The combination of the two technologies is intriguing and it is noticeable that advertisers in *The Autocar* and in *The Aeroplane* had a tendency to conjoin the two means of transport in their illustrations so that both benefited from a joint feeling of modernity. This is seen to great effect in the Hudson Terraplane, a modern streamlined American car built, in London, in a factory on the Great West Road. This was an aeroplane for the ground, a 'terra' plane. In its American advertising Hudson went further, using the flying ace Amelia Earhart to advertise its products.[55]

Peter Adey's description of the inequalities at Hendon can be clearly seen in the map of the display, but concentrating on the differences in the seating, means of transport and view tends to diminish the impact of the attendances of large numbers of people in the cheap two shilling seats. This was half the price of a trip round the airfield at a much less prestigious event. About 45 per cent of the audience were crammed into the lower-priced seats.[56] In these less prestigious surroundings a more boisterous and traditional carnival atmosphere reigned. Here, 'newsvendors were allowed to shout about crashes at the display and to obtrude offensive and misleading posters' and 'candy and fruitmongers are allowed to howl among the spectators'.[57]

In 1934, a complementary series of air displays were convened by the Air League of the British Empire, with the approval of the RAF, to open up local RAF airfields to the public.[58] This was called the Empire Air Day. They were rather low-key compared to the RAF Display Day, but their objective was the same, to encourage air-mindedness and to generate money for the RAF benevolent fund. The approach taken for Empire Air Day was, though, different. Rather than being concentrated around spectacular flying at a single aerodrome, the idea of the Empire Air Day was that every RAF aerodrome would open its doors to the public and would allow them to get very close to the aircraft and to meet and talk with air force personnel. *Flight* magazine described it as 'our first line of defence doing its daily routine, more or less' and an opportunity for the public to see 'what all this air talk was about'.[59] Admission charges were much lower than at the RAF Display Day, one shilling for adults and sixpence for children.

In 1935, total attendances across the United Kingdom were 149,000. Forty-five aerodromes were opened, with the smallest having a disappointing thirty-eight visitors and the largest, Hendon, having 18,000. These events were very much local affairs with the air-minded attending their local RAF station. As such, suburban London, which had more than its fair share of stations, contributed about 30 per cent of the total audience with about 44,000 visitors. Hendon was to the fore, but visitors also came to other suburban stations such as Northolt, Kenley, Hornchurch and Biggin Hill.

Suburban spectacle – Croydon, Lindbergh and Johnson

Some of the most important contributions to air-mindedness in the 1920s and 1930s were those made by individual flyers in pursuit of speed and distance records. Speed records were encouraged by competitions such as the King's Cup and the Schneider Trophy and were, in their way, an extension of the manly ideals seen in the early flying of the First World War. The King's Cup was a popular spectator event at both the start/finish airport and at the intermediate way-points. For example, in 1930, provision was made for the accommodation of forty thousand spectators and five thousand cars at Hanworth airfield.[60] Interestingly, this would suggest that a quarter of the crowd came by car.

The arrivals and departures at London's airfields of pilots engaged in breaking distance records attracted unprecedented public interest and attendance. The flyers who captured the public imagination to the greatest extent were the American pilot Col. Charles Lindbergh and Britain's Amy Johnson, and the locus of this attention was Croydon Airport.

Lindbergh, is of course, famous for his first solo crossing of the Atlantic from Roosevelt Field (owned by R.J. Reynolds, see Chapter 9) to Le Bourget in Paris, which he completed in May 1927. By so doing, he became an international celebrity, as well known as a Hollywood star; one of the later consequences of this fame was the kidnap and murder of his son in 1932. His successful journey led to a wave of unprecedented excitement and celebration on both sides of the Atlantic, the synchronicity of which was an indication of the arrival of a more closely aligned popular culture across the western world, powered by communication technologies.[61]

Lindbergh's next step of his journey after receiving the medal of the *Légion d'honneur* was to fly to London to receive the Air Force Cross from the King, together with many other presentations and receptions. This involved a short flight from Paris to Croydon accompanied by planes carrying reporters and photographers from Britain's national papers. Croydon Airport prepared for Lindbergh's arrival by arranging for the police to direct motor traffic and by arranging for some men with a stout rope to protect his plane, *The Spirit of St. Louis*, from the crowd.[62]

Despite the rope, Lindbergh's arrival on Sunday 28 May 1927 did not go according to plan. Throughout the day people came to Croydon to witness *The Spirit of St. Louis* at first hand. Some took the opportunity to have a flight themselves and Surrey Flying Services were very busy taking up joyriders. *Flight* magazine recorded that 'from an early hour on Sunday, large numbers of people arrived at the aerodrome so as to be in good time …' Many came by car, but trains, trams and 'buses from all points leading or near to Croydon were packed throughout the afternoon, while bicycles and pedestrians largely contributed to the steady influx.'[63]

This preponderance of pedestrian and bicycle traffic indicates the largely local and suburban origin of this crowd. In total, over a hundred thousand people came to Croydon on this unusual day. Local knowledge of the airport allowed some of the crowd to force their way onto the airfield by breaking down a fence at the far side of the field from the airport's terminal building. *Flight* reported that 'Motor cars and what few police could be spared were at once rushed to meet them … it was obvious to many that there was going to be trouble'.[64] Even before Lindbergh's arrival, this section of the crowd broke into the central part of the airfield, making it difficult for Lindbergh to land safely, and, when he did so, surrounded him and his plane. Lindbergh's arrival was, then, witnessed by a mostly local suburban crowd of well-wishers and celebrity spotters. By 1927, those who lived in the area neighbouring Croydon Airport had become extremely familiar with the world of flight and flying.

Three years later, these scenes were repeated at Croydon with the return of Amy Johnson from her record-breaking solo flight to Australia. Johnson was, compared to many women fliers, home-grown, unglamorous and sub-urban.[65] For the next decade, Johnson was one of the most famous people in Britain, but she was worshipped for the first time in South London. Johnson had taken off from Croydon on 5 May 1930 with no crowds and with little public interest. As her journey continued, publicity arranged by *The Daily Mail*, showing her as a modern, imperial heroine brought her to the national consciousness.

Her arrival at Croydon was witnessed by the type of suburban air-minded crowd seen in Lindbergh's arrival, a live outside broadcast from BBC radio and newsreel companies.[66] Pathé recorded the large crowds at Croydon standing ten to fifteen deep outside the Aerodrome Hotel. Johnson's fame was such by this point that Pathé announced her in the titles simply as 'Amy'.[67] Movietone's newsreel was altogether more modern and sophisticated. It included a soundtrack, still quite a novelty in 1930, and featured dramatic footage of Johnson's arrival against at Croydon just as the sun was setting at the airport. There was less emphasis on the crowd in this report and more on the formalities and speeches.[68]

The local press commented on the suburban nature of the welcome:

> Amy Swoops to Croydon. Aerodrome magnet for young and old – Air Queen's Homecoming. Visitors to London made a special journey to Croydon. Northern dialects mingled with the Cockney accent. And, of course, Croydonians assembled in their hundreds; accompanied by large contingents from Purley, Wallington, Carshalton, Sutton and Cheam … four thousand cars parked, whilst the whole length of Purley Way is lined with humans all cheerfully facing a three-hour wait for their heroine.[69]

Johnson's journey from Croydon to the West End was a suburban pro-cession via Norbury, Streatham, Brixton and Kennington. *Flight* recorded her journey:

> Miss Johnson was driven round the aerodrome in a car, while the mobile floodlight showed her to the waiting crowd in the main public enclosure on the Plough Lane side of the aerodrome. Then she drove at little more than a foot pace through the streets from Croydon to Grosvenor House Hotel in Park Lane. It was drizzling on and off, and the car was an open tourer. But the patient waiting thousands along the 12 miles of route certainly deserved a glimpse of her whom they had come out to see. So Miss Johnson stood up in the car and bowed to the people practically all the way.[70]

It is difficult over a distance of eighty years to explain Johnson's popu-larity fully. Her bravery and fortitude were admired and she formed a part of the period's obsession with new technologies and new frontiers. Her gender was of great interest but she was not the only well-known female flyer. Despite being, in reality, an extraordinary person, Johnson, who came from a well-off but distinctively suburban background in Hull, pro-jected a note of ordinariness that was very appealing to the newly formed lower middle classes in London's outer suburbia.[71] This was due to her unglamourous appearance at this point in her career, and to the girl next door projection made for her by her sponsors at *The Daily Mail*.[72] Her slow parade through London's suburban streets allowed for a direct connection between the accentuated air-mindedness of outer London and a reflected validation of ordinary suburban virtues.

Resistance to suburban air-mindedness

As has been shown, airports and airfields were very popular places for visitors in the 1930s. Flying was less popular with the local residents who lived near to airport boundaries. The suburban idyll was interrupted here by the modernity of flight. Complaints were made about low flying, night flying and Sunday flying by local residents who had lived in the area for many years, but also by the residents of new suburban estates who must have been aware of the likelihood of disturbance in buying a house near an airport.[73] The consequences of being so close to an airport could be danger-ous and deadly, a theme explored in Chapter 9.

Not everybody in London thought the RAF displays at Hendon a suitable form of entertainment. In 1935, three communists were arrested for pasting over posters for the event with a bill that read: 'Air Pageants Today! Death and Destruction Tomorrow! Gas Masks, Blackouts, A trebled RAF – There is no protection. If you want peace, fight against the war preparations now! Down with the National Government!'[74] Locally, Hendon Peace Council – a left-leaning Christian group – also campaigned against the air display and its proselytising of a rearmament agenda.[75]

This active resistance was a reflection of a much wider concern over the possible implications of an escalating competition for air dominance in Europe in the 1930s. It had been made clear by Stanley Baldwin in 1932 that 'the man in the street should appreciate that there is no power on earth that can prevent him from being bombed … the bomber will always get through'.[76] The idea was brought to public attention in a more vivid way in 1936 by a major film, *Things to Come*.[77] This showed the death and destruction that would come to major cities such as London in a war of the near future. London's suburbia and its ordinary houses would be in the front line of the next war.

Neville Chamberlain now has a reputation based on appeasement and political failure, but in the late 1930s this ordinary man was a hero in the suburbs for his tireless work to avoid another war. His flights to Berlin departed and returned to Heston Airport, on the fringe of West London's suburbia, and his arrival there was greeted by thousands of suburban residents who had found hope that their new houses were no longer under the threat of being destroyed by German bombers.

Conclusion

Although air-mindedness was a national campaign in Britain in the 1920s and 1930s, it had particular resonance in the London suburbs. Greater London had more airfields than any other part of the country, which was a consequence of London's commercial and political importance and, for the RAF, because of the capital's likely targeting in any future war.

Suburban London was home to Britain's two largest and earliest aerodromes. Hendon aerodrome was the most important location for flying in the period before the Great War, hosting flying clubs and air displays. Croydon Airport came to prominence in the 1920s, providing a variety of modernities, such as the glamorous Imperial Airways flights to Paris and beyond and as the natural departure and homecoming point for the air heroes and heroines of the 1930s. Outer London was also a centre for the aviation industry between the wars; many light industrial factories could be found near London's airfields. Official air-mindedness campaigns found their apogee at Hendon, where the RAF Display Day, a national demonstration of Britain's attempt to dominate both commercial and military aircraft manufacture, was held. The vast crowds and attendant publicity ensured that Hendon was seen as a special locus for enthusiasm for everything in the air.

Hendon, Croydon and London's other airfields had to be suburban. Early dreams of airports on the roofs of railway stations in central London soon proved themselves unfeasible; long runways and clear horizons could be found only in outer London. Airfields were often located next to or near to major arterial roads providing fast vehicular access to new green-field sites. In this way, airfields were connected to the development of motoring in London's suburbs. Cars were always much in evidence at all the major air events and displays. The two technologies were also intertwined in commercial representations: both the car and the plane were used as visual short cuts in advertisements to portray a luxurious and modern life; aerial terms crossed over to the car industry so as to emphasise the futuristic quality of their products.

It did not take long for clear horizons to begin to be crowded by rows of suburban houses, as competition for the landscape of London's interwar suburbia got under way. The new residents of these houses grew very accustomed to the world of the aerodrome and airport. Some of them had their mobility and experience of modernity transformed by being early passengers in five-bob flips round the airfield, or in a more sophisticated flight over London that gave them an unusual, totalising view of the city and their home in the suburbs. Even those suburbanites who had not flown were able to embrace the modernity of the air; their mobilities did not change, but their attitude to the world was opened up through a close appreciation of flight. They turned up in their cars or on their bicycles to view the planes at Croydon.

The image of a massive airship, passing noisily over the back garden of a semi-detached house, on its way to Croydon evokes the relationship between domesticated suburban life and flying in Greater London that was highly specific to this time and place. This relationship reached its height when Amy Johnson, a homely figure from Hull, arrived at Croydon and was fêted by hundreds of thousands of Londoners in a journey from the airfield through the south London suburbs.

Notes

1 'Airports' were, strictly, airfields with customs facilities, such as Croydon and Heston. 'Aerodrome' was a term used in Britain to describe a large airfield. I have used 'airfield' as a generic term for these two former types and smaller areas that could, in the early days, be literally the size of one field.

2 F. K. Mason, *Hawker Aircraft Since 1920*. 2nd ed., London 1971.

3 J. W. R. Taylor (ed.), *Fairey Aviation*, Stroud 1997.

4 A. Dowsett, *Handley Page: A History*, Stroud 2003.

5 R. T. Riding (ed.), *De Havilland: The Golden Years 1919–1939*, Sutton 1981.

6 D. Cluett, J. Nash, R. Learmonth, *Croydon Airport: The Great Days, 1928–1939*, Sutton 1980.

7 1931 Census, visionofbritain.org.uk [accessed 25 March 2012] and L. P. Abercrombie, *Greater London Plan 1944*, London 1945, p. 188.

8 C. Boff, *Boys' Book of Flying. The Latest in the Air*, London 1937, p. 173.

9 W. Allen (ed.), *Looping the loop: Posters of Flight*, Carlsbad, Calif., 2000, Plate 60.

10 C. Cruddas, *Those Fabulous Flying Years: Joy-Riding and Flying Circuses Between the Wars*, Tunbridge Wells 2003.

11 T. Chapman, *Cornwall Aviation Company*, Falmouth, 1979.

12 Royal Borough of Kingston upon Thames, Archives and Local History Service, KX40.

13 C. Cruddas, *Those Fabulous Flying Years*, appendices.

14 P. Adey, *Aerial Life: Spaces, Mobilities, Affects*, Oxford 2010.

15 British Movietone, *Modern Circus Drops into Town*, Story: 1761, 1932.

16 *The Surrey Comet*, 23 September 1933.

17 C. Cruddas, *Those Fabulous Flying Years*, appendices.

18 *Flight*, 27 August 1936.

19 Reminiscences of Seymour Johnson, Sutton Local History Service, undated.

20 Letter from Mrs B. Wood, *Wallington and Carshalton Advertiser*, 14 March 1986.

21 Reminiscences of Seymour Johnson, Sutton Local History Service, undated.

22 British Pathé, *Get Airminded Cheaply!*, reel: 877.28, 1931.

23 Reminiscences of Mrs J. Newbold, *Wallington and Carshalton Advertiser*, 21 February 1980.

24 Letter from W. Hudson, *The Advertiser*, 12 October 1980.

25 Reminiscences of Geoffrey A. Perrott, Sutton Local History Service, undated.

26 British Pathé, *Graf Zeppelin*, reel: 683.05, 1932.

27 *Flight*, 8 July 1932.

28 For example, C. Boff, *Boys' Book of Flying; Chums Annual 1934–35*, London 1934; E. Hawks, *The Marvels and Mysteries of Science*, London 1939.

29 Letter from Mrs B. Wood, *Wallington and Carshalton Advertiser*, 14 March 1986.

30 Letter from K. Elmer, *Wallington and Carshalton Advertiser*, 9 March 1990.

31 Air Ministry, *Guide to Croydon Aerodrome (the Air Port of London)*, London 1929.
32 Memo from Air Ministry to the Treasury, 13 March 1929, The National Archives, TNA T161/1383.
33 Memo from Air Ministry to the Treasury, 14 April, 1930, TNA T161/1383.
34 D. Cluett, J. Nash, R. Learmonth, *Croydon Airport: The Great Days, 1928–1939*.
35 John Stroud, *Air Pictorial*, July 1975.
36 Reminiscences of Geoffrey A. Perrott, Sutton Local History Service, undated.
37 D. Cluett, J. Nash, R. Learmonth, *Croydon Airport: The Great Days, 1928–1939*, p. 42.
38 J. Sowerby, *I Got on My Bicycle*, London 1939, p. 195.
39 Statistics extracted from a number of papers in TNA T161/1383.
40 Croydon Airport, Statement showing number of visitors, May 1929 to April 1930, TNA T161/1383.
41 P. Adey, 'Architectural Geographies of the Airport Balcony: Mobility, Sensation and the Theatre of Flight', *Geografiska Annaler: Series B, Human Geography*, 90:1, 2008, pp. 29–47.
42 Air Ministry, *Guide to Croydon Aerodrome (the Air Port of London)*, London 1929.
43 *Popular Flying*, February 1938.
44 *Flight*, 24 March, 1938.
45 1931 Census, visionofbritain.org.uk; [accessed 25 March 2012] and L. P. Abercrombie, *Greater London Plan 1944*, London 1945, p. 188.
46 *Flight*, 27 January 1938, p. 94.
47 *The Times*, 1 July 1935.
48 Charities Accounts, TNA AIR 2/4440.
49 *The Aeroplane*, 3 July 1935.
50 *The Times*, 27 June 1935.
51 *Flight*, 27 June 1935.
52 *The Times*, 18 June 1935.
53 *Popular Flying*, August 1935.
54 P. Adey, *Aerial Life: Spaces, Mobilities, Affects*, p. 63.
55 T. Comden, home movie, 1932, http://youtu.be/C8ZstFnvBGc [accessed 10 April 2012].
56 Charities Accounts, TNA AIR 2/4440.
57 *The Aeroplane*, 3 July 1935.
58 TNA AIR 20/594.
59 *Flight*, 31 May 1934.
60 *Flight*, 30 June 1930.
61 *The Times*, 30 May 1927.
62 R. Learmonth, *First Croydon Airport, 1915–1928*, Sutton 1977, p. 74.
63 *Flight*, 2 June, 1927.
64 *Flight*, 2 June, 1927.

65 M. Gillies, *Amy Johnson*, London 2003. Later in the 1930s, Johnson became a more urbane and sophisticated figure as her celebrity began to wane.

66 *The Times*, 5 August 1930.

67 *Air Port of London. Amy's Wonderful Welcome Home*, Pathé reel: 721.16, 1930.

68 *Amy Johnson's Arrival at Croydon*, British Movietone, Story: 801, 1930.

69 *The Wallington and Carshalton Times*, 7 August 1930, quoted in D. Cluett, J. Nash, R. Learmonth, *Croydon Airport: The Great Days, 1928–1939*, p. 162.

70 *Flight*, 8 August, 1930.

71 M. Gillies, *Amy Johnson*.

72 See B. Rieger, *Technology and the Culture of Modernity in Britain and Germany, 1890–1945*, Cambridge 2005.

73 D. Cluett, J. Nash, R. Learmonth, *Croydon Airport: The Great Days, 1928–1939*, p. 95.

74 TNA MEPO 2/4204, June 1935.

75 D. Oliver, *Hendon Aerodrome – A History*, Shrewsbury 1994, p. 94.

76 *The Times*, 11 November 1932.

77 *Things to Come*, Dir. W. Menzies, 1936.

Part III

Roads

New mobilities in construction

In December 1920, *The Times* served up a surprise to its readers. In recent years, they had been treated to news of the Russian Revolution and the break-up of the old world order at the Versailles Conference. It now seemed that revolutionary ferment was getting closer to home; first with a disruptive miners' strike and then with a new, disturbing headline, 'Buildings seized by the unemployed – Town Halls now guarded'.[1] Unemployed workers in London had occupied a dozen public buildings: drill halls, town halls and swimming baths. One of the buildings under workers' control was Edmonton Town Hall. Police and officials were eventually able to restore order and the council was, finally, able to hold a meeting. As the meeting progressed, the unemployed workers packing its public gallery made their feelings clear on the debate below. One announcement that the audience loudly applauded was that Middlesex County Council had decided to begin the construction of a new arterial road.[2] These new roads were to be the conduits that enabled the development of new forms of suburban mobility.

Two years after the end of the First World War, Britain was failing to make a quick adjustment to a peacetime economy. The government considered unemployment such an issue that David Lloyd George, the Liberal prime minister, prepared a cabinet scheme to generate jobs. A recent demonstration where the unemployed and what *The Times* described as 'the unemployable and, mischief-makers' marched up and down Whitehall had also heightened public awareness of this issue.[3] Lloyd George's scheme had three main initiatives to increase the employment of ex-servicemen. These were a housing programme, the admission of men into the iron and steel industry and, most interestingly for the purposes of this book, the development of a London and provincial arterial road scheme.

Thus began the interwar arterial road programme that was to transform London's landscape over the next twenty years. In the popular imagination, and in recent academic enquiry, the most significant period of road development in Britain was the construction, from the 1950s onwards, of a motorway network.[4] However, in its own way, the interwar programme was as important in its building of hundreds of miles of high-quality arterial roads, bypasses and tunnels in Britain's largest cities and, in particular, in London. Without the interruption of the Second World War, and the delays incurred in the reconstruction of the British economy, the arterial road programme would have developed into a motorway programme as planners had *autobahnen, autostrade* and motorways very much in mind in the 1930s.[5]

Construction

For all their association with interwar modernisation, the arterial roads had a much earlier conception in the busy streets of Edwardian London. At the beginning of the twentieth century, London's roads were filled with an uncontrolled jumble of horse-drawn carts, carriages, buses and taxis, early cars, trams and bicycles. Traffic jams on poorly made, narrow streets were common and made for extended journey times; long-distance journeys from the capital to the provinces were particularly problematic. The building of the inner ring of Victorian suburbia had added 1.6 million people to London's population in a period of twenty years.[6] These newcomers were housed in a densely packed set of regular streets formed alongside the main exits to the capital. Once traffic had negotiated this newly built suburbia, the next hazard was provided by the narrow streets of the small towns on London's periphery. These towns, soon to form contiguous suburbs in Greater London, had traffic jams of their own. At Kingston, Croydon, Brentford, Bromley and Barnet, traffic was frequently at a standstill.

The arrival of the car was the initial catalyst that drove much discussion on the building of new roads. In the early 1900s, traffic patterns changed dramatically as motorised vehicles competed for space with traditional horse-drawn transport. A survey undertaken in Westminster shows the rapid growth in motor traffic that occurred in London in the first decade of the twentieth century. It shows that in a five-year period, over 30 per cent of vehicle journeys switched from horse-drawn to motorised transport. In addition, reflecting London's growing size and activity, total journeys had increased by 15 per cent.

Between 1903 and 1916, both national and local government involved themselves in a series of commissions, investigations, plans and conferences. Decision-making on a road-building programme was particularly difficult because of the number of different authorities involved in the process. The Chancellor of the Exchequer, David Lloyd George, remarked in 1909, 'I believe that no main road has been made out of London for eighty years. We have no central road authority.'[7]

These discussions were complicated. In short, following the Royal Commission on London Traffic that reported in 1905, the London Traffic Branch of the Board of Trade drew up a plan of arterial roads and bypasses that set out, in protean form, the network of roads built between the wars.[8] As the result of pressure from various London local authorities, the Local Government Board held a series of conferences from 1913 to 1916 to determine the exact line of route for these various arterial roads.

The cabinet scheme for the development of London's arterial road network came into operation with an estimated initial budget of £10.4 million.[9] The scheme was designed so as to place as many unemployed men as possible in work. This was achieved by eschewing mechanisation so that large numbers of manual labourers could be hired and, by putting men on to short-time working, to provide employment to the maximum number of individuals. By January 1922, national arterial road schemes were providing employment for just fewer than ten thousand persons.[10] These labourers were really earning their money as they worked with picks and shovels to build the road and did not have access to 'mechanical excavators, trench cutting machines, concrete mixers, compressors and pneumatic drills'.[11] In all, 266 miles of arterial road were constructed in Greater London before the beginning of the Second World War.

These developments were matched and exceeded by road-building programmes in Italy, Germany and the USA. In Italy and Germany, road-building efforts were concentrated on motorway projects to reinforce the presentation of national development fostered by their fascist governments. In the USA, the emphasis was placed on arterial parkway systems that excluded common carrier traffic and promoted leisure and commuter driving.[12]

In all, 266 miles of arterial road were constructed in Greater London before the beginning of the Second World War. Some of the better-known

Table 6   Major arterial and bypass roads in Greater London

Road	Date started	Date completed	Length (miles)
Western Avenue	1921	1943	12.6
Watford Bypass	1926	1928	13.0
Barnet Bypass	1926	1928	18.0
North Circular Road	1923	1934	19.0
Great Cambridge Road	1923	1924	11.0
Eastern Avenue / Southend Arterial Road	1921	1924	29.5
East Ham and Barking Bypass to Tilbury	1924	1928	20.5
Bexleyheath Bypass	1928	1928	5.5
Eltham/Sidcup Bypass	1926	1926	18.5
Orpington Bypass	1928	1928	6.7
Bromley Bypass	1927	1927	2.0
Croydon Bypass	1911	1924	4.0
Sutton Bypass	1936	1936	5.0
Kingston Bypass	1927	1927	9.5
Chertsey/Chiswick Arterial Road	1932	1937	5.0
Great West Road	1914	1925	8.0

Adapted from R. Jeffreys, *The King's Highway*, p. 229.

roads together with their completion dates and lengths are shown in Table 6. These new arterial roads were very different from their prewar antecedents, allowing in their early years, before ribbon development and the introduction of speed limits, for modern high-speed motoring. Each mile of new road cost the government £60,000.[13]

In contrast to the old trunk roads that followed ancient routes and field boundaries with consequent tight and dangerous bends, the new roads were planned by architects and mostly ran in straight lines with carefully engineered gentle bends. The eccentric cambers of the old road were replaced by positive cambers that ensured that rain would run off and provide easier cornering. The road itself was formed in either concrete or asphalt, providing consistent predictable driving that was a welcome change to the wooden blocks, setts or cobbles of their predecessors.[14]

The old roads were of varying width, but were mostly narrow. They were particularly narrow when they passed through towns and villages and when a bridge was required to cross over a railway line or a river. Junctions were haphazard affairs, often with poor visibility. Their replacements were originally thirty feet in width, but, as traffic increased, were expanded into dual carriageways, sometimes accompanied by cycle paths and service roads. In these cases, the overall width of an arterial road could be as much as one hundred feet. These roads were planned so as to bypass town centres and employed roundabouts and full-width bridges, which allowed for a more consistent and much less dangerous drive.

The different surfaces of the road produced quite different driving encounters. Concrete, a surface that was cheap and efficient in installation, produced an aesthetic effect that appealed to the industrial/modernist sensibility. It was laid in great slabs with tar used to seal the gaps between them. The spirit of modern motoring was disrupted somewhat by the regular thump of car tyres hitting the joints between the slabs. Motorists soon learned to be particularly cautious of concrete in the rain where it combined with oil and petrol left on the road to produce a slippery and dangerous surface although some observers preferred this surface because it 'secured visibility at night'.[15] Concrete was eventually superseded by asphalt, a material still in use today. It was noisy but provided plenty of grip for the car; its dark surface made driving on the unlit road at night more dangerous than on concrete.

The improved quality of the engineering of the arterial road enabled the drivers of modern closed cars to change the manner of their driving. Improvements to the suspension and handling in the cars themselves also contributed to an increased sense of driving security. The result was driving at higher speeds than had been previously seen on public roads. The early 'scorching' of Edwardian motoring had, with rapidly rising car use, been reduced to a slow and frustrating driving experience. In effect, the development of the arterial road provided for a re-emergence of the unconstrained open road of this earlier period (see Figure 5).

As will be seen in Chapter 6, reactions to the aesthetics of the arterial road network were contested and complex. As far as their practical possibilities were concerned, many observers, were, at first, optimistic. Harold Clunn gushed:

> The great new arterial roads leading out of London constructed since the Great War, are amongst the finest in the world … [they] have made the Home Counties seem like one vast playground laid out almost at our doors. To the busy Londoner in search of relaxation a new world has thus been opened up, which, for the average individual of fifty years ago, was almost as difficult of access as Switzerland or China. The Home Counties, clothed in all their summer glory, may be imagined as a portfolio of the finest views of domestic scenery in the world, not less rich in architectural and historical interest than in natural beauty.[16]

5

Western Avenue
The National Archives, MT/34 (Open Government License 2.0)

Clunn thus positioned the arterial road as a conduit to the countryside, showing how London's motorists and cyclists could exploit the arterial roads to speed their journey. His readers seemed to have got the message very quickly. Newspapers were soon reporting traffic jams on arterial roads on summer Sundays and bank holidays. As we saw in Chapter 2, car volumes grew steadily in the interwar period. Clunn was an example of the many different authors and filmmakers who recognised that the road had a new role to play in British life.

Road-mindedness

Chapter 4 describes the relationship between suburbia and the spirit of air-mindedness that was so prevalent in the late 1920s and early 1930s. Air-mindedness was a government-sponsored programme led by the Air Ministry that aimed to educate all sections of British society on the importance of the air in the development of a modern economy and in maintaining a strong imperial and martial presence in the twentieth century.

Proselytising the benefits of Britain's new roads was not co-ordinated by the MoT, but was the result of the combined efforts of the car industry, road lobbyists such as the AA and the RAC and the efforts of a number of independent writers. They together produced a campaign that amounted to a road equivalent of air-mindedness. I have called this 'road-mindedness' and, although the term is a little clumsy, it describes well one of the prevalent attitudes of the interwar period. It had strong connections to London's suburbia since as, we have seen, so much of the interwar road programme was directed at building bypasses and arterial roads in outer London.

The literature of road-mindedness falls into three categories. First, the rise of the car prompted a number of histories of the road, which had a tendency to include a forward-looking last chapter on the modern road. The second was the interwar road novel where the road was used to signify a metaphorical modernity; and finally, the travelogue explaining how England could be seen anew by road and car.

The new histories of the road were led off in 1923 by the poet and commentator Hilaire Belloc in *The Road*. This is a beautifully produced book, set in an attractive art nouveau font, the whole effect only slightly spoiled by it being sponsored by the British Reinforced Concrete Co. Ltd. Belloc was writing just before construction of the arterial roads began, but he was prescient enough to recognise that the car was bringing about a significant alteration in Britain's relationship with the road. He identified that 'a … great change is upon us'.[17] He was also far-sighted enough to recognise the need for fast arterial roads and motorways. With an eye to his sponsors, he proposed, sensibly enough, that one of the fundamental requirements of such a road was a very strong foundation'.[18]

T. W. Wilkinson produced a history of the British road in *From Track to By-pass* in 1934. This concluded with a forward-looking section that considered the recent road-building developments in suburban London. Wilkinson was particularly struck with the difficulties encountered in completing the North Circular Road: 'As the Lea Valley is liable to flooding, the engineers threw across it an impressive viaduct, the greatest in the country'.[19] This was followed in 1939 by the rather less optimistic Geoffrey Boumphrey's *British Roads*. By then, the problems of ribbon development had been fully revealed and Boumphrey took Britain to task for its failures in allowing suburban houses to be built alongside arterial roads.[20]

Novelists were keen to use the road as a metaphor for modernity throughout the interwar period. The car itself was also a constant theme in novels of the period, and I have referenced literature on the road and the car throughout this book. For example, *the* best seller of the period, J. B Priestley's *The Good Companions*, describes the picaresque stories of various members of a touring musical troupe with dramatic changes in a character's life being signalled by cars, lorries and the open road. Mobility is provided by hitching lifts down the Great North Road or by buying a small car.[21] Train journeys are shown as mundane and dull. Another bestseller, *South Riding* by Winifred Holtby, uses the prospect of a new road to reflect on societal change.[22] Elizabeth Bowen's *To the North* is a more metropolitan novel and uses the new suburban arterial road network as a location for speed and danger. The driver in this book is female and empowered and this was a common device in interwar novels.

The final category of road-mindedness literature can be found in the travelogue book, which was a popular form of writing between the wars. A visit to a second-hand bookshop will still show large numbers of this type of work, reflecting the vast numbers that were sold at the time. The most famous of these is *In Search of England* by H. V. Morton which was published in 1927 and by 1935 was already in its twenty-second edition.[23] Its novelty was provided by its expectation that England could be rediscovered from the inside of a car. In a similar vein were offerings from S. P. B. Mais and, as we have seen, Harold Clunn.[24]

Road-mindedness was not restricted to the written word. A number of documentary films of the 1930s emphasised the road as a modern engineering marvel that was capable of transforming Britain. In some of these films the motivation of the makers was very apparent. For example, Daimler, a car manufacturer, was the sponsor of Paul Rotha's film *Roadwards* of 1933.[25] Later in the decade, two films were made that, rather than making a plea for more road use, were asking for a more rational use of the road with greater planning and control. This can be seem in Sidney Cole's *Roads Across Britain* of 1939 and in Cavalcanti's 1937 film *Roadways*.[26]

This latter film, which was produced by the General Post Office (GPO) Film Unit, formed part of the British documentary movement of the 1930s and sets out an agenda for modern Britain. The film portrayed government-built arterial roads as an example of the benefits of state intervention and planning and pointedly contrasted them with the dangers of unconstrained and unregulated capitalism. *Roadways* is very much of its time, part of a response to the failures of the depression, promoting statism, planning and control. The roads are shown as a network, equivalent in their way to the rail system or the national grid, a conjunction of technology and interconnectivity that epitomised a national modernity.

The film begins in a GPO depot, where parts and supplies are being dispatched to all parts of the country. The superintendent calls out each delivery of modern electrical equipment. 'One bundle of connectors, Birkenhead 290'. This depot is shown to be a central hub in a new network of a different set of connections, which were the new arterial and bypass roads. The film shows an ordered, controlled delivery system and the narrator softly says 'whether their course is North, Liverpool or Glasgow, or West to Bristol and Plymouth. A day's journey takes them through the new world of the modern roads.'[27] As is later made clear, this new world was beginning to replace the railways as the primary means of rapid travel, with an important difference: road journeys were point-to-point, flexible and individual.

Both road lobbyists and more independent commentators used literature and film to demonstrate the capacity of motoring for modernity and progress. The widespread consumption of these sources, more so for the books than the films, helped produce a changed mindset that allowed roads to be seen as modern and necessary, which, in turn, allowed the car to be seen as desirable and normal.

The arterial road in suburban formation and overdevelopment

The building of housing estates in response to, or sometimes in advance of, new railway services has been strongly emphasised in much British suburban history, with the formation of Metro-Land by the Metropolitan Railway being one well-known example. In studies of suburbia in the United States, the streetcar and the railway are shown as key to nineteenth- and early twentieth-century development. After 1918, the emphasis switches to the influence of the car, reflecting the early and widespread adoption of motoring in that country.[28] This aspect of the positioning of suburban estates has received much less emphasis in the analysis of British suburbia, but developers were not shy of demonstrating the relationship between new houses and new arterial roads. There was a strong association made between the good life in suburbia and motoring. This is seen in a 1935 advertisement for a smarter semi-detached house (its twin was artfully removed from the illustration). The inclusion of a luxurious car and a garage's double doors was given particular emphasis to distinguish this house from thousands of other similar homes. Its location next to the main London to Brighton road was seen as a selling point rather than, as it would be today, a detraction.[29]

An analysis of the exact dates of the construction of suburban houses alongside the Kingston Bypass, in the late 1920s and early 1930s, shows, for example, that housebuilding would start from roads adjacent to a new arterial road, in a similar manner to those provoked by the introduction of a new railway station. This analysis shows that the earliest new housing developments occurred, in some cases, at the furthest distance to the railway station and very near to the arterial road. This conclusion is in marked contrast to most readings of the relationships between suburban development and transport, where a new rail link is seen as the exclusive catalyst for the building of housing estates.[30]

Housebuilders were also attracted to roadside sites because they recognised that suburban society was becoming increasingly less dependent on the railways for communication. One 1934 house advertisement, in a common approach that matched the bucolic with the modern, proclaimed 'Surbiton, London's most select suburb. Wimpey's splendidly built houses are a credit to the neighbourhood, semi-detached and soundly built with room for a garage. A delightful situation, close to Kingston By-pass surrounded by beautiful unspoiled countryside.'[31]

The over-building of houses adjacent to main arterial roads was known as ribbon development. The circumstances that brought it about were complicated and interlinked. Ribbon development is not a modern phenomenon. In Southwark in the sixteenth century, coaching inns, shops and houses lined the road leading from London Bridge. Clearly, the market will respond to the opportunity to build alongside a busy new road. As has been shown, London in the interwar period experienced a phenomenal growth in suburban population and housing with both London County Council and firms of speculative builders creating low-cost houses in their hundreds of thousands. Viewed from today, when planning is highly controlled, it appears odd that developers could build unconstrainedly on these new roads, making them inefficient and unsightly and slowing down fast traffic by allowing cars to join from side streets. It also seems strange, from today's perspective, that housing developers found it an attractive proposition at all, as we associate these sites with noise and dirt. In fact, in Britain in the interwar period, all of the prerequisites for ribbon development were in place.

The first element that permitted ribbon development was the depressed state of agriculture. Arterial roads typically cut their way through open fields and market gardens on London's outer fringes. At the end of the First World War, landowners faced a combination of estate duties and depressed prices for agricultural land, so the opportunity to sell their fields to a developer presented a profitable one-off transaction.[32] The second element was the attraction of light industrial development to south-east England; a roadside location made sense for the new factories, head offices and display rooms that started to line the arterial roads on the point of exit from built-up London. This was partly because of the advantages of marketing to passing drivers in these prime locations, partly because of the ease of access to a fast road and partly because arterial road sites were often the earliest recipients of reliable electricity supplies.[33] The third element was in the legislation that compelled councils laying out a new road to install services, such as the sewage pipes, alongside it.[34] This cost, in another location, would normally be borne by the builder, so an arterial road site had an immediate advantage.

There were two key reasons for the failure to prevent ribbon development. The first reason was the government's reluctance to act under powers that they had gained in the establishment of the Road Board in 1909 to purchase roadside land within 220 feet of the highway. As Geoffrey Boumphrey put it, 'the power was never exercised, since the new roads were made, not by the MoT, but by the local authorities'.[35] The MoT would have had neither the funds nor the political will to intervene in a topic that could easily be seen, if one wanted to, as something that should be dealt with locally. Second, the local council who made the planning decision had to negotiate the line of route through many properties, and allowing the local landowner to reap some of the development benefits was the oil needed to grease the political machinery. Ribbon development was the result almost everywhere.

After ten years of heated debate over its causes, the Restriction of Ribbon Development Act of 1935, which empowered the MoT to forbid building within 220 feet of the road, largely halted ribbon development.[36] John Sheail records that this Act was brought about by the intervention of a delegation of MPs to Ramsay MacDonald in 1934. MacDonald told them, 'I want complete control ... the delay in tackling the problem has been criminal'.[37]

'Californian' factories on the Great West Road

It was the ribbon development of housing that caused the most concern. Factories, in contrast, were thought more suitable neighbours for fast motor roads.[38] A location on the arterial road provided factory owners with easy access to a road-based distribution network, connection to bus services and cycle paths for employees and the possibilities of marketing to well-off motorists. Most arterial roads had factories and warehouses located on them, and the North Circular Road still provides visual evidence of this. It was, though, the 'Golden Mile' of factories that lined the Great West Road that were the best known as they were built in a modern, glamorous American style.[39]

'Very odd, being new it did not look English, we might have suddenly rolled in to California'.[40] J. B. Priestley's well-known observation on the Americanisation of London's suburban landscape is used here to introduce the particular roadscape of the Great West Road. American and British manufacturers were attracted in great numbers to London's western arterial roads. Joan Skinner has explained how this attraction developed and how technological developments and aesthetic and architectural choices provided for a very specific roadscape of elegant white factories.[41] For the purposes of this chapter, two buildings are considered: Wallis, Gilbert and Partners' Firestone Factory of 1928 and F. E. Simpkins' Currys headquarters of 1936.

Thomas Wallis was a British architect, but was heavily influenced by the practices employed in the construction of modern American factories. As early as 1914, Wallis had built a business relationship with the American engineers Kahncrete and its subsidiary the Trussed Steel Concrete Company to help them expand into Britain.[42]

Wallis's first factory on the Great West Road was for Firestone. The location appealed to the company because it was a green-field site with plenty of space to build a large factory and associated offices.[43] The new road provided easy access to both London's West End and its car showrooms and garages and to Britain's road network such that it was. The white façade of the factory was a nod to modernist design; the decoration featured the highly fashionable Egyptian motifs of the period.[44]

Firestone, an American tyre company, had decided to manufacture in Britain, in part to avoid paying £50,000 a year in tariffs on its exports from the USA.[45] The Home Secretary attended the opening of the factory, which was addressed by Harvey S. Firestone Sr using the medium of a transatlantic radio broadcast that was then relayed over a public address system. Here, modernity was layered on modernity, with a radio broadcast, floodlighting and a modern electrified factory with assembly lines, canteens and health facilities all positioned on the new arterial road.

After Firestone's arrival, a number of American organisations followed its lead and established London outposts of their empire, completing the ribboning of the 'Golden Mile' section of the Great West Road with white façaded factories. Currys, which was famous for bicycles, but also sold camping gear and wireless sets, moved its sales headquarters on to the Great West Road. The positioning of the building as a marketing and advertising device is clear from the faintly defensive tone of Currys' in-house magazine: 'It is indeed true that nowhere in the whole of the British Isles is there a road which will advertise Currys to the world as the Great West Road. The Directors are to be commended upon this wise choice of site for our Headquarters.'[46] Chapter 8 considers how the Golden Mile was transformed by being viewed from a car.

Cycle paths and resistance to the domination of the car

Cyclists found arterial roads particularly attractive; they were smooth and fast and a pleasant contrast to their predecessors. A cycle-trade visitor from South Africa was struck by how many cyclists used these roads. 'I was amazed when I saw the large number of club cyclists on the main roads last weekend.'[47] He went on to mention the wisdom of providing cycle paths on arterial roads.

The modernist planners of London County Council and its adjacent counties took a logical approach to solving the problem of the everyday fatal encounters between cyclists and cars.[48] The introduction of cycle paths would separate two types of traffic, one dangerous, one vulnerable, that operated at very different speeds. Middlesex County Council introduced cycle paths into the design of the Western Avenue extension that was built in 1934. The council described them as follows:

> The cycle tracks have been constructed on the grass swards on both sides of the carriageway of the arterial road between Hanger Lane and Greenford for a length of 2½ miles. They are 8 ft. 6 ins. wide, and have been constructed in concrete at an approximate cost of £7,000. It is believed that this is the first occasion upon which a County Council, with the assistance of the MoT, has included cycle tracks in the design of a great traffic artery .... For workers travelling between their homes and the factory, for children proceeding to and from school, for holiday-makers intent on a country jaunt, these tracks should prove a boon and a safeguard.[49]

Not all cyclists appreciated the suggestion that cyclists should be separated from cars through the provision of cycle paths or tracks. This was a heated debate in the 1930s in which cyclists tried to preserve the right to ride on the road that they had won in the decades before the adoption of the car. The debate was summed up by 'Attaboy', a writer on cycling:

> There is a lot of talk today of tracks. Motorists in fact are most anxious that cyclists should have special tracks all to themselves – *for their own safety!* (The kindly thoughts of motorists where cyclists are concerned are wonderful to hear). It does not occur to the thoughtful people, that at every intersection the cyclist must dismount – or brave the ever-faster motorist on the road … Cyclists, themselves, can be a confounded nuisance to each other on tracks. In suitable stretches, tracks would soon be monopolized for racing – just as roads have been by cars …. I have at times been informed by persons connected with motoring, scouts, garage men and drivers – that I have no legal right at all to complain of other users of the road because *I do not pay a tax.* The idea is that the motorist owns the road, and merely suffers others to use it.[50]

At a meeting of the National Cyclists Union in 1934, Mr F. P. Low, presiding, stated that 'we told Mr. Hore-Belisha [Minister of Transport] that he has no power to compel us to use cycle paths. Nor has he.'[51] This emotive response was typical of what David Patton describes as 'a consistent theme of discrimination of being the underdog. Although cyclists were extremely numerous, they alternately felt ignored, misunderstood, threatened and victimised.'[52] Cyclists sometimes took direct action. In one example in 1935, five hundred cyclists met in Hyde Park and then cycled to Western Avenue, and, ignoring the cycle path, cycled up and down the main carriageway in 'club' formation (i.e. three or four abreast) thus blocking the traffic.[53]

John Sowerby also showed his disdain for cycle paths, but in this instance for practical not ideological reasons. He recorded his views on the cycle paths alongside the Great West Road: 'I set sail up the Great West Road to find it a perfect mess for miles with new cycle paths being made (and quite time too, for those one yard wide pink atrocities were no good). Those pink paths had a surface like a rubbish heap, cement full of cracks and pot-holes. No wonder that few cyclists used them.'[54]

Later in the year, he was using newer, better cycle paths, but still retained his feelings towards his and others' right to use the road: 'Then the Great West Road, where more and more of the cycle track is in commission – rode partly on this, but did not desert the road entirely (Hope I never shall either, not for the finest track ever made) the roads remain ours.'[55]

Conclusion

In the nineteenth century, the railway line transformed the town and the countryside, developing, in London, an inner ring of suburbia. New railway lines powered a further wave of suburban development in the 1920s, changes that replicated those of eighty years earlier. In the interwar suburbs, it was the development of a road network that was new and remarkable. The potentials for fast and autonomous connections between towns by road and for exciting high-speed driving in the suburbs were new elements in the generation of modernity.

The origins of the arterial road and bypass network were Edwardian but, because of the First World War and economic depression, building did not begin in earnest until the mid-1920s. In its early years, this network of arterial and bypass roads provided a powerful, well-engineered, modernistic environment that could be explored at high speed by the wealthy drivers of the period. By the 1930s these modern roads formed part of an imperial competition with those built in Germany and Italy.

Laissez-faire planning policy resulted in ribbon development. This had two effects. First it provoked the building of housing alongside the roads that formed new areas of suburbia that were less dependent on the train than their predecessors. Second, these houses spoiled the modernist aesthetic of the new roads and filled them with low-speed local traffic. So, instead of being a suburban motorway, they became full of bicycles, delivery vans and local buses. Where planning was implemented in a coherent way, it was possible for the arterial roads to appear modern and even glamorous. This was best seen in the 'Golden Mile' of the Great West Road, where the white moderne and deco factories produced a startling roadscape.

The building and subsequent compromise of the new roads excited a great deal of public discourse in the form of a literary and documentary film campaign. Writers and filmmakers proselytised the possibilities of the new road in a campaign of road-mindedness and railed against ribbon development, contrasting Britain's experience unfavourably with its European rivals. Road-mindedness found wider expression in the way that new roads were frequently featured in interwar novels, often as a metaphor for modern life or for wider freedoms.

For cyclists, the arterial roads became a location of contestation and resistance. It was not a resistance to modernity that was in play but a demand for cyclists to play an equal part in it. Before the rise of the car, cyclists had won the right to the road and did not wish to be confined to new cycle paths because of this principle and because of the paths' poor state of construction. Interwar cycling associations were surprisingly militant on this issue and the topic provoked much argument. This contestation is still being played out on Britain's roads eighty years later.

The arterial road also became a locus of contestation between modernist planning and early conservationism. Although new roads were a sign of modernity in life and literature, being Britain, a negotiation was required between the past and the future. This is discussed in the next chapter.

Notes

1 *The Times*, 3 December 1920.
2 Part of this chapter has been reproduced or modified from M. J. Law, 'Stopping to Dream: the Beautification and Vandalism of London's Inter-war Arterial Roads', *The London Journal*, 35:1, 2010, pp. 58–84, published by Maney Publishing on behalf of The London Journal Trust.
3 *The Times*, 20 October 1920.
4 See P. Merriman, *Driving Spaces: A Cultural-historical Geography of England's M1 Motorway*, Oxford 2007; P. Merriman 'A Power for Good or Evil: Geographies of the M1 in Late Fifties Britain' in D. Gilbert, D. Matless, B. Short (eds), *Geographies of British Modernity: Space and Society in the Twentieth Century*, Oxford 2003; J. Moran, *On Roads*, London 2009; Le Corbusier in *The City of To-morrow and Its Planning*, London 1929.
5 See R. Jeffreys, *The King's Highway*, London 1949.
6 B. Weinreb and C. Hibbert (eds), *The London Encyclopaedia*, London 1987, p. 632.
7 D. Lloyd-George quoted in R. Jeffreys, *The King's Highway*, p. 23.
8 See for example, C. Buchanan, *London Road Plans 1900–1970*, London 1970, and R. Jeffreys, *The King's Highway*.
9 R. Jeffreys, *The King's Highway*, p. 93.
10 The National Archives, TNA, LAB 2/729/ED5351/1920, approximate date as memorandum entitled 'note on working short-time on arterial road schemes' is undated.
11 R. Jeffreys, *The King's Highway*, p. 148.
12 See C. Mauch and T. Zeller (eds), *The World Beyond the Windshield: Roads and Landscapes in the United States and Europe*, London 2008.
13 R. Unwin, *Greater London Planning Committee Report*, London 1929, Memorandum No. 2, p. 27.
14 R. Jeffreys, *The King's Highway*.
15 S. P. B. Mais, 'The English Highway', *The Geographical Magazine*, May 1937.

16 H. P. Clunn, *Face of the Home Counties*, London 1936, p. 2.

17 H. Belloc, *The Road*, London 1924, introduction.

18 H. Belloc, *The Road*, p. 198.

19 T. W. Wilkinson, *From Track to By-pass*, London 1934, p. 233.

20 G. M. Boumphrey, *British Roads*, London 1939.

21 J. B. Priestley, *The Good Companions*, London 1929.

22 W. Holtby, *South Riding. An English Landscape*, London 1936.

23 H. V. Morton, *In Search of England*, London 1927.

24 S. P. B. Mais, 'The English Highway'; H. P. Clunn, *Face of the Home Counties*.

25 *Roadwards*, Director, Paul Rotha, British Independent, 1933.

26 *Roads Across Britain*, Director, Sidney Cole, Realist Film Unit, 1939; *Roadways*, Director, A. Cavalcanti, S. Legg and W. Coldstream, GPO Film Unit, 1937.

27 *Roadways*, 1' 07".

28 K. T. Jackson, *Crabgrass Frontier: The Suburbanization of the United States*, Oxford 1985.

29 From P. Oliver, I. Davis, I. Bentley, *Dunroamin: The Suburban Semi and Its Enemies*, London 1981, back dust-jacket.

30 From M. J. Law, unpublished MA dissertation, Birkbeck College, University of London, 2006. House completion dates taken from maps.kingston.gov.uk [accessed May 2006].

31 *Surrey Comet*, 28 April 1934.

32 See J. Stevenson, *British Society, 1914–45*, Harmondsworth 1984.

33 See J. Marshall, *The History of the Great West Road: Its Social and Economic Influence on the Surrounding Area*, Hounslow 1995.

34 G. M. Boumphrey, *British Roads*, p. 149.

35 G. M. Boumphrey, *British Roads*, p. 149.

36 The Restriction of Ribbon Development Act, 1935, 25 & 26 Geo V Ch. 47.

37 R. MacDonald quoted in J. Sheail, *Rural Conservation in Inter-war Britain*, Oxford 1981, p. 133.

38 J. Piper, 'London to Bath', *Architectural Review*, May 1939, p. 230.

39 A colloquial term for this stretch of the road: see J. Marshall, *The History of the Great West Road: Its Social and Economic Influence on the Surrounding Area*.

40 J. B. Priestley, *English Journey*, London 1934, p. 4.

41 J. Skinner, *Form and Fancy: Factories and Factory Buildings by Wallis, Gilbert & Partners, 1916–1939*, Liverpool 1997.

42 J. J. Snowdon and R. W. Platts, 'The Work of Wallis, Gilbert & Partners', *The Architectural Review*, 5 July 1974.

43 J. Skinner, *Form and Fancy*.

44 J. Marshall, *The History of the Great West Road*.

45 *The Times*, 17 October 1928.

46 *Currys Magazine*, August 1936.

47 *Bicycling News*, 26 August 1937.

48 See Chapter 9 for details of suburban accidents.

49 Brochure of Official Opening of Western Avenue by Leslie Hore-Belisha, 14 December 1934. London Metropolitan Archives MCC/CL/L/CON/03/05842.

50 Attaboy, pseud. [John R. Hetherington], *Cycling for Fun. With a dash of cricket for makeweight and a preface for motorists, etc*, Birmingham 1936, p. 14.

51 *The Times*, 19 November 1934.

52 D. L. Patton, 'Aspects of a Historical Geography of Technology: a Study of Cycling, 1919–1939', *Cycle History – Proceedings of the 5th International Cycle History Conference*, San Francisco, 1995.

53 *The Times*, 26 August 1935.

54 J. Sowerby, *I Got on My Bicycle*, London 1939, p. 65.

55 J. Sowerby, *I Got on My Bicycle*, p. 239.

6

Negotiating modernity –
Beautification and contestation

The incursion of the city into former countryside became a key element in the contestation that occurred between planner/preservationists and the relatively uncontrolled developments of the speculative builder.[1] This was an example of the broader contest between the unconstrained capitalism that so typified the nineteenth century and the planning agenda forged during the First World War.[2] It was heightened by the apparent failure of the capitalist system in the depression of 1929 and onwards and the much wished for, but mostly imagined, benefits ascribed, by some, to the state planning of the Soviet Union.

The arterial road was a focal point for the interwar debate about beauty that was, in itself, a synecdoche for a much wider contestation over the development and appearance of a new England that simultaneously needed both to remember the recent past and to embrace a modernistic future.[3] These new suburban roads were an important symbol in the interwar negotiation of modernity as part of the debate over beauty, as an emblem of national progress in competition with Germany and Italy, and as an icon of modern life in literature.[4]

Two organisations were central to this debate, the Roads of Remembrance Association (RRA) and the Roads Beautifying Association (RBA). The RRA and RBA attempted to connect the bare, modern road to a vision of England, formed from the beauty of the traditional English countryside and garden, in memory of the fallen of the Great War. These well-meaning defenders of England's amenities fought a campaign against both council incompetence and vandalism perpetrated by the youth of London's new suburbia. The appearance of London's arterial roads was eventually determined not by the beautifiers or the vandals but by the phenomenon of ribbon development, the *bête noire* of conservationists and one of the issues that led to the formation of the Council for the Preservation of Rural England (CPRE).

Rural beauty and the modern road

Activists and commentators in the 1920s often spoke of the need for beautification. In 1930, the geographer Vaughan Cornish attempted a summary of how he saw English rural beauty: 'Agricultural England is a country of gentle undulations where rivers flow quietly in winding curves, a land well timbered by deciduous trees of rounded form, of fields divided by a bushy fence, all in a climate of soft skies, where the song of birds is heard throughout the year'.[5]

Of course, the appearance of the English countryside had been highly contrived through the process of agricultural development, enclosure and hedging. The leading town planner Patrick Abercrombie described it as follows:

> Roads, hedges, fields, woodlands, villages, are all part of an elaborate, if unconscious, remodelling of the earth's surface, which has taken centuries to mature. The result as everyone agrees and as foreigners never fail to remark is singularly beautiful.[6]

This view of the countryside had formed part of the picturesque imagination since the eighteenth century and, as a visual tradition, formed, for some, a key element of Englishness in the early twentieth century. The impact of the First World War added a melancholic nostalgia for England before the fall, reinforcing this idea of rural English beauty.[7] In the 1930s, Stanley Baldwin used this referencing of 'deep' England as a nationalist political theme to evoke England's relationship with its countryside and to distinguish it from the characteristics of other European countries that had abandoned traditional values.[8] H. V. Morton also expressed this backward-looking view of English beauty, writing for example, 'This village that symbolises England sleeps in the subconscious of many a townsman'.[9] This interpretation of the traditional and rural was the type of beautification called for by the RRA and the RBA and was, in effect, an attempt to resist and disguise the modernity of the arterial roads and cloak them with trees and shrubs so that they appeared more rural, more pleasing to the eye, and therefore more English.

The positioning of the planners/preservationists was somewhat different.

While appreciating beauty, as Abercrombie showed in the passage quoted above, they proposed an ordered and planned countryside that could embrace modern elements such as the electricity pylon or the arterial road and remain beautiful. Clough Williams-Ellis concluded that as 'the great network of smoothed-out concrete roads is completed' there was little point in travel to the countryside as it was becoming indistinguishable from the town.[10] He pleaded for the need to appreciate 'the beauty about us, that is the beauty of country, town and village, the normal visible setting of our ordinary, everyday lives'.[11] Neither Williams-Ellis nor Abercrombie was a strict architectural modernist, but both were highly appreciative of the need for planning and a return to order that was such a feature of that movement. For example, Williams-Ellis is famous for his romantic village at Portmeirion, but also collaborated with John Summerson on a highly appreciative study of modernist architecture in *Architecture Here and Now* (1934), and Abercrombie's *County of London Plan* (1943) has been seen as 'an English reworking of Le Corbusier's ultra-modernist radiant city'.[12]

The new roads' appearance was strikingly modern. As discussed in the previous chapter, there had been no new major roads in England for generations, so the old roads were lined with mature trees, cottages and houses. They were narrow and had only recently been tarred to reduce the dust caused by cars. The contrast with the new arterial roads, cutting their dramatic way across the countryside, was extreme. The concrete blocks of the road were bright and white and, on a sunny day, some found them attractive. For example, Williams-Ellis described the modern road as follows:

> There is surely something rather noble about the broad white concrete ribbons laid in sweeping curves and easy gradients across the country – something satisfying in their clean-planed cuttings and embankments.[13]

Even C. H. Bressey, the traditionalist chief engineer of the Roads Department of the MoT, commented that the roads were 'not necessarily beautiful in themselves' but that 'a new highway striking a bold course over hill and dale gives an exhilarating feeling of freedom and expansion'.[14]

Unfortunately, for the more featureless sections of London's outer suburbia, the new road might take a more banal turn. Fenced in by barbed wire and flanked by fields of cabbages, the new road could look bare and ugly. H. J. Massingham described this type of road as 'debilitating' because of 'partly the continuous and superfluous curbstone [*sic*], partly the equidistance of the pettifogging little trees, partly the wire railings on either side, and partly the unnatural breadth and lack of flexibility in the road itself.[15] In strong agreement was Stenson Cooke, the secretary of the AA, who commented that 'Some of the arterial ways certainly want beautifying'.[16]

Beautification and special interest groups

Into this picture of competing visions for the arterial road stepped a number of special interest groups who lobbied throughout the late 1920s and the 1930s for the beautification of the road and the removal of ribbon development. In 1921, one of these groups, the London Society, published its plans, *London of the Future*, and was prescient about the need for beautification and the dangers that lay ahead.

> In laying out new roads, at any rate, additional land might, as a rule, be easily acquired without undue expense for the purpose of ornamental planting; and some control should be exercised over the frontages of these main approaches, to prevent their being disfigured by squalid and unsightly erections.[17]

Another organisation thinking on similar lines to was the Roads of Remembrance Association, which came into being during the First World War. In 1920, the RRA held a public meeting to debate the use of roads as war memorials. One speaker suggested that 'a great cross could be drawn across the face of England formed by one magnificent new road running north and south, east and west'.[18] After this, the RRA was quiescent and then reappeared as an active lobby group in 1927. In that year, the secretary of the RRA, Mrs W. H. Morrison, visited the Board of Education to ask for an introduction to the MoT as part of her plan to reactivate the association. Mrs Morrison made an impact on the Board of Education but not in the way that she, perhaps, had expected. In a note to the MoT, her interviewer commented that:

> Mrs. Morrison is not a very clear or coherent person, but so far as I understand her object, it is to get trees and shrubs planted alongside the roadsides, especially of the new arterial roads and to provide seats for wayfarers, village signs and other decorative devices, including statuary ... In my private opinion, the scheme is not likely to achieve much result.[19]

Despite the doubts of the Board of Education, the RRA was a well-sponsored organisation and had established a committee of the great and good with six peers, five Members of Parliament and several knights. One other prominent committee member was Megan Lloyd George, the daughter of the sponsor of the arterial roads scheme, and soon to become a Member of Parliament herself.

The RRA set itself the following mission: 'To secure the beauty of new highways, especially of new arterial roads – in remembrance'.[20] This adornment would include trees, park strips, fountains, milestones and statues. It is likely that the identification of park strips refers to the American parkway system where the road was beautified and separated from housing and other roads. The idea of milestones had come to the RRA via the example of the *Voie Sacrée* at Verdun, which formed part of the process of remembrance there. Mrs Morrison considered that statues could form part of the remembrance: 'apart from new work, there are in private parks forms and figures of artistic and historic interest which owners may be willing through this Association to present for adornment of the highway'.[21]

Other groups were also interested in embedding remembrance into the nation's transport infrastructure. One early attempt was made by the Society for Raising Wayside Crosses which was wound up in 1919 owing to lack of public support.[22] In addition, the London Society's plans included a new bridge at Charing Cross that would be 'as worthy a memorial of the Great War at the beginning of this century as Waterloo Bridge is a worthy memorial of the Great War at the beginning of the last century. A great "Place" there should be at either end, with memorials to those who have fallen.'[23]

The RRA's interest in statuary is also associated with the installation of a statue, *La Delivrance*, in October 1927 on a site adjacent to the North Circular Road in North London. Press reports of its unveiling do not mention the RRA, but the ceremony was led by David Lloyd George and RRA committee member Megan Lloyd George so there is a circumstantial connection; certainly the RRA used *La Delivrance* prominently in its brochures.[24] The statue represented the deliverance from the Germans in the battle of the Marne in 1916, rather than strictly being a memorial to the fallen.

The RRA was making a connection between formal ceremonial ways with memorials celebrating the lives of heroes and the new arterial roads. By converting these newsworthy highways into roads of remembrance, the RRA thought that it could provide permanent and frequently observed memorials to the fallen, positioning them within people's everyday lives.

Simultaneously, the RRA promoted a simple bucolic beauty for the roads that fitted with its members' conventional tastes.

In the meantime, an anonymous private donor added to the arterial road network's roadside statuary by donating a piece of land and a bronze statue for the Kingston Bypass. *The Times* accompanied the announcement of the installation of the statue with a poem by Mrs M. E. Mason entitled 'The New Road'. The poem looks forward to the provision of open fields for city children.

> Here in the spring –
> There will be daisies
> And buttercups of gold
> To make a fairy chain ...[25]

This sort of mawkishness seems to have been an unfortunate corollary to the provision of beautification on the new roads. The RRA chose, for example, an appropriate poem by Lucy Larcom for its stationery.

> He who plants a tree
> He plants love
> Tents of coolness spreading out above
> Wayfarers he may not live to see
> Gifts that grow are best
> Hands that bless are blest
> Plant! Life does the rest.[26]

The idea of statues on the road did not meet with universal acclaim. *The Daily Mirror* presented a cynical response through a humorous column. The anonymous commentator was unusually prescient about the future appearance of the new arterial roads:

> They forget that your hardened motorist gets used to anything. He wouldn't halt at the statues. He wouldn't stop to dream, by the splashing fountains. He wouldn't bathe in the pools. A hostelry now–a 'p u b' in a word might be better. Or a cocktail bar. Or a cinema. I bet even those he'd get tired of. He'd know them all on the Great North Road.[27]

Although the RRA did not achieve much in the way of implementation of statuary on the arterial roads, it was, for a time, successful in placing tablets of remembrance on new trees on the Kingston Bypass. These oval tablets were made of cast zinc, measuring nine inches by five inches. The relatives of the fallen subscribed for each tablet and the RRA attached them to iron guards around the new trees to form part of an overall planting scheme for this road.[28] The London Society reported to its members that:

> So far, the majority of trees have been dedicated to the honour of men who made the Great Sacrifice Pro Patria – the two sons, for instance of Mrs. M I. Illingworth and of Mrs. Alec Tweedie: the sons of Sir William Simpson and Lord Aberconway; and among many others, to the 19 year old lad, a pilot of the air service, who in the defence of London, 1917, was brought down near Robin Hood Gate.[29]

The next development in the beautification process was the formation of the Roads Beautifying Association. In November 1925, the MoT held a conference with county councils to discuss tree-planting on arterial roads in response to the Roads Improvement Act of 1925. This conference proposed a large oak or elm be planted every ten yards on the road to produce an avenue of trees. This was an unfortunate selection, as the leaf fall of these deciduous trees promoted skidding.[30] In April 1928, Dr Wilfrid Fox, a wealthy dermatologist and keen amateur horticulturalist, began a correspondence with the MoT on the possibility of forming a group to supervise the beautification of the roads.[31] Fox was proposing a body that would be constituted of qualified horticulturalists who would be able to advise county councils on how to best plant the new arterial roads, so that the planting was appropriate, maintainable and safe for motorists.[32] A friend described Fox, after his death, as 'patient, humorous and kind, incapable of pettiness and devoid of self-importance'.[33] These qualities are evident in his correspondence where he showed himself to be perfectly happy for others to lead his new association if they were more qualified than he was.

The ministry's initial response was to let Fox know of the activities of the RRA and of a group with similar aims, but which did not restrict itself to road beautification, 'The Men of the Trees'. The Men of the Trees was an organisation formed in Kenya in 1922 by Richard St Barbe Baker with the intention of promoting tree planting and campaigning against deforestation. In 1924, St Barbe Baker established a Men of the Trees Society in Britain.[34] Fox was, in fact, well aware of the activities of both groups, and he wished, in forming the RBA, to do something specifically horticultural for the new roads and not have to be bound by the requirements for remembrance. In May 1928, the secretary of the Men of the Trees wrote to Dr Fox to say that they had unanimously decided to join forces with the proposed RBA in the task of beautifying the roads and suggested that six members, including St. Barbe Baker, join the RBA committee.[35]

Fox proposed that nurserymen and representatives from Kew Gardens, the Royal Horticultural Society, the RAC and the AA should be added to the committee. The minister of transport, Colonel Ashley, agreed that he would become president of the RBA. Ashley's wife was a keen amateur horticulturalist and already a member of The Men of the Trees and was to become an influential participant in arterial road beautification projects for the RBA.[36]

Fox produced a manifesto for the RBA to send to county councils in Britain. In it, he stated that:

> it is felt that many of the new roads which have been recently made, although necessary to the community for the purposes of transport – have to a certain extent destroyed the natural beauty of the countryside, and it is only right that an effort should be made to replace this for future generations.[37]

The final step in the formation of the RBA was the agreement from the RRA that it would like to appoint a representative to the RBA council. In August 1928, Fox wrote to Colonel Bressey at the MoT. This letter confirms the suspicion of other preservationists that the RBA was a 'front' organisation for the Ministry in that Fox was anxious to make sure that the Ministry would not object to the RRA representative joining, not the action of an independent association.[38] This is borne out by an examination of RBA's funding, which came from the Road Fund (i.e. the MoT), private subscriptions, oil companies, the Royal Horticultural Society, the British Road Federation and the AA.[39] In this letter, Fox also confirms the Ministry's views of Mrs Morrison. While welcoming a representative from the RRA, Fox hoped 'to God that it won't be Mrs. Morrison'. On a more positive note, the RBA had already begun to develop a planting scheme for the Kingston Bypass.

The RBA's ideas for planting were based on sound horticultural practice rather than a didactic attempt to beautify the road in a self-consciously English manner. This scheme discarded various English trees because they were deciduous and their fallen leaves would be dangerous for traffic. The RBA did not choose fruit trees, as they might harbour pests and encourage people to stop for fruit picking. The RBA was also happy to consider foreign shrubs and trees for its plans. It recognised that it might be criticised by conservative horticulturalists who would have preferred only native plants in the scheme and who considered that foreign plants would look too 'gardeney'. Fox saw his role as to plant for future generations. He wrote 'there is a chance now of striking out in a new line and showing what can be done in the way of roadside planting'.[40]

An example of an RBA arterial road-planting scheme reveals Fox's particular interest in trees, befitting someone who, in 1937, would found the Winkworth Arboretum.[41] At the western end of this plan, next to the Hogsmill River, Fox suggested *Populus eugenei* (poplar) as it would survive in damp ground.[42] At each crossroads, Mrs Ashley proposed planting Lombardy poplars, tall and straight, to mark the junction. The use of these trees was a particular *idée fixe* of Mrs Ashley and although they helpfully identified junctions, they also gave drivers something to crash in to.[43] In the middle of the plan, Fox selected *Prunus* (cherry) to produce a flowering avenue in spring. At the north-eastern edge of the plan, Fox proposed the planting of *Carpinus betulus* (hornbeam), 'a good wind-resisting tree' suitable for this exposed part of the road.[44] Fox's choice of trees and large shrubs rather than municipal lawns and flowers reflects both his practical nature and the recent return in interest in gardening circles to the landscapes of the Georgian period, rejecting Victorian formalism.[45]

Other countries were also undertaking similar efforts to landscape their new roads. In Germany, the Nazi government used official *autobahn* landscape architects for the role taken informally by the RBA in Britain. These landscape architects encouraged the use of native plants to encourage a sense of *heimat*.[46] In contrast, in Italy, the designers of the emerging *autostrade* system were not interested in landscape and concentrated their attention on producing beautifully engineered infrastructure, such as bridges.[47] In the USA, road-building efforts were concentrated on the parkway, which was pioneered in suburban New York State as early as 1906.[48] This was the epitome of new road development in a pastoral setting. The parkway, bordered by trees, shrubs and grass, was a road reserved for light motor traffic that developers could not build on. This provided the motorist with an efficient and aesthetically pleasing leisure drive.[49]

Over the next few years, the RBA would present and supervise the implementation of planting schemes for many arterial roads and bypasses. Within three years of formation, the RBA was able to claim optimistically that 'the Greater London Arterial Roads for the most part bid fair to develop into attractive avenues displaying for several scores of miles a wide variety of ornamental and flowering trees'.[50]

This presented quite a gloss on the RBA's actual experiences. The planting and maintenance of the trees and shrubs were, in fact, the responsibility of the relevant county council. The RBA had to rely on the actions of the councils as it had insufficient funding of its own to execute schemes, which led to frustration for the RBA as poorly qualified council gardeners planted trees incorrectly or failed to maintain them so that they quickly died.[51]

Suburban vandalism

The RBA's frustrations were not limited to poor planting. Its efforts were also undermined by the work of vandals. In the writings of Williams-Ellis and C. E. M. Joad and others, their concern over badly behaved visitors from the town littering and spoiling the countryside is clear.[52] They set out a moral geography that would, ideally, permit access to the country-side only to those citizens who had been educated in proper conduct.[53] This concern was not just limited to intellectuals. A cartoon in *The Daily Mirror* from 1929 identified an equivalent popular concern over littering, vandalism and the transgression of the town dweller into the countryside. An early conservationist is pictured asking a motorist who has thrown his picnic rubbish out of the car window, 'I'm collecting meat tins – may I add yours to my collection?' [54]

In the new suburbia of the arterial road, the problems of vandalism were particularly associated with teenagers. Although in the popular imagina-tion, teenage vandalism is first associated with the teddy boys of the 1950s, concern over juvenile delinquency stretches back to the Victorian period when, for the first time, the criminal justice system treated youths differ-ently from adults. By the 1920s, special courts, borstals and probation officers were in place to deal with juvenile crime. Such crime was associated in the minds of concerned citizens with poverty and urban deprivation. To find an example of suburban vandalism is more unusual, but is a reflection of the scale of suburbanisation of London at this time and perhaps the boredom of life in these new houses.[55]

The planting on the Kingston Bypass took place in late 1928 and early 1929. In all some ten thousand trees and shrubs were planted on this road.[56] Almost immediately, vandals started disrupting the planting. The RBA, much concerned by this new development, wrote to the MoT to sug-gest that they should put up some notices stating the following:

> These trees (or shrubs) are planted with public funds for the benefit of the community, and it is hoped that individuals will not only refrain from damaging them, but will look upon themselves as guardians of their own

property, and will prevent others from breaking, or in any way damaging the trees.[57]

In February 1929, *The Times* reported that there had been extensive damage to trees on this bypass. A Surrey County Council official doubted that the damage was the work of small children as six-foot-high wire protected the trees.[58] In May 1929, vandals destroyed 70 young trees and hundreds of bulbs on the same road. The RBA responded by appointing an ex-policeman as a 'watcher' on the road.[59]

The RRA had become the Roads of Remembrance Committee of the RBA by this stage, and had planted eight hundred trees for remembrance purposes. Two hundred trees had been allocated to donors and labelled for them; of these 120 were damaged. The RBA and the ministry agreed, unrealistically, that a useful response to the vandalism would be to get a local dignitary, Sir Archibald Sinclair, to write to *The Times*:

> I have observed with regret the damage which is being done by thoughtless people to the trees which have been planted along the side of the road, most of them bearing memorial tablets. Not only are the trees themselves damaged but the tablets have been broken and in many cases thrown away. Most of these memorials are to men who fell in the war, and I write this letter in the firm belief that this damage would stop if it could be brought home to the perpetrators that their conduct is the equivalent of the desecration of tombstones and an insult to the memory of those who died for their country.[60]

In this plea, Sinclair was aiming to reinforce the resolve of scoutmasters and teachers to the young people in their care. Sinclair assumed that young people were responsible, which seems plausible as adults almost universally observed remembrance at this time.[61]

The continuing destruction of the trees and shrubs on the Kingston Bypass led the RBA to consider it almost normal behaviour, to the point that when it did not occur it became a matter of comment. After a tour of the newly planted Eastern Avenue, the RBA wrote the following to the MoT: 'The one striking point was that no damage appeared to have been done to any of the trees or shrubs which spoke well for the inhabitants of this neighbourhood'.[62] Colonel Bressey of the Ministry responded in a letter to Wilfred Fox comparing the Eastern Avenue to Kingston: 'I drove that way this morning, and was very gratified to see how entirely immune from damage the trees and shrubs have been. It makes it all the more difficult to understand the wanton destruction that has taken place along the Kingston By-Pass.'[63]

The RBA let its frustration with vandalism show in its instruction manual *Roadside Planting*:

> Much of the disappointment caused by the failure of road planting schemes is due to wilful damage, either by local inhabitants wantonly destroying the trees and shrubs, or by motorists and others breaking the flowering branches when in bloom to take home, or digging up the smaller shrubs and plants and carrying them away, presumably to plant in their own gardens. It must be confessed that the English population is lacking in the primary instincts necessary for the creation and maintenance of agreeable surroundings to a greater extent than any other nation in western civilisation.[64]

In 1927, Stanley Baldwin, in his speech at the opening of the Kingston Bypass, had expressed the hope that appealing to gentlemanly behaviour might prevent drivers despoiling the roads: 'There ought to be an unwritten code that to defile any of these great roads, either by ugly surroundings, by hoggish behaviour along them, or by upsetting or spilling litter on them, should be a bar to a man from entering any decent club or any decent home circle'.[65]

Baldwin, typically invoking an appeal to English gentlemanly conduct, was both anachronistic and out of touch. The adolescent vandals who defied convention by ripping up the tablets of remembrance would have been unlikely to respond to a request to observe the manners of a gentleman's club. It is more likely that their influences came from the American gangster movie they saw at their weekly visit to the cinema.[66]

Baldwin in referring to 'ugly surroundings' on the road was commenting on the emergence of ribbon development. In 1930, as the RBA was contemplating how its planting schemes might look in fifty year's time, the forces of speculative building were already massing to contest their beautification and turn their pastoral visions into a suburban nightmare.

The actuality of ribbon development physically rooted up the planting schemes of the RBA far more efficiently than a group of teenage vandals could manage. The early signs of ribbon development in the countryside along main roads formed one of the aspects of 'beastliness' that provoked Patrick Abercrombie to write his highly influential call to arms, *The Preservation of Rural England*, in 1926.[67] This proposed a federation of voluntary and professional groups to fight for a separation between the urban and the rural and led directly to the formation of the CPRE later that year. Ribbon development, later seen as a key campaigning point, was in fact only one of many provocations discussed in the paper, which included thoughts on quarries, playing fields and the preservation of ancient monuments. If the CPRE was to act as the federal leader of preservation and beautification interest groups, it would have seemed natural that the RBA would affiliate itself under its umbrella. This did not turn out to be the case, with the two organisations competing for funding and media attention.

The CPRE did not welcome the formation of the RBA and saw it as a distraction from its own efforts to introduce preservationism with modern planning. Its view is summed up in this draft of a letter to the prime minister: 'It ought to be totally unnecessary to create a society to beautify roads any more than to beautify home-fronts. The control over the margin of the roads should obviously be part of the design of the road itself.'[68]

The sponsorship of the AA was a key prize for direct funding and access to a wealthy membership list. Dr Fox was at first nervous that the AA was already associated with the CPRE: 'I think their [the AA] attitude will be a good deal guided by the CPRE as they have already rather enthusiastically espoused their cause'.[69]

This proved not to be the case and the AA and the RBA, for example, went on to publish booklets together jointly,[70] Fox was less successful at using the BBC as a medium for disseminating their message, as the BBC was already tied up with the CPRE and had broadcast a series of its talks.[71]

In *England and the Octopus* in 1928, CPRE founder, Clough Williams-Ellis, used a disease metaphor to protest against ribbon development: 'In the buildings that quickly crop up on either hand there is nothing at all noble or satisfying. Whether bungalows or garages, tea shops or villas their nastiness is assured … the disfiguring little buildings grow up and multiply like nettles along a drain, like lice upon a tape worm.'[72]

In a similar vein, two examples of the continuous stream of criticism of ribbon development throughout the 1930s were provided by C. E. M. Joad, who thought that the new citizens of the ribboned arterial road 'spread like locusts over the land', and H. J. Massingham, who wrote that 'the rural scene was plastered and littered with the fungoid growths of the Machine Age, villas, booths, shacks and shanties'.[73]

What all of these commentators missed, and it is only now visible through hindsight, is that, for the lower middle classes, in conjunction with the desire to return to an imagined rural England in the new suburbia was a parallel and equally strong desire for the modern. This did not successfully translate into the building of many homes in the modernist architectural idiom but was a strong feature in the internal design of the houses themselves. The key ingredient for this domestic modernity was electrification in its introduction of the telephone, radio, lighting, heating and washing, transforming the experiences of the preceding generation. In a similar way, the arterial road with its exciting and new high-speed vehicles provided another, in this case visual, sense of the modern. To live on the arterial road was, in itself, a modern and exciting experience.[74] Alan Jackson reports that roadside houses were more expensive than those on side streets.[75] Paul Vaughan recalls this theme from his childhood on the Kingston Bypass in the 1930s: 'There was a certain excitement and even prestige about our proximity to this tumultuous new highway. You felt au courant, up to date, as along its modern dual carriageway bowled the compact little motors adventuring to the coast for the day.'[76]

This excitement in the arterial road was, of course, more appealing to the young than to the traditionally minded. The satirical columnist Robert Lynd caught the mood, remarking tartly that 'The storm of noise that rises and falls all through the night along an arterial road might prevent some of us elders from sleeping, but to the new generation it may well be a lullaby'.[77]

Although it was incomprehensible to the preservationists, ribbon development was, in fact, rather popular with the lower-middle-class purchasers of houses fronting the arterial road or in the streets running off it. Their new houses provided them with modernity inside and out, somewhere to park the car and quick access to a fast road for trips to the country or for commuting to their new job in a light industrial factory. It was only at the end of the 1950s and with the associated rapid growth in car ownership that the full impact of life on the arterial road was revealed in terms of noise and pollution.

Ribbon development had a dramatic impact on the final appearance of London's arterial roads. For example, within ten years of the RBA's planting and beautification of the Kingston Bypass, ribbon development had changed its appearance in a dramatic fashion. By 1939, concrete and those epitomic features of the 1930s suburban landscape, an Odeon cinema and a large Charrington public house, had replaced the acers and Lombardy poplars. This was replicated throughout London's arterial road network.

Conclusion

The activities of the RRA and the RBA present an important insight into the way in which the road became a focal point for the contestation of the appearance of England's landscape in the years after the First World War. This was part of a much wider debate about what suburbia should look like and was influenced by the controversy over modernism, which in its architectural form was finding some traction in a small number of well-publicised public and private buildings. The Victorian and Edwardian obsession with gothic and arts and crafts styles was carried through into suburban house design in the interwar years, much to the despair of intellectuals. They derided the Tudorbethan semi-detached, but these houses were extremely popular. Arterial roads, financed from the public purse, were developed as engineering rather than as aesthetic projects. The resultant clean, efficient and, to some eyes, ugly new roads presented a strikingly modernistic appearance. It was inevitable that they would provoke a response.

The RBA proposed to disguise the nature of the roads by the introduction of beautifying planting schemes. This, if successful, would have conferred an even greater emphasis on suburbia as an imitation of 'real' countryside. The planner/preservationist leaders of the loose federation that was the CPRE saw things in a different and more modernistic light, seeing not a lack of beauty but a lack of order.

In Greater London, suburbanisation and its associated vandalism defeated both the RBA and the CPRE. This vandalism shows that the desire for proper citizenship for town-dwellers in the countryside was matched by similar concerns when the city met the country in the new suburb. Moving from individual to corporate vandalism, the unfettered growth of tearooms, roadside advertising, houses, factories and other forms of ribbon development led to the arterial roads becoming disordered and unpleasant, the Restriction of Ribbon Development Act coming too late in the day to save them. The RBA did not see, in the new arterial roads, a binary of excitement and danger but a different coupling of ugliness and incursion. The teenage suburban vandals' resistance was, if anything, directed towards the old guard and the patriotism of the Great War.

In effect, the patrician members of the RBA were attempting to negotiate and interpret this suburban modernity through visions of England's past. As Martin Daunton and Bernhard Reiger have suggested, this was a common reaction to the English encounter with modernity in the interwar period.[78] These debates over the appearance of the road signified a much wider contemporary concern about the transition of the English landscape from the bifurcated town/country of the Edwardian age to a more complex, hybrid suburbanised England of the interwar period. The resultant ribboned sprawl that characterised the roadsides of the period testifies to the emergence of a new, more disrespectful and, for many observers, less pleasant English culture that foreshadowed many changes to English life after the Second World War.

Notes

1 D. Matless, *Landscape and Englishness*, London 1998. In this, David Matless identified the planner/preservationist, who wished to preserve the countryside through planning, as a key figure in the interwar debate on landscape.
2 Part of this chapter has been reproduced or modified from M. J. Law, 'Stopping to Dream: the Beautification and Vandalism of London's Inter-war Arterial Roads', *The London Journal*, 35:1, 2010, pp. 58–84, published by Maney Publishing on behalf of the London Journal Trust.
3 See D. Matless, *Landscape and Englishness*; Peter Mandler, 'Against Englishness: English Culture and the Limits to Rural Nostalgia', *Transactions of the Royal Historical Society*, 7, 1997, pp. 155–175, and S. Kohl, 'Rural England: an Invention of the Motor Industries?' in R. Burden and S. Kohl (eds), *Landscape and Englishness*, New York 2006.
4 The road as a symbol of modernity is most closely associated with Marshall Berman in *All That Is Solid Melts into Air: The Experience of Modernity*, London 1983, and, originally, with Le Corbusier in *The City of To-morrow and Its Planning*, London 1929, and in S. Giedion, *Space, Time and Architecture: The Growth of a New Tradition*, Oxford 1962 [1941].
5 V. Cornish, *National Parks and the Heritage of Scenery*, London 1930, p. 73.
6 L P. Abercrombie, 'The Preservation of Rural England', *Town Planning Review*, 12:1, 1926, pp. 5–56.
7 The extent to which the connection between the rural and Englishness was the product of a 'small, articulate but not necessarily influential avant-garde' is discussed by Peter Mandler in 'Against Englishness: English Culture and the Limits to Rural Nostalgia, 1850–1940', *Transactions of the Royal Historical Society*, 7, 1997, pp. 155–175.
8 See D. Gilbert and R. Preston, 'Suburban Modernity and National Identity' in D. Gilbert, D. Matless B. Short (eds), *Geographies of British Modernity: Space and Society in the Twentieth Century*, Oxford 2003.
9 H. V. Morton, *In Search of England*, London 1927, p. 2, and S. Kohl, 'Rural England: an Invention of the Motor Industries?' in R. Burden and S. Kohl (eds), *Landscape and Englishness*, pp. 185–206.
10 C. Williams-Ellis, *England and the Octopus*, London 1928, p. 21.
11 C. Williams-Ellis, *England and the Octopus*, p. 23.

12 M. Miller, 'Abercrombie, Sir (Leslie) Patrick (1879–1957)', *Oxford Dictionary of National Biography*, Oxford 2004; online edn, Jan 2008 [www.oxforddnb.com/view/article/30322, accessed 16 December 2008.].

13 C. Williams-Ellis, *England and the Octopus*, p. 162.

14 Roads Beautifying Association, *Roadside Planting*, London 1930, foreword.

15 H. J. Massingham, *London Scene*, London 1933, p. 97.

16 S. Cooke, quoted in *The Daily Mirror*, 22 October 1928.

17 London Society and A. Webb, *London of the Future*, London 1921, p. 26; see also D. Gilbert, 'London of the Future: the Metropolis Re-imagined after the Great War', *Journal of British Studies*, 43:1, 2004, pp. 243–268.

18 *The Manchester Guardian*, 25 March, 1920.

19 TNA, MT 39/60, letter from Board of Education to the MoT, 16 December 1927.

20 TNA, MT 39/60, RRA letterhead, 1928.

21 TNA, MT 39/60, letter from Mrs Morrison to Sir Henry Maybury, 19 January 1928.

22 A. King, *Memorials of the Great War in Britain: The Symbolism and Politics of Remembrance*, Oxford 1998, p. 74.

23 London Society and A. Webb, *London of the Future*, p. 26.

24 *The Times*, 21 October, 1927.

25 M. Mason, 'The New Road', *The Times*, 28 December 1928.

26 TNA, MT 39/60, letter from RRA to Sir Henry Maybury, 19 January 1928.

27 *The Daily Mirror*, 4 January 1929.

28 *The Times*, 29 March 1930.

29 *The Journal of the London Society*, 148, June 1930, p. 86 (Robin Hood Gate was the starting point for the Kingston Bypass as it left London).

30 *The Times*, 24 February 1926.

31 TNA, MT 39/60, letter from MoT to Dr Wilfred Fox, 10 April 1928.

32 See also P. Merriman, *Driving Spaces: A Cultural-historical Geography of England's M1 Motorway*, and E. Ford, 'Byways Revisited', *Landscape Design*, 234, 1994, pp. 34–38, on the formation of the RBA.

33 Letter from W.L.S. in *The Times*, 28 May 1962.

34 R. Burleigh, 'Baker, Richard Edward St Barbe (1889–1982)', *Oxford Dictionary of National Biography*, Oxford University Press, 2004 [www.oxforddnb.com/view/article/50369, accessed 7 December 2008].

35 TNA, MT 39/60, letter from Mrs Grant-Duff to Dr Wilfrid Fox, 10 May 1928.

36 TNA, MT 39/60, letter from RBA to MoT, 16 July 1928.

37 TNA, MT 39/60, W. Fox, *Draft RBA Manifesto*, undated but probably August 1928.

38 TNA, MT 39/60, letter from RBA to MoT, 8 August 1928 see D. Matless, *Landscape and Englishness*, p. 55.

39 P. Bassett, *A List of the Historical Records of the Roads Beautifying Association*, Birmingham 1980.

40 RBA, *Roadside Planting*, p. 4; although *Roadside Planting's* authorship is anonymous, Wilfrid Fox's voice is clearly discernible in the text.

41 www.nationaltrust.org.uk [accessed 4 March 2009].

42 Surrey County Council, Surrey History Centre, Papers relating to Kingston By-Pass (1928), Manuscript 4284 1–4.

43 *The Times*, 1 November, 1928.

44 RBA, *Roadside Planting*, p. 153.

45 B. Elliott, 'Historical Revivalism in the Twentieth Century: a Brief Introduction', *Garden History*, 28:1, 2000, pp. 17–31.

46 For a detailed reading of the landscaping of the autobahn, see T. Zeller, 'Building and Rebuilding the Landscape of the Autobahn, 1930–70' in C. Mauch and T. Zeller (eds), *The World Beyond the Windshield: Roads and Landscapes in the United States and Europe*, London 2008; T. Zeller, *Driving Germany: The Landscape of the German Autobahn, 1930–1970*, Oxford 2007; W. Rollins, 'Whose Landscape? Technology, Fascism and Environmentalism on the National Socialist Autobahn', *Annals of the Association of American Geographers*, 85:3, 1995, pp. 494–520.

47 For the *autostrada* see M. Maraglio, 'A Rough Modernization' in C. Mauch and T. Zeller (eds), *The World Beyond the Windshield*.

48 *Time Magazine*, 28 June 1937.

49 For the parkway see T. Davis, 'The Rise and Decline of the American Parkway' in C. Mauch and T. Zeller (eds), *The World Beyond the Windshield*.

50 RBA, *Annual Report of the RBA*, 1931, London 1932.

51 TNA, MT 39/60, letter from RBA to MoT, 7 May 1930.

52 C. Williams-Ellis, *England and the Octopus*, and C. E. M Joad, *The Horrors of the Countryside*, London 1931.

53 D. Matless, *Landscape and Englishness*, p. 62.

54 W. K. Haselden, cartoon from *The Daily Mirror*, 14 May 1929.

55 See J. Savage, *Teenage: The Creation of Youth Culture*, London 2007, and V. Bailey, *Delinquency and Citizenship: Reclaiming the Young Offender, 1914–1948*, Oxford 1987.

56 *The Times*, 4 February, 1929.

57 TNA, MT 39/60, letter from RBA to MoT, 22 October, 1928.

58 *The Times*, 27 February 1929.

59 *The Manchester Guardian*, 13 May 1929.

60 A. Sinclair, letter to *The Times*, 28 March 1930.

61 See A. King, *Memorials of the Great War in Britain*.

62 TNA, MT 39/60, letter from RBA to MoT, 7 May 1930.

63 TNA, MT 39/60, letter from MoT to RBA, 9 May 1930.

64 RBA, *Roadside Planting*, p. 17.

65 *The Times*, 29 October 1927.

66 J. Richards, *The Age of the Dream Palace: Cinema and Society in Britain, 1930–1939*, London 1989. Richards reports that opinions varied as to whether violent films at the cinema were promoting teenage vandalism. See

also B. Rieger, *Technology and the Culture of Modernity in Britain and Germany, 1890–1945*, Cambridge 2005.

67 L. P. Abercrombie, 'The Preservation of Rural England', *Town Planning Review*, 12:1, 1926, pp. 5–56.

68 London Society's drafting of a CPRE letter to the Prime Minister, Museum of Rural Life, SR CPRE C/1/104/2, undated but likely to be from November 1929.

69 TNA, MT 39/60, letter from Dr W. Fox to MoT, 16 July 1928.

70 For example, *The Roadside Halt, a joint Plea by the Automobile Association and the Roads Beautifying Association*, London 1935.

71 TNA, MT 39/60, letter from BBC to RBA, 5 July 1929.

72 C. Williams-Ellis, *England and the Octopus*, p. 162.

73 C. E. M Joad, *The Horrors of the Countryside*, p. 143, H. J. Massingham, *London Scene*, p. 95.

74 See N. J. Thrift, *Spatial Formations*, London 1996, for a discussion of British electrification, motoring and modernity.

75 A A Jackson, *Semi-detached London: Suburban Development, Life and Transport, 1900–39*, London 1973, p. 124.

76 P. Vaughan, *Something in Linoleum*, London 1994, p. 58.

77 R. W. Lynd, 'Life on an Arterial Road', *The New Statesman and Nation*, 14 October 1933.

78 M. J. Daunton, and B. Rieger, *Meanings of Modernity: Britain from the Late-Victorian Era to World War II*, Oxford 2001.

Part IV

Journeys

7

Pleasure and peril at the
suburban roadhouse

The new arterial road system provided for the possibility of high-speed motoring from London into its suburban periphery.[1] As driving became fashionable and an opportunity to display wealth and status, it was inevitable that entrepreneurs would begin the process of converting their garages, tearooms and filling stations into roadhouses that catered for their customers' drinking and entertainment as well as their practical needs. The popularity of the high-speed journey to the roadhouse soon came to the attention of Pathé, a newsreel company, who saw the phenomenon as an exciting topic for their filmed news magazine. The scene can be imagined as follows.

It is almost dark on a London summer's night in 1933. Turning on to the Kingston Bypass, the cherry-red Swallow SS1 two-seater sports car accelerates on to the bright white concrete of the new road. The driver and his passenger, perhaps not his wife, both in evening dress, have had cocktails in town and are now in hot pursuit of the latest fashion, dancing at one of London's new roadhouses. After some exhilarating high-speed driving, the Ace of Spades roadhouse comes into view. Brightly floodlit and flashing neon, its Tudor exterior conceals a jazz-moderne dance floor set beside an oversized outdoor swimming pool. The SS1 is parked amongst other fashionable marques in the roadhouse's large car park. An aeroplane passes overhead. Turning a Brilliantined head skywards, the driver can just make out the profile of a newsreel cameraman filming precariously from the side of the plane. The plane banks sharply, and the camera records the empty road, the black ace symbol at the bottom of the floodlit pool and the lights of the restaurant. Walking to the poolside, the driver and his partner see a second cameraman filming as a man in full evening dress dives into the pool from the top board. Once in the water, he wrestles with three lady swimmers in bathing suits and hats to the laughter and applause of the audience.[2]

The roadhouse was portrayed in this way as both sensational and fashionable. The realities of the roadhouse in interwar England were, inevitably, more complex. Roadhouses were located on the network of arterial roads and formed an element of J. B. Priestley's 'third England' that he considered democratic, inauthentic and Americanised.[3] The roadhouse was a locus of the developing motoring culture and both generated and responded to new mobile experiences for the wealthier middle classes. The construction of a large number of roadhouses in the 1920s and 1930s altered the interwar roadscape of the Home Counties. Priestley nominated 'Californian' factories as the most surprising new addition to the road but, if fog had not obscured his view on his journey into London, he might have seen several roadhouses and added them to his list of exciting developments. Vast in scale and in their variety of attractions, architecturally striking, set next to large car parks and swimming pools, roadhouses were an important contributor to the forces changing the semi-rural outskirts of London.

The roadhouse provides important insights into the history and sociology of leisure in the period. Roadhouses were spatially liminal, positioned at a distance from the newly burgeoning London suburbs somewhere between town and country. Their attraction to a wide range of motorised customers also made them sociologically liminal, blurring established class boundaries. The journey to the roadhouse became a key element in the development of interwar class distinctions occasioned by owning a car. At first, this journey was for the privileged few but later, as the roadhouse became increasingly déclassé, for many more.[4] The roadhouse (as both the site of new forms of behaviour and an increasingly significant feature in the imaginary of interwar England) also provides evidence of the relationship between independent mobility and social and sexual transgression.[5]

The roadhouse was a product of and contributor to distinctive forms of suburban modernity, reliant on the new highways and electric power and lighting to make a new site for leisure, marked by distinctively new cultural and social practices. Yet, like other facets of interwar modernity, there were also efforts to connect with a longer history of Englishness, most obviously in the adoption of 'Olde English' architectural forms.[6] Contemporary commentators, who increasingly conflated the modern with the United States, often treated the roadhouse as a transplanted American form. Discussions of the hybridisation of American cultural products by European audiences have tended to emphasise partial resistance to American economic and cultural hegemony by the disempowered.[7] By contrast, the recipients of such American cultural transmissions in the interwar roadhouses were middle-class and relatively wealthy and powerful.[8]

The arterial road roadhouse

As discussed in Chapter 2, the car provided an opportunity for class distinction and the acquisition of status through consumption and display. As motoring became more popular, local businessmen responded by building garages, tearooms and roadhouses. In the late 1920s, the term 'roadhouse' took on two meanings. First, it was used to describe the newly built, very large brewer's pubs aimed at the increasingly motorised lower-middle classes (see Chapter 10); second, and particularly in the relatively wealthy South East of England, there emerged a different type of roadhouse that was a highly distinctive and sizeable place of entertainment.

This chapter examines this latter type of roadhouse. However, even at the time, definition was problematic. One writer of a guide to inns and roadhouses considered that 'It is very difficult to say what is and what is not a Road House. I suppose the popular conception of the phrase is an attractively designed building possessing a swimming pool and restaurant where you can dance.'[9] The short-lived Roadhouses Association also concluded that 'a thoroughbred roadhouse should have petrol in its veins' i.e. that its origins should be 'based around the garage and petrol pump'.[10] As part of the fashion for the outdoors and physical fitness, roadhouses provided large swimming pools, which together with lunches and afternoon teas and tea dances catered for daytime customers. One such pool was advertised with 'its crystal clear waters scientifically filtered and purified and kept at a temperature of 70F'.[11] In the evening, roadhouses also provided dining, dancing and entertainment. This was an important aspect of interwar social life, and roadhouses offered expensive sprung dance floors, West End orchestras and appearances by film stars, singers, dance acts and comedians.

The location of roadhouses was associated with motoring for pleasure, where day trips to the coast or the countryside were enlivened with a stop at a roadhouse for lunch, or where a specific outing was made for an afternoon of swimming or an evening of dancing. Although it is possible to identify roadhouses throughout Britain, the majority were in the Home Counties.[12]

Table 7 Leading roadhouses

Roadhouse name	Date of opening (if known)	Location
Ace of Spades	1927	Kingston Bypass
The Thatched Barn	1933	Barnet Bypass
The Showboat	1933	A4 in Maidenhead
The Berkeley Arms	1932	A4 in Cranford
Ace of Spades	1926	Great West Road
The Spider's Web	Before 1934	Watford Bypass
Kingfisher's Pool		Woodford Green
The Clock	1929	Welwyn
The Spinning Wheel		Hoddesdon
The Bell	1931	Beaconsfield

Developers built roadhouses on many of the new suburban arterial roads and bypasses including the Kingston Bypass, the Great West Road and the Barnet and Watford Bypasses (see Table 7). Within Greater London, this was largely a western phenomenon reflecting the relative wealth of Surrey, Middlesex and Hertfordshire.

The roadhouse's architecture, operations and spatial organisation

As the roadhouse developed, its design became increasingly sophisticated. Early examples reflected a nostalgic Englishness in their appearance and, typically, these roadhouses did not yet provide entertainment. A 1924 example was in the form of an enormous thatched cottage.[13] An examination of this early roadhouse illuminates, at a micro-geographic level, the divisions within the middle class, and its design shows a kind of cultural apartheid. The elite customers were members of the chauffeur-driven carriage trade who made use of the restaurant and lounge while their chauffeur used a separate waiting room. Superior owner-drivers could also use this restaurant with its adjacent wine store. Those whose wealth allowed them access to a car but whose social standing was less certain could choose the café and its choice of beers.

At the end of the 1920s, larger, grander roadhouses were constructed that featured dance floors, swimming pools and gardens providing sport and games. Roadhouse owners increasingly drew a distinction between club members and the public. Roadhouses had to have club membership in order to subvert entertainment and liquor licensing laws that would not have otherwise permitted extended opening hours for late-night dining and dancing. The architectural design of the roadhouse became more varied and reflected the general skirmishing between the nostalgic and the modern that was a feature of British building at this time.

The Ace of Spades was the most famous of all interwar roadhouses and is the archetype for the more developed roadhouse.[14] Cinema newsreels portrayed it as a kind of sophisticated suburban nightclub. It was located on the Kingston Bypass and provided an alternative night out for the metropolitan set that was easily accessible from central London. It had a flying field and encouraged aviators to visit by offering free meals to those who arrived by plane.[15] With its huge open-air swimming pool featuring an ace motif in its tiling, and its restaurant, dance floors and clubrooms, it provided entertainment throughout the day and night on a massive scale. A report noted that 'its restaurant was a success from the first and now keeps open for twenty-four hours a day. It will accommodate from seven to eight hundred persons. There is a ballroom with space for 350. Dances are held every evening' (see Figure 6).[16]

The Ace of Spades was a contrasting combination of petrol pumps and Tudor elevations, mimicking other roadhouses that were conversions of genuine Elizabethan barns. The filling station owners first constructed a restaurant; as this became successful, they added a private members' club-room and a swimming pool. In contrast to the mock-Tudor of the public areas, E. B. Musman, a leading hotel architect, built the clubroom in the deco style. This room attracted the attention of *The Architectural Review*, which described how the 'dance floor surround is covered with black rubber and the dance floor is laid in maple. The ace of spades is introduced as a central panel to the floor. The bar is finished in black cellulose with aluminium strips and a peach mirror.'[17] Clearly, this room was at the height of fashion, carrying many art deco design cues.

The Ace of Spades also featured in that important element of interwar popular culture, the romantic novel. It was the model for Monica Ewer's serialised novel *Roadhouse*, originally written in 1934 for female suburban readers of *Home Notes* magazine and later published as a book.[18] Ewer presented her roadhouse as a glamorous and exciting location set in a new landscape of the bypass and connected to the West End by the new road. Ewer played out an unremarkable story of a naive young woman, patronised by dissolute urban types, who used her common sense and resourcefulness

6

Opening night at the Ace of Spades, 1931
Photo by Sasha/Getty Images

to best them. *Roadhouse*, although a pot-boiler of a novel, is full of telling details on the customers and manners of a roadhouse of this period.

Osbert Lancaster, who wrapped his disdain for the vulgar middle-class world of the interwar period in mild satire, made a more sceptical response to the Ace of Spades. In *Progress at Pelvis Bay*, Lancaster records the traduction of a small Victorian seaside town by a variety of clumsy attempts at modernisation. The journey from town to Pelvis Bay along the arterial road featured a stop at the Hearts are Trumps roadhouse.[19] Lancaster cleverly pins all the horrors of the roadhouse in one cartoon. By suggesting a church on the horizon he shows the liminal positioning of a roadhouse on the bypass, amidst empty fields. The swimming pool has gothic turrets, the garage is open all night and, in a clubroom, cabaret starts at midnight. Lancaster's illustration could be mistaken for reportage apart from his satirical descriptive addition of a first-aid station and a funeral parlour.

In contrast to the garage-based Ace of Spades, The Showboat Roadhouse in Maidenhead was purpose-built as a fashionable motoring destination. Maidenhead had been a popular excursion for Londoners since Victorian times and had a number of river-based clubs catering for a metropolitan audience. Exploration of the river and fashionable boating were an important Edwardian theme, featured in, for example, the writing of Jerome K. Jerome and Kenneth Grahame. As the road came to the fore in the interwar period it was appropriate that Maidenhead should be the location for a grand roadhouse with the river replaced by the London to Bath road (later, the A4).

The Showboat, which opened in April 1933, was of moderne design, mixing aspects of modernist architecture and deco styling, the whole resembling the bridge of an ocean liner.[20] Its architect, Eric Norman Bailey, had established his reputation in designing cinemas using similar themes. This was a highly ambitious development; the local paper described the new addition to Maidenhead's attractions as 'The Palm Beach of Maidenhead' and 'in the nature of the latest innovation the roadhouse'. Its features were listed as: a large ballroom, an ample tearoom, a fine bathing pool, diving stages, dressing boxes and lavatories, a roof garden, a sun roof, sixteen modern service flats, a public restaurant, a billiard room, a hairdressing salon and a large free car park.[21]

This strikingly new roadhouse also featured in the weekly newsreels. A newsreel on the Showboat shows young couples and families enjoying the sun deck, sunbathing in their swimming costumes and various cabaret acts performing in the ballroom (see Figure 7). The owners of the Showboat recognised that there was sufficient wealth and leisure time among residents of the Home Counties to provide them with customers day and night throughout the year. Its wide membership allowed women and children to use its facilities and distanced it from the gendered Edwardian atmosphere of the golf club.

A third, monumental, roadhouse was the Thatched Barn on the Barnet

The Showboat Roadhouse, 1933
Footage supplied by British Pathé

Bypass. This was a purpose-built Elizabethan creation designed to attract passing motorists heading north on the A1 and to pull in a London-based audience to its members' club. Massive in scale, it sported a thatched roof and half-timbered elevations. It featured a 46–metre pool and a car park that could accommodate one thousand vehicles. Its restaurant could seat four hundred guests. Other attractions for members were tennis and squash courts, a gymnasium and a golf school. In effect, the Thatched Barn was an early country club in the American sense. As a guidebook put it, 'There is dancing every evening to a well-known band and a cabaret every Saturday evening. The place's position, half an hour's run from town, makes it an ideal object for an evening's expedition.'[22]

The Thatched Barn was probably the largest Tudorbethan structure ever built, fascinating and grotesque in turn (see Figure 8). The guidebook's author estimated the cost of construction of this monument to metropolitan leisure and wealth as £80,000. This was an enormous sum, considering that the price of a smart, large suburban house of the period was about £2,000.

The owners of the roadhouses came from diverse backgrounds, although

The Thatched Barn Roadhouse, circa 1935   **8**
Author's collection

one writer considered that ex-naval officers were particularly suited to running roadhouses.[23] D. C. Wadhwa, an Indian architect and builder, owned the Showboat. It has been suggested that the Thatched Barn was built for Mrs Kate Meyrick, the infamous owner of several illegal West End nightclubs. By the late 1920s, the Home Office had hounded her out of Central London and she was, perhaps, looking for an opportunity to diversify beyond the geographical writ of the Metropolitan Police, but by the time the Thatched Barn had opened she had died.[24] In 1935, the ownership of the Thatched Barn passed to Jack Isow, a well-known Soho nightclub owner.

Roadhouses of the smaller variety provided an opportunity for enthusiastic local businessmen, *The Daily Mirror* celebrated this on two occasions, showing how both former builders and mill workers had risen to roadhouse prominence.[25] Roadhouses were attractive businesses for entrepreneurs riding the wave of south-east England's prosperity who were prepared to invest substantial sums to attract the custom of the newly motorised.

The roadhouse experience

The roadhouse was sufficiently newsworthy and novel to require explanation to wider audiences. In a two-year period, from mid-1932 to mid-1934, roadhouses featured in Pathé's weekly newsreel magazine on six occasions. Similarly, *The Daily Mirror*, with a working-class and lower-middle-class readership, asked, in 1933, 'What is a roadhouse?'[26]

Marketing for the roadhouse as a nightclub was, initially, aimed at a metropolitan audience; roadhouse advertising was quick to describe how short the run from town was and how well-made the road. The targeted roadhouse customer was mobile, wealthy, sophisticated and well dressed. Images from the opening night of the Ace of Spades clubroom in 1931 show an audience in evening dress, white tie for the men and evening gowns for the women. Monica Ewer, writing in *Roadhouse*, described the clientele of a fictionalised but clearly recognisable Ace of Spades as 'the great cara-vanserai, crowded with city folk, rich, idle, sophisticated their clothes from Paris'.[27] She conjured up a romantic vision of a roadhouse in suburbia, but peopled by customers who had clearly driven from the Embassy Club in Old Bond Street. Ewer portrayed the young in their tiny sports cars: 'There was a bustle of new arrivals, sports cars disgorging laughing young people, some in berets and jumpers, some in full evening dress'.[28] Her fictional account is borne out by roadhouse pricing. Roadhouses charged between three and five shillings for lunch, or dinner and dancing for two at ten shillings and sixpence, restricting access to wealthier customers.[29]

The reality of the roadhouse experience was, inevitably, somewhat different from its newsreel portrayals. One hundred and fifty years earlier, the Vauxhall pleasure gardens, situated in the suburbs outside the newly developed West End were a place for 'intrigue, play and for experimenting with social roles'.[30] In a similar vein, the roadhouse, where the wealthy journeyed from central London to a suburban pleasure ground, also presented a complex and compromised set of class-based encounters. Before the First World War, club membership would have been restricted to the upper middle classes, members of the same social set. In contrast, the act of driving a car and being able to afford club membership was enough to gain access to the interwar roadhouse. In his memoir of the 1930s, René Cutforth observed that wearing Brylcreem in your hair was the sole entry requirement for the Ace of Spades:

> There was more champagne than bitter drunk at the Ace of Spades but, all the same, it was considerably unbuttoned for the period: almost anybody could get in there so long as he had his hair appropriately slicked back … with perhaps a little Ronald Colman moustache, a single breasted flannel jacket, a pair of not too outrageous plus fours.[31]

Accounts of the roadhouse by commentators, novelists and newspaper reports show how these class contests played out. In January 1933, Guy Waliken, his brother and his friend Wallis and their girlfriends from

Loughborough Junction, a respectable working-class London suburb, spent the evening at the Hammersmith Palais, a good location for an unsophisticated night out. Near midnight, they drove to the nearby Ace of Spades where drinking and dancing continued until 4 am. It was into the inner sanctum of the newly opened clubroom that Wallis, at 1.30 in the morning, climbed through a window to watch the cabaret. On his return, perhaps ejected for not being a member or, perhaps, just for being drunk, he dropped his plate of bacon and eggs down a flight of stairs. At which point, when he was asked to leave, a fight broke out with the waiters and chefs. The staff were of Italian origin and drew the comment from Wallis that 'I am not going to have a half-caste waiter talk to me like that' although he denied saying that 'he was not going to have back-chat from a dirty foreigner'.[32] In the car park, the cooks held Wallis as the waiters gave him a severe beating.

Jack Isow's ownership of the Thatched Barn provided a direct link between the world of Soho's illegal clubs, gambling and the roadhouse. Judith Walkowitz has shown how Isow, a Russian Jew, built up a large property portfolio of clubs and restaurants, the best-known being the Shim-Sham Club and Isow's Restaurant that attracted visiting American celebrities.[33] Under the previous owners, the Barn had maintained an anti-semitic membership policy. One victim of this was Victor Rothschild, who, in 1934, was ordered off the premises on admitting that he was Jewish.[34] Isow, understandably, welcomed Jewish customers and was the victim of an anti-Semitic protest in 1936, when oil was poured into the swimming pool and a note pinned to the front door read 'Britons awake, we will not fight for the house of Rothschild'.[35] Isow's liberal interpretation of the licensing laws caught up on him when in 1937 he was sent to jail for three months, for allowing non-members to drink at the Barn and for providing gaming machines for customers' use.[36] 'One-arm bandits' were surprisingly prevalent in the 1930s, with one estimate that there were between 200,000 and 300,000 such machines in operation in Britain in 1938.[37]

These incidents were in marked contrast to the portrayal of roadhouses as sophisticated haunts for bright young people. Outside of the members' clubroom, the roadhouses' clientele was considerably more mixed than was shown in newsreel reportage. The class of the audience was a preoccupation in reports and literature. Michael Arlen, in his 1924 novel of the fashionable London set, *The Green Hat*, skewers the class concerns in describing a late-night motor trip to a Maidenhead river club, a precursor to the bypass-based roadhouse: 'I've heard there's a River-Night-Club arrangement about here, Very exclusive. We know, excludes all who can't crowd in' … 'I knew it was the River Club as soon as I picked up a bus ticket scented with Bacardie [*sic*] Rum'.[38]

Arlen's example of class anxiety was a reflection of wider concerns of democratisation and the accelerating blurring of class boundaries. This anxiety was a continuing theme from the Victorian period where universal education and the emergence of a lower middle class with disposable income allowed a wide group to emulate the habits of the wealthier sections of society. As John Carey has argued, the intelligentsia were increasingly concerned by changes in social attitudes after the war.[39] The arrival of hire purchase agreements, a second-hand market for cars and the increasing number of motor-coach parties allowed access to the roadhouse to a much wider class of person.

Both newspaper articles and novels suggest a broadening of the roadhouse clientele towards the end of the 1930s. Newspapers of the period reflected a general concern over morality and the roadhouse. As the roadhouse audience changed to encompass the readers of *The Daily Mirror*, the roadhouse became a dangerous place for 'nice girls'. Under the title 'If I had been a cad' one reporter noted how easy it was to 'pick up a girl and take her to a roadhouse if you say you have a car'.[40] In his 1939 novel *Let the People Sing* J. B. Priestley expressed the reaction of an old and, now, redundant England on visiting a roadhouse: 'Humph! So this is the place, eh! said Sir George not yet stirring from the car. Hardly my style y'know … brand new Americanized, lower-middle class.'[41]

As well as encouraging class transgression, the roadhouse was also used as a place of encounter for queer men. The Ace of Spades appeared on a list of possible all-night destinations on a coach-trip poster aimed at this secretive section of society.[42] The queer intent of the poster is indicated by coded words such as 'bohemian' and 'unconventional'. As Matt Houlbrook has shown, at this time homosexual activity was severely punished, but flourished in private clubs and London's parks and 'cottages'. It is intriguing to think that a roadhouse would be a sufficiently private space for a night out for London's queer men.

After the initial period of roadhouse glamour had passed, British novelists began to portray roadhouses as dangerous. It is suggestive that a writer of a leading roadhouse guide felt the need, at all, to dispel any suggestion that British roadhouses were transgressive: 'In the course of my travels I sensed a feeling in some quarters that the very words "road house" meant something naughty. This atmosphere should be dispelled. The roadhouses I have used and described in this book are perfectly respectable places.'[43]

This writer may have protested too much, or perhaps only those road-houses featured in the guidebook were respectable. In their social history of the interwar period *The Long Week-end*, Robert Graves and Alan Hodge suggested that roadhouses were 'large elaborate inns which provided meals, drink, dancing, a night's lodging and no awkward questions asked' and that 'one or two of them had a reputation as being "bagnios" in the Italian sense'.[44]

Novelists used the roadhouse to represent an anonymous meeting point for a variety of disreputable 'types'. Outside of conventional constraints, the female bright young thing could meet with the cad in his red cad's car or encounter criminals of all sorts. Here is the archetypal interwar theme of individuals in a modernistic landscape anonymising and disguising themselves, and thereby producing social anxiety. Alison Light has written persuasively on this idea in her examination of Agatha Christie's crime stories where the detective unmasks the disguised and provides resolution.[45] In Victorian fiction and life, the crowded city produced anonymity, but by the 1930s new mobilities also produced anonymity in the suburb. The conjunction of a powerful car and fast new roads provided the means for couples to visit several clubs in the town and the country in the same evening. When the newsreel cameras intervened, they exposed the roadhouse and it became known to the world. In one newsreel, a straying husband had to protect his anonymity by hiding his face with a convenient dinner plate.[46]

Edgar Wallace positioned a new roadhouse as a rendezvous for a criminal gang in his novel, The *Coat of Arms* and, later in the period, Graham Greene used the roadhouse as a focal point for bringing together rival groups of agents of an enemy power in *The Confidential Agent*.[47] Greene's evocative description of the late 1930s roadhouse portrays it as a place of danger and intrigue. Greene's roadhouse was a conversion of a Tudor house on the Dover Road. On a foggy night, a chauffeur corners the confidential agent in the gentlemen's toilets and the agent narrowly escapes a beating. In *Brighton Rock*, Greene again uses a roadhouse in a key scene. Here his Brighton razor gang travel up the London Road to the 'Queen of Hearts', 'the best roadhouse this side of London'.[48] They enjoy the typical facilities of the period, dancing, dining and swimming with the addition of sex in the car park. This was not an option that featured in roadhouse marketing, but as most roadhouses did not offer overnight accommodation may have been a popular choice.

A number of factors allowed the roadhouse to become a site for sexual transgression. The First World War brought about a transition in British society that had produced a sea-change in the behaviour of young women. Women were no longer chaperoned in public, and some drove. Behind the media's fascination for flappers in short skirts was a wider social liberation that increasingly tolerated women travelling independently, drinking cocktails, smoking, wearing make up and attending nightclubs.[49] Women were also becoming more aware of contraceptive techniques that enabled sex outside of marriage to become less dangerous.[50] Tim Cresswell has examined the long history of the link between mobility and immorality; this was particularly apparent in the reaction to popular use of the car.[51] It was in the United States that the effects of the car on public morality were first noted. It was here that increasing family wealth gave young people, in significant numbers, their first access to a car. Peter Ling has explored this theme, identifying concerns about the impact of motoring on sexual behaviour in the 1920s in America, where outrage resulted from the lewd conduct of courting couples parked in their cars.[52] In Britain, access to cars for young drivers took a little longer to arrive but, by the early 1930s, the sight of young men driving sports cars was a common one. Peter Thorold has examined British associations between motoring and sex in this period. He considers that 'from the start the car challenged carefully nurtured conventions' and quotes Osbert Sitwell's comment that 'mine was the first generation in which young men were allowed to take their sweethearts for drives'.[53]

The introduction of the pressed-steel closed-bodied saloon car provided an increased incentive to use the car for amorous activity. They were enclosed, dry and lockable and were far more private than their open predecessors. Photographs of roadhouses show both types of car in the car park. This innovation and the anonymity of the roadhouse provided an opportunity for one of the changes in social behaviour that so characterised the period. A courting couple or a husband and his mistress could choose from a variety of roadhouses in the London area where they would not be known or observed.

The roadhouse and the Americanisation of the suburban landscape

J. B. Priestley identified a number of key elements that contributed to the Americanisation of suburban England that included arterial roads, cocktail bars and swimming pools.[54] The roadhouse, which featured all three of these components, thus occupied a central position in the long-running debate about the impact of American popular culture on British life. Other observers regarded aspects of American popular culture as degenerate and dangerous. For example, Tim Cresswell has shown how the British ballroom dancing establishment considered American dance steps too sexual and modified them for British audiences.[55]

The pervasive influence of American popular culture was sufficiently strong for an informal English roadhouses association to deny any connection with America in the introduction to its guidebook:

Students of the less fastidious sort of transatlantic film and fiction, on whose ears it will doubtless fall with a dreadful and sinister significance, must make what they can of the publisher's personal assurance that every house described in the following pages is of blameless repute and irreproachable decorum.[56]

The idea that the American roadhouse was dangerous and immoral stems from the role of the roadhouse during Prohibition in the United States. These unprepossessing roadside bars and diners provided dancing to a jukebox and access to alcohol outside the city limits and the attention of the city police force. Warren Belasco writes that hoteliers considered American roadhouses to be 'centers of debauchery'.[57] American roadhouses were attractive locations for popular gangster and detective stories such as *The Roadhouse Murder*.[58] More importantly, for English audiences, Hollywood took up the theme in movies such as *The Secluded Roadhouse*, *Road House*, *Roadhouse Nights* and *The Roadhouse Queen*.[59] These movies reinforced the roadhouse as a transgressive location where gangsters, detectives, jazz musicians and bootleggers could meet.

Major Rawdon Hoare, just returned to Britain from many years abroad, writing in *This Our Country*, observed the roadhouse phenomenon on a journey down the Great West Road. Hoare found the behaviour of roadhouse customers infuriating, observing two young men, wearing berets, driving to Maidenhead with their girlfriends on their laps. Stopping at the Ace of Spades, sister roadhouse to the Kingston Bypass establishment,

Hoare is attended at the filling station by a 'rather Americanized looking lad'.[60] He found the Ace of Spades of particular interest:

> I had seen – since my return – other magnificent petrol stations; I had seen places that were not unlike American roadhouses. But here on the Great West Road was a combination of the two – super petrol filling and a café that will eventually (I have no doubt) become a roadhouse. But why the youth with a rather feeble attempt at an American accent? I asked him where he came from, 'the East End of London' he said.[61]

Monica Ewer also suggested that roadhouse customers took 'their slang from America and their morals from Bloomsbury'.[62] It is intriguing that the *Maidenhead Advertiser* identified the Showboat, without explanation, with Palm Beach in Florida. The reporter had assumed that provincial newspaper readers would understand this reference to American modernity as presented to them in the cinema. Of course, America was the exemplar for much London fashion in dress, popular song, movies, dance and musical theatre. The Showboat itself was named after the successful 1927 Broadway musical.

English roadhouses provided examples of hybridisation in the way that roadhouses anglicised and re-presented American culture to their audience.[63] This hybridised product was then often jarringly set against a highly nostalgic Tudorbethan background. For example, at the Ace of Spades, photographs show customers in evening dress and fashionable cocktail dresses in the recently constructed Tudor restaurant with its traditional Windsor chairs and linen cloths. In the clubroom there were cocktails from a chrome and glass American bar and a stage for the evening cabaret.[64] Roadhouse cabaret provided, like the architecture, a strange brew of the American and the English. One newsreel shows shimmying girls in swimsuits, aping Busby Berkeley routines, but somehow looking gauche and suburban in their peroxide shingled hair, together with the Southern Sisters, a plain-looking trio, who sing 'It Don't Mean a Thing (If It Ain't Got That Swing)' in plum, faintly Americanised accents. Betty Astell, a British film star, entertains the audience with 'Heigh-Ho, Lackaday', from the Broadway musical *Dearest Enemy*. Duke Ellington's song 'It Don't Mean a Thing' had gone through two translations, first in Harlem for white New Yorkers and then once again for a London audience. This American source material was counterpointed by British music hall acts such as the Houston sisters and the not very quick-talking radio comedy duo Collinson and Dean. The night's entertainment might conclude with some exotic dancing or demonstrations of the tango.[65]

British audiences inevitably filtered American cultural products through their own experiences and aspirations. This was clearest for young working-class audiences in the period. If the recipient was unsophisticated then imitation was the most likely result. In the case of the roadhouse petrol pump attendant, pretending to be American provided him with the distinction and excitement he sought. Richard Hoggart famously saw this reflected in the mimetic responses to the milk bar after the Second World War.[66] More radical working-class readers were likely to use the material in a way that provided meaning for their lives. Ken Worpole has shown that British working-class readers identified more strongly with American literature, with its authentic portrayals of working life, than they did with British offerings.[67] For the British middle classes the receipt of American popular culture was more ambiguous as they negotiated relationships between the wealth and fashion of America and their strong senses of nostalgia, empire and Britishness. The processing of American sources for the British middle classes was complex, as microscopic differences in tone drove so much of middle-class behaviour.[68] An example from one of the roadhouse newsreels demonstrates this. Betty Astell's performance of 'Heigh-Ho' shows her looking like Jean Harlow with peroxide hair and a slinky evening gown but singing the Broadway hit in a strangely modulated Oxford accent. The image and the sound seem to come from two disparate sources.[69] The visual identity of a Hollywood star was clearly fashionable, modern and daring, but to sing in a straight copy of an American accent was considered vulgar.

The roadhouse's architecture, cocktails, cabaret, music, dancing and swimming pool all had American antecedents and were all subject to modification that produced a new hybrid experience for its customers. This hybridisation process was also in play in the activities, practices and mobilities of its customers. The key to roadhouse use was a journey in a car. One writer of the period thought that driving to a leisure destination was an American idea. He commented, 'We now find gaudy shacks working under the American title of "road-houses"'.[70] 'They [the roadhouses] have supplied a modern need which the Londoner did not know until New York impregnated him with it, the need of some place to go.'[71]

The assumption that New York was now the source of metropolitan conduct is suggestive that economic and cultural leadership had transferred across the Atlantic. It is also recognition of new mobilities, powered by consumption for its own sake, restlessness, increased access to cars and better new roads. Hollywood rather than New York, with its portrayals of American roadhouses and of location shots of driving in suburban Los Angeles, is the more likely source of transatlantic influence. Hollywood provided British mass audiences with movies showing a motoring-based suburban culture, country clubs and the latest musical and dance crazes as well as more specific representations of roadhouses themselves. This influence on London's culture changed the entertainment that roadhouses provided and also the roadhouse audience's behaviour, speech and dance steps.

As suburbia expanded, new housing surrounded roadhouses that once occupied a distinct space between town and country. This can be seen at the Ace of Spades. In the early 1930s, aerial photographs show it adjacent to the arterial road bordered by farmers' fields.[72] By the end of the decade, these fields were covered in typical interwar housing developments attracted by the quick access to the fast motor road. At the same time, and perhaps because of the encroachment of lower-middle-class suburbia, the roadhouse became less fashionable with the urban elite and started to look for its customers nearer to home, advertising its facilities in local papers.

Conclusion

During the 1930s, the roadhouse became an iconic and sometimes infamous destination for the motorist. Roadhouse owners needed space and speedy communications to Central London; consequently, they positioned their establishments on the new arterial roads just beyond what was, in the late 1920s, the limit of suburban development. Land was cheap there, planning restrictions few and journey times short. Disconnected as they were from village or suburb, only a car could provide the necessary access. Roadhouses sat at the borderline between country and town, adding their striking presence to outer London's emerging landscape of new roads, electricity pylons, telegraph poles and suburban houses. What could be more modern than to drive at speed to swimming and dancing? This experience presaged Britain's motorised future and helped obliterate memories of Victorian constraint.

The successful roadhouses were, for a few short years, a key destination for the fashionable driver. The roadhouse, acting as a locus of leisure and consumption, produced place from space. The thrill of visiting the road-

house was not limited to its cabaret and swimming pools. Despite the pro-
testations of its owners, and the glamorising presentation of the roadhouse
in newsreels, the reality of roadhouse experience was more questionable
than the publicity proposed. The roadhouse, beyond the conventions of
the West End, provided greater opportunity for class interaction than was
usual for the period. The roadhouse subverted and compromised traditional class roles in its anonymous setting by allowing entry through access
to a car and the 'right' clothes. Anonymity also powered the roadhouse's
reputation as a source of transgressive behaviour by connecting obscure
suburbia and the protection of a closed-roofed car in the car park.

The roadhouse phenomenon produced a form of displaced metropoli-
tanism. Many writers have located Soho as the metropolitan or cosmopoli-
tan centre of interwar London. This area was, between the wars, the site of
illegal, homosexual, multi-racial and cross-class encounter.[73] Proponents of
Soho's transgressive entertainments also set it in opposition to London's
suburbia; for example its critics were marginalised as 'suburban nobod-
ies'.[74] This idea was perpetuated throughout the twentieth century; Frank
Mort has shown that commentators saw Soho as a release from suburban
constraint as late as the 1990s.[75] Car driving connected the suburban
roadhouse with clientele more used to Soho for a night out. Roadhouses
were positioned in a liminal space between the 'real' countryside and the
burgeoning suburbs. When the suburbs encroached on the roadhouses, an
effect particularly noticeable with the Ace of Spades, they lost their cachet
and were relegated to being a night-spot for the smarter sort of suburban
pleasure-seeker.

The roadhouse divided commentators of the period on the nature
of its origins. The owners fiercely defended its Englishness; others were
convinced that it had an American source. The answer lies somewhere
between these points, reflecting the diversity of the roadhouses themselves, which featured a strange hybridisation that juxtaposed nostalgic
and modern elements; even the most Tudor of premises would offer an
American-style cocktail bar. Beyond architectural form, the association
of luxury, leisure, dancing and music Americanised the experience of the
roadhouse. The social mixing was also a reflection of the more open and
democratic American society portrayed on British cinema screens in the
period. Roadhouse cabaret artists hybridised their performances to make
them more appealing for British audiences and to forestall accusations of
vulgarity.

Roadhouses were an item of popular interest from about 1929 to the mid-1930s at which point fewer and fewer newspaper reports appeared as they became increasingly familiar to the public and more suburbanised in location and clientele. Literary accounts show that roadhouses were already becoming less fashionable in the late 1930s, and were increasingly represented as seedy or dangerous. The fascination with roadhouses did not survive for long after the Second World War, the necessary disposable income and easy mobility not being much in evidence in the austerity years.

Notes

1 This chapter was substantially based on M. J. Law, 'Turning Night into Day: Transgression and Americanization at the English Inter-war Roadhouse', *Journal of Historical Geography*, 35, 2009, pp. 473–494, published by Elsevier.

2 Based on the Pathé newsreel *Outer London Clubs and Cabarets – 'The Ace of Spades'*, reel: 1086.02, 7 August 1933. The car is as imagined by the author but was a popular choice of model and colour.

3 J. B. Priestley, *English Journey*, London 1934, p. 401.

4 S. O'Connell, *The Car and British society: Class, Gender and Motoring 1896–1939*, Manchester 1998.

5 P. Ling, 'Sex and the Automobile in the Jazz Age', *History Today*, November 1989, sets out the connection between motoring and sexual transgression, and T. Cresswell, *On the Move: Mobility in the Modern Western World*, London 2006, provides the theoretical positioning for the topic.

6 See for example, D. Gilbert and R. Preston, 'Stop Being So English: Suburban Modernity and National Identity in the Twentieth Century' in D. Gilbert, D. Matless and B. Short (eds), *Geographies of British Modernity: Space and Society in the Twentieth Century*, Oxford 2003.

7 For example in J. Fiske, *Understanding Popular Culture*, London 1989, and D. Hebdige, *Subculture: The Meaning of Style*, London 1979.

8 See R. Kroes, R. Rydell and D. Bosscher (eds), *Cultural Transmissions and Receptions: American Mass Culture in Europe*, Amsterdam 1993, particularly Kroes' essay 'Americanisation, What Are We Talking About?' portraying Americanisation as a semiotic black box.

9 W. G. Macminnies, *Signpost to the Road Houses, Country Clubs and Better and Brighter Inns and Hotels of England*, London 1935, p. 136.

10 Anon., *Roadhouses and Clubs of the Home Counties, 1934*, London 1934, p. 1.

11 W. G. Macminnies, *Signpost to the Road Houses*, p. 47.

12 The research for this book identified approximately forty-five Home Counties roadhouses, although the difficulties of definition make this exercise

problematic. The most important roadhouse outside of the Home Counties is, perhaps, the Maybury in Edinburgh (1936) in modern style by Patterson & Brown.

13 RIBA archive at the Victoria and Albert Museum PA887/1 (1–5).

14 Anon, *Roadhouses and Clubs of the Home Counties*.

15 *Flight*, 6 July 1933.

16 G. Long, *English Inns and Road-houses*, London 1937, p. 179.

17 *Architectural Review*, May 1933, p. 186.

18 M. Ewer, *Roadhouse*, London 1935.

19 O. Lancaster, *Progress at Pelvis Bay*, London 1936.

20 I. J. C. Brown, *The Heart of England*, London 1935, p. 73.

21 *The Maidenhead Advertiser*, 13 April 1933.

22 W. G. Macminnies, *Signpost to the Road Houses*, p. 141.

23 W. G. Macminnies, *Signpost to the Road Houses*, p. 4.

24 F. Boyce, *SOE: The Scientific Secrets*, Stroud 2003, p. 22, and R. Davenport-Hines, 'Meyrick, Kate Evelyn (1875–1933)', *Oxford Dictionary of National Biography*, 2004, www.oxforddnb.com/view/chapter/66827 [accessed 29 August 2008].

25 *The Daily Mirror*, 10 July 1935 and 23 April 1936.

26 *The Daily Mirror*, 25 July 1933, 'What Is a Roadhouse?'.

27 M. Ewer, *Roadhouse*, p. 34.

28 M. Ewer, *Roadhouse*, p. 27.

29 Anon., *Roadhouses and Clubs of the Home Counties*, Trying to convert these values into present-day terms is problematic but 5s would be equivalent to about £45 based on relative earnings. See www.measuringworth.com.

30 M. Ogborn, *Spaces of Modernity*, London 1998, p. 119.

31 R. Cutforth, *Later Than We Thought: A Portrait of the Thirties*, Newton Abbot 1976, p. 28.

32 *The Times*, 30 March 1933.

33 J. R. Walkowitz, *Nights Out*, London 2012, pp. 235–246.

34 *Jewish Telegraphic Agency*, 29 August 1934.

35 *The Daily Mirror*, 18 May 1936.

36 *The Times*, 27 February 1937.

37 M. Clapson and BACTA, *Amusement Machines*, London 2000.

38 M. Arlen, *The Green Hat*, London 1924, p. 203.

39 J. Carey, *The Intellectuals and the Masses: Pride and Prejudice Among the Literary Intelligentsia, 1880–1939*, London 1992.

40 *The Daily Mirror*, 2 December 1935.

41 J. B. Priestley, *Let The People Sing*, London 1969 [1939], p. 298.

42 M. Houlbrook, *Queer London: Perils and Pleasures in the Sexual Metropolis, 1918–1957*, Bristol 2005, p. 71.

43 W. G. Macminnies, *Signpost to the Road Houses*, p. 5.

44 R. Graves and A. Hodge, *The Long Week-end: A Social History of Great Britain 1918–1939*, London 1941, p. 380. 'Bagnios' is used here as a euphemism for brothels.

45 A. Light, *Forever England: Femininity, Literature and Conservatism Between the Wars*, London 1991.

46 Pathé newsreel *London's Famous Clubs and Cabarets – The Ace of Spades Club* Reel: 1072.14, 24 April 1933.

47 E. Wallace, *The Coat of Arms*, London 1931; G. Greene, *The Confidential Agent*, London 1939.

48 G. Greene, *Brighton Rock*, Harmondsworth 1970 [1938], p. 132.

49 See R. Graves and A. Hodge, *The Long Week-end*.

50 See R. McKibbin, *Classes and Cultures: England, 1918–1951*, Oxford 1998.

51 T. Cresswell, *On The Move: Mobility in the Modern Western World*.

52 P. Ling, 'Sex and the Automobile in the Jazz Age'.

53 P. Thorold, *The Motoring Age: The Automobile and Britain 1896–1939*, London 2003, p. 133.

54 J. B. Priestley, *English Journey*, London 1934, p. 401.

55 T. Cresswell, '"You Cannot Shake That Shimmie Here": Producing Mobility on the Dance Floor', pp. 55–77. *Cultural Geographies*, 13:1, 2006.

56 Anon., *Roadhouses and Clubs of the Home Counties*, p. 3.

57 W. J. Belasco, *Americans on the Road: From Autocamp to Motel, 1910–1945*, Cambridge, Mass. 1979, p. 149.

58 A. Skene, *The Roadhouse Murder*, Sexton Blake Library (Second Series) #405, London 1933.

59 *The Secluded Roadhouse*, 1926; *Road House*, 1928; *Roadhouse Nights*, 1930; *The Roadhouse Queen*, 1933.

60 R. Hoare, *This Our Country: An Impression After Fourteen Years Abroad*, London 1935, p. 35.

61 R. Hoare, *This Our Country*, p. 36

62 M. Ewer, *Roadhouse*, p. 34.

63 C. Waters, 'Beyond Americanization: Rethinking Anglo-American Cultural Exchange Between the Wars', *Cultural and Social History*, 4:4, 2007, pp. 451–453.

64 *The Architectural Review*, May 1933, p. 186.

65 Pathé newsreels: *Roadhouse Nights*, reel 1058.14, 18 July 1932; *Outer London Clubs and Cabarets – 'The Ace of Spades'* reel: 1086.02, 7 August 1933; *Outer London's Clubs and Cabarets – 'The Bell'*, reel, 1076.07, 17 July 1933; *Outer London Clubs and Cabarets – 'The Showboat'*, reel 1088.18, 18 September 1933; *'The Order of the Bath'*, reel: 1174.06, 8 August 1938.

66 R. Hoggart, *The Uses of Literacy*, London 1957.

67 K. Worpole, *Dockers and Detectives: Popular Reading, Popular Writing*, London 1983.

68 R. Samuel, 'Middle Class Between the Wars', *New Socialist*, January/February 1983, pp. 30–36.

69 Pathé newsreel, *'The Bell'*, reel: 1076.07, 17 July 1933.

70 T. Burke, *London in My Time*, London 1934, p. 36.

71 T. Burke, *London in My Time*, p. 199.

72 *Flight*, 6 July 1933.

73 J. R. Walkowitz, *Nights Out*; M. Houlbrook, *Queer London: Perils and Pleasures in the Sexual Metropolis, 1918–1957*; F. Mort, *Capital Affairs: London and the Making of the Permissive Society*, London 2010.

74 J. R. Walkowitz, *Nights Out*, p. 61.

75 F. Mort, *Capital Affairs*, p. 227.

8

Modern motoring and the enclosed body

London's suburbs developed in radial lines leading out from the railway and tram termini. At a time when Saturday morning working was the norm, and when leisure time was consequently restricted, the emphasis of life in the suburb was, for men and the emerging young female clerical worker, based around commuting to work. From Monday to Saturday, suburb was synonymous with dormitory. On Sunday mornings suburban life revolved, for most, around church attendance and for the rest of the day respectable forms of entertainment.[1]

The Edwardian suburban worker led a highly structured radial life, shuttling back and forth between the home and the office in a regulated and controlled way. These sleepy suburbs were explored during the week on foot and by bicycle by women and children, enjoying the parks or the nearby parade of shops in the high street. The dormitory suburb was positioned by a wide variety of authors as being truly asleep, placing it in direct contrast with the modern, metropolitan life found in Central London, an idea that was ruthlessly exploited for humour and disdain.

Not every rapid journey generates modernity. In suburban commuting by train the repetitive and routine nature of the journey deprives it of meaning. The expected modernity of time-space compression associated with fast trains to the metropolis was, in this way, disabled. This idea is very familiar to anyone who has commuted in this way; I identify with it closely through many years of personal experience. Tim Cresswell has described this effect as where 'such be movements appear to be below the level of conscious scrutiny'.[2] By the late 1920s, the independent mobility brought about by the wider adoption of cars transcended this unconscious movement of railway commuting to generate an encounter with the sub-urban arterial road that produced new experiences and meanings. The car provided suburban mobility that was independent of the railway in both direction and time of travel, changing the nature of suburban life. This experience of modernity was mediated by the nature of the road, the form of the car and the controls imposed on drivers.

This chapter first considers how motoring changed in the car's material form and in its drivers' destinations. It then looks at how the car became domesticated and suburbanised and isolated from the kinaesthetic and embodied experiences of early motoring. It then suggests that the peculiar roadscape of the suburban arterial road, when seen from a closed car, generated contradictory reactions that can be seen together as presenting a form of modern motoring.

Journey to the modern: motoring in the interwar years

The first three decades of motoring in Britain were mostly confined to the activities of a small number of wealthy car owners. It was, in reality and in the imagination, a masculine endeavour; the few famous and daring women motorists were acclaimed because they were so unusual. Driving a car in this period was an exercise that required physical strength and mechanical knowledge, qualities that were mostly limited to male owners and chauffeurs. Cars were unreliable, temperamental and had to drive on roads that were not designed for their use. Motoring, before the First World War, was experimental and experiential and was directed towards establishing speed and distance records. In the 1920s, it moved away from this earlier preoccupation and was primarily undertaken for the purposes of leisure, particularly touring the countryside and visiting the seaside. Cars were still owned only by those in the wealthier sections of society, and, for the very richest, continued to be chauffeured. The emphasis on good weather driving meant that most cars did not need a roof.

Motoring was thus connected to two important features of interwar life, nostalgia for a prelapsarian England and an enthusiasm for the outdoors. These came together in the exploration of rural England by car. John Urry sums this up as 'the inter-war transformation of the car, from alien threat to a "natural" part of the rural scene'.[3] This idea was at a peak in 1925 as car sales began to rise and ownership widened. As one writer put it, with a definite sense of agency, 'How little we knew of England before cars came to show it to us'.[4] This change in focus for the drive, from the speed or endurance trial to a family outing to explore the countryside, pointed to the increased feminisation and domestication of interwar life.[5] This idea can be placed alongside the contemporaneous increased suburbanisation of Britain and the middle-class withdrawal from the public sphere to the private and domesticated world of the suburban garden.[6]

The open car

The experience of motoring for drivers and passengers was largely determined by whether they were driving in an open or in what later became its dominant form, the closed car. Motoring before 1925 meant, for the vast majority, driving in an open car, which had been the dominant design of cars from their inception. An open car had coachwork built on a drive-train of chassis, engine, gearbox and wheels, which was often produced by a separate manufacturer. The coachwork was typically built on a white ash wooden frame, the exterior made of sheet steel or aluminium panels.[7] Craftsmen would then paint the coachwork using traditional methods dating back to the days of horse-drawn coaches. Weather protection was provided, to some extent, by folding flexible covers. Initially, the open style of car was a result of the need to reduce weight so that early low-powered engines could propel the car at a reasonable speed. The First World War encouraged technological developments, but the styling of cars changed little between 1914 and 1918.[8] From the end of the war up to the mid-1920s cars became more sophisticated, longer and lower but, largely, open in design. At this time, closed cars were confined to the most luxurious, sedate and formal vehicles.

The key sensory experiences of driving in an open car were those of wind and speed. Osbert Sitwell described this in his autobiography *Great Morning*:

> They would sit together, the two of them, the man at the wheel, the girl beside him, their hair blown back from their temples, their features sculptured by the wind, their bodies and limbs shaped and carved by it continually under their clothes, so that they enjoyed a *new* physical sensation, comparable to swimming; except that here the element was speed, not water.[9]

Sitwell presents an evocative picture of independent travel unconstrained by railway timetables away from an intruding public gaze, so that driving at speed could be intimate and private. Interwar writers were quick to recognise the romantic possibilities for placing a male driver and female passenger into an open car and to use the sensual aspects of motoring to provide a metaphor for unconsummated or, perhaps, just unwritten sexual encounters. Another example taken from literature emphasises the association of pleasurable, transcendental, sensual experience of wind and speed with motoring: 'The wind in their faces increased from a capful to half a gale to a full gale, very nearly a hurricane. Lord Horenden's spirits rose with the mounting speed. His lips curved into a smile of fixed and permanent rapture.'[10]

Before the construction of the arterial road network, the feeling of driving was intense. The roads were poorly surfaced and full of bumps and holes. The cars were not isolated from the road; suspension systems were crude and not much improved from cart springs, and sitting was uncomfortable on long journeys. The net effect was a shaky journey even at low speeds. Many writers pictured the open car driving in the beautiful British countryside on a sunny spring day or on a balmy moonlit night. Britain's climate assures us that this was not the case on the majority of days. Open cars were cold and draughty, and let the rain in. Windscreen wipers were primitive, heating non-existent. The effect of driving on a cold rainy night would have been extremely unpleasant and, as a result, many drivers used their cars only in the summer months.

In an attempt to understand how this felt, I drove an open interwar small sports car for a day, on some narrow and windy and not particularly well-made roads in the border region in Scotland. Although the limited number of companies who are prepared to rent out valuable old cars determined the location, this quiet area was representative of countryside motoring in the 1920s. I drove a 1937 MG Midget, which, although from later in the period, is a typical open car in that it has metal panels on a wooden frame sitting on a chassis. It is simply constructed with the engine and gearbox separated from the passengers by a thin bulkhead.

Driving this car felt very much like riding a bicycle down a hill. There was an incredible sensation of speed; the handling was imprecise, the suspension primitive, feeling every defect in the country road. Double-declutching made changing down difficult, producing a wrist-jarring shake and a nasty noise when mistimed. The brakes were very soft and unresponsive and required hand and foot brakes to be operated simultaneously. In short, driving this car was exhilarating, terrifying and exhausting. Driving after a rainstorm increased the perception and reality of danger with all the car's defects exaggerated. On a dry, good-quality A road, the ride was transformed and fast driving was possible and enjoyable.

The Midget has, not entirely surprisingly, a tiny seating area for the driver and passenger. It is very cramped, requiring some careful manoeuvring to get in and out. With the covers on, the overall feeling was of claustrophobia. During a downfall, rain poured into the car, as we did not have the side protectors fitted, and the covers did not fit properly. The MG is a very noisy car, producing a huge roar from the engine in second and third, combining with surprising noises from double-declutch failures. It was hard to hear yourself speak, my voice was hoarse from shouting to my passenger. The sightlines from the car with the hood down provide a 360–degree view of the landscape. With the hood up, vision from inside the car becomes restricted to a narrow slot looking forward. The feeling of claustrophobia could be relieved to some extent by rotating the car's windscreen for ventilation. With the hood down, the full smell of town and country becomes available to the driver, although it is always overlaid with the smell of petrol and oil coming from the engine compartment.

The closed car

Motoring leisure was transformed in the later 1920s when the open car was replaced in popularity by the closed car; which is the car that we drive today, if we exclude the convertible, which, in Britain, is a minority choice. The body of the interwar closed car was made from sheet steel that was pressed in moulds and then fixed together using newly developed spot-welding techniques. A windscreen, a rear window and side windows that could be raised and lowered using a lever provided vision.[11] A British example from the period is shown in Figure 9.

As has been shown, car ownership in the suburbanised South East of England grew rapidly. It penetrated into the lower reaches of the middle classes, and touring in the car changed into a popular and normalised part of the middle-class way of life. These newly purchased cars were, in the vast majority, closed saloon cars. The present-day popular perception of interwar motoring is often represented by an open sports car, an image that is, in fact, misleading; by 1929, 90 per cent of car sales were of the closed-body type.[12] This seismic change in the production and consumption of cars was noted at the time, one correspondent claiming that 'We are rapidly approaching the time when the term car will mean a closed vehicle only'.[13] In the same issue of *The Autocar*, F. Gordon-Crosby observed: 'It is a noticeable fact that the closed body in one form or another is very largely superseding the ordinary open type of car for both town use and touring. No doubt the treacherous and bad weather of the last year or so

A closed car   **9**
Author's photograph

is responsible for this preference.'[14] Gordon-Crosby may have been right,
but alongside protection from the weather the closed car provided a radi-
cally changed and more sophisticated form of motoring that was warmer,
quieter and cleaner.

In order to experience and fully understand the differences between
open and closed cars I spent a day driving an Austin Goodwood, a four-
door saloon car from the late 1930s. It was considerably more sophisticated
than the open car of a decade earlier. It featured a four-speed gearbox with
synchromesh on gears two to four. It had an electric starter, electric windscreen wipers, a speedometer, oil and battery gauges, wind-up windows
and adjustable seats.

Instead of collecting the smells of the outside, the Austin Goodwood
smelled of itself. On opening the car's doors on a sunny day, there was
a strong, pleasant smell of its leather seats. Ventilation was poor with
all the windows closed, so little of the summer scents from the outside
world came into the cabin. With its low roof and small windows, it was
very claustrophobic inside the Austin's small cabin. The leather seats were
slippery and shiny, making my passenger sway from side to side when the
car was at speed; I had to hold on hard to the steering wheel. The car was
very skittish on the poorly constructed country roads, but was much more

predictable when on a smooth metalled road. The gears crunched despite the synchromesh; the steering was imprecise, and the car did not encourage me to drive at over 50 mph.

In comparison to the Midget, the Austin was much more insulated from noises from the car and the outside world. In an open car, the driver is not really conscious of the interior of the car; the focus of attention is the road ahead. In contrast, the Austin had a dark and gloomy interior with brown 'Bakelite' switches, and an instrument panel illuminated by a soft yellow light. Being in the car felt like sitting in an old-fashioned sitting room, with a Bakelite radio in the corner.

Mass-production techniques for closed cars provided a level of comfort previously available only in luxury coach-built saloon cars that were around ten times as expensive. *The Times* published an article that attributed the preference for the closed body to a feminine influence on design. Under a subtitle of 'The Enclosed Body', Mrs Tom Thorneycroft stated that 'I now do not even want a car that can open'.[15] Male motorists were also keen to distinguish themselves from the goggles, hats and dusty days of early motoring:

> In the interests of good health it is necessary to have some protection from dust and tar spray which one encounters on the very few fine days that we get at any time of year. By motoring in this manner, I am able to wear respectable clothes and call on either business or social friends without looking like a 'third-class mechanic' or a 'golliwog'.[16]

This claim to social distinction was a key element in the transition from open to closed-bodied motoring. As motoring moved away from its original, enthusiastic and wealthy participation where dirt and dust showed that you were adventurous and authentic, it became increasingly important to distinguish yourself by your choice of car and appearance, both themes that Sean O'Connell has written on comprehensively.[17] For the uncertain middle classes, to be mistaken for a mechanic would be shameful. Presumably, the wealthy owners who dominated motoring in the early, open days were sufficiently confident not to care what they looked like; ownership of a car was in itself sufficient, at that time, to demonstrate your social standing.

This social distinction worked both ways. The use of the closed car by wider social groups was not universally welcome. Some saw driving closed cars as a sign of degradation. This debate was held in the correspondence columns of *The Autocar* throughout 1925. One reader distinguished the 'real' motorist who enjoyed the open car on the open road from the new-comer in his or her closed car.[18] This reaction is, perhaps, typical of early adoptors of a technology or fashion who see their interest mimicked and then spoiled by the ill-informed masses. Traditionalists saw driving in an open car as a healthy practice compared to being closed in. An anonymous reader took the argument further by conflating the adoption of the closed car with racial weakness:

> Surely the [English] race must be getting very delicate not to be able to drive in open cars … To see hale and hearty people driving about in luxurious coaches makes me think the race is in decline.[19]

This provoked a response from another reader, who employed his view of English racial superiority to justify the use of closed cars:

> Does it necessarily mean that sensitiveness to climate is deteriorative? Is the fuzzy-wuzzy who can stand tropical sun on his unprotected wool head less degenerate than the white man who cannot? … The sensitiveness of the body seems to increase with that of the mind but is this not really progress rather than decay?[20]

As well as demonstrating how readily the English interwar middle-class writer was prone to adopt imperialist and racist metaphors to support the most domestic of debates, this exchange of correspondence was missing the point. What these correspondents were really witnessing was the transition of motoring from an exciting outdoor pastime, based largely on masculine, Edwardian ideas of racing and exploration, to the mass-consumerist version of motoring which valued comfort and protection from the elements, and provided distinction not by how far or how fast but through styling and gadgetry.

For another section of society, interwar intellectuals, the closed car could be seen as further evidence of suburban ordinariness. For example, John Betjeman, an aesthete far removed from the hale and hearty brigade of motorists, wrote disdainfully, in 1933, of a suburban colleague at the *Architectural Review*. 'I do not wish to be unpleasant about the Regans, but they are not our sort. They all live in Wimbledon, have closed saloons … and are not interested in anything but getting money which they do not know how to spend.'[21]

The closed body enabled genuine mass-production to begin, forcing down car prices and simultaneously providing a modern comfortable experience for the motorist whose idea of endurance driving would be confined to a day out in Brighton. The replacement of the open car with the closed car could be seen, through the lens of technological determinism, as an example of newer, more efficient technology replacing outdated craft-based expensive skills. The correspondence columns of *The Autocar* indicate that a social construction of technology was also in play. Fresh air was a problem for one group and a boon for the other.[22]

The suburbanisation of the closed car

Increasingly the interiors of cars, now protected from the elements, came to resemble the suburban houses of their owners. Mrs Thorneycroft, for example, commented on interior fittings for the readers of *The Times*:

> In an open car leather covered seats are a necessity, but in a closed car other materials can be used, such as Bedford cord, corduroy etc. These are very nice to sit on, but difficult to keep clean. Real leather seats with thick detachable linen covers which wash, seem to be the most satisfactory.

This domesticated dressing of the car was also reflected in the use of another technology that distinguished suburban life in the 1920s and 1930s, the wireless. By 1925, the wireless was already a part of the touring experience, although listening-in could take place only on reaching a destination. This was, typically, a beauty spot. This was, of course, just the type of philistine behaviour that outraged social commentators such as C. E. M. Joad and Clough Williams-Ellis. Playing jazz dance tunes and listening to the cricket scores and stock prices in the middle of the beautiful countryside was, for them, beyond the pale.

On arrival at the beauty spot, reception was achieved only by casting a long wire aerial over a tree branch as if you were fly-fishing. New technology, in the form of super-heterodyne valves, had made tuning so easy that *The Autocar* reported that 'a wholly untutored woman in Great Britain can pick up American broadcast programmes with it'.[23] In contrast with the fishing line approach, by 1935 the in-car radio had now become available and fitted into the glove compartment with a tuning dial on the dashboard; drivers could receive up to fifty different stations. This allowed music on the move, and reinforced the closed car as a domesticated but mobile experience.[24]

The closed car was a lockable and secure environment for driving. This provided particular advantages for women. The privacy and protection afforded by the closed car allowed women to drive alone, knowing that they would be safe inside the car and also be protected from the male gaze and cat call. As Cotton Seiler puts it, 'the closed car removed many of the physical barriers to being alone in a car'.[25] Seiler has also shown that Ford's advertising in the United States, when directed at women drivers, emphasised this important feature of closed cars.

Another aspect of the closed car's privacy and security was the opportunities it provided for sexual encounter. Lockable doors and a closed body would, for the nimble, produce a mobile and safe place that was not easily obtainable for otherwise respectable people in the 1930s. Peter Ling explains how 'the automobile aided this process, especially when car manufacturers shifted from open-top to closed body models, improved interior upholstery and included a heater as a standard feature'.[26]

The introduction of the closed car changed the experience of motoring leisure and the relationship between the driver and the world he or she passed through so rapidly. First and foremost, the closed car restricted the vision of the driver and passengers. In an open car, drivers were afforded a 360–degree view of the landscape. In contrast, the view from the closed car was much reduced. The roof restricted the view of the sky, the windscreen provided a narrow slit though which to see the world. This narrowness was caused by difficulties and expense in producing safety glass and by a general lowering and streamlining of the appearance of cars in the 1930s. This view was restricted further when it was raining, as the simple and slow windscreen wipers of the period were inefficient compared to those we use today.

Closed cars insulated their drivers. The roar of the engine and the noise from the tyres was muted and deadened. With the windows closed, the sounds of the world outside of the car were almost eliminated. Conversation between drivers and passengers became relaxed and gentler. The shouting and sign language of the roaring open car was superseded by the more domesticated interior of the closed car where listening to music on the car radio became a possibility.

Finally, the sense of speed so apparent in the literary and actual experiences of driving in an open car was transformed by the change in car design. The open car generated a rush of wind on the driver's face. The full view of the landscape around the speeding car produced an exciting and definitive feeling of movement. Sitting in a closed car changed this; the driver was isolated from the weather as the wind moved over the streamlined car. This isolation was accentuated by the restricted view through the windscreen. By changing the relationship between the driver and the outside world in this way, the closed car also changed the relationship between the driver and the car.

The attenuated sensory experiences of the closed car became a choice and then a dominating motoring fashion in the late 1920s; simultaneously, in Greater London, the development of the arterial road network provided a space for closed car drivers to carry out new practices that would become, before the Second World War, a recognisable modern motoring.

Journeys along the arterial road

Although the closed car driver was insulated from landscape and the sensory world, his or her driving did not take place in empty space; a key element of the experience of motoring was how the car and driver encountered the road itself. As new arterial roads were introduced, the nature of driving changed with it.

The choices of camber and surface afford widely different driving possibilities. As was shown in Chapter 5, a traditional road from 1919 would allow for a more haphazard, slower and dangerous driving experience. An arterial road, with its wide, well-engineered, gentler curves and because of its level predictability, generated fast driving. Improvements to the suspension and handling in the cars themselves also contributed to an increased sense of driving security. The result was driving at higher speeds than had been previously seen on public roads. The early 'scorching' of Edwardian motoring, had with rapidly rising car use, been reduced to a slow and frustrating driving experience. In effect, the development of the arterial road provided for a re-emergence of the unconstrained open road of this earlier period.[27]

Interwar motorists used these new roads for testing the top speed of their cars. One passenger, reminiscing about this period, remembered the Kingston Bypass as a testing ground: 'A fast road in the pre war days, I was driven in 1935 from the Ace of Spades roundabout to Hinchley Wood in a big Bentley sports car driven by my father's apprentice. The speed we attained then was 72 mph, fast then on the road. So road racing was even carried out then eh?'[28]

The many literary illustrations of this novelty showed its possibilities for transcendence, for example, on the Barnet Bypass: 'They cleared London and ran out into the country, Cecilia blinked; they were doing seventy on a straight stretch of road. Julian drove in silence; she raised her face happily to the sun.'[29] Further market downmarket from Cecilia, Patrick Hamilton described a similar affective experience that associated the modernity of flight with driving:

> And now they had passed Gunnersbury, and had turned up to the right, and were ripping up the wide, smooth, deserted spaces of the Great West Road ... Gee! it was like a racing track–no wonder he put on speed. It was like being in an aeroplane! 'Go on. Let her rip!' cried Rex from behind, and 'Yo-ahah-eye-atee!' yodelled the young man.[30]

Hamilton's fictional drivers formed a spirited assemblage, where the road's width and smoothness differentiated the journey from older road experiences.

As the interwar period progressed, the ribbon development of large sub-urban housing estates compromised London's arterial roads. Junctions were regulated by the introduction of roundabouts, pedestrian crossings and traffic lights to reduce the likelihood of accidents. The motorist was further constrained by the introduction of white lines and arrows to suggest positioning on the road. The driver had been repositioned on the road, but the closed car also changed the driver's perspective from inside the car. As has been shown, the closed car directed the driver's attention to a small area of windscreen. The introduction of constraints in driving on the arterial road increased the need for the driver to look forward, and in Britain, to the left.

The resultant positioning of the driver can be thought of as the driver sitting still in the car while a series of images rush towards him or her. Tim Dant describes this as the driver looking 'out from their seat in the car through a quadrant at the world rushing towards her at a variety of speeds'.[31] This tendency began to be reflected in arterial road architecture, where buildings and advertising were displayed to catch the attention, front and left, of the driver. In this way, a modern way of seeing the world was combined with a new and compromised way of engaging with the road itself. So, here in the 1930s was a fully developed example of what we now think of as modern motoring.

A potentially sublime motoring experience

Chapter 5 described how the Great West Road, of all London's arterial roads, provided a ribboned landscape that was modern, exciting and

Americanised. When experienced at night and seen through a closed car's windscreen the effect became particularly filmic and conveyed a little of Hollywood's portrayal of Los Angeles for London's suburban drivers.

> We might have suddenly rolled … into one of the main avenues of the old exhibitions, like the Franco-British exhibition of my boyhood. It was the line of new factories on each side which suggested the exhibition … At night they looked as exciting as Blackpool.[32]

Although J. B. Priestley's *English Journey* is well known for its identification of Americanisation, his referencing of the Franco-British exhibition at the White City suggests an alternative perspective, which is to consider the 'Golden Mile' of the Great West Road as a suburban display for Londoners to experience. The Franco-British exhibition of 1908 celebrated the signing of the entente cordiale in 1904 and was one of a series of international exhibitions of the period influenced by the 1893 World's Columbian Exposition in Chicago.[33] A feature of these events was the construction of white-painted buildings, illuminated and decorated with electric lights. The 1924 Empire Exhibition at Wembley used similar techniques and also enjoyed a tremendous popular success.

As Priestley's comments demonstrate, the factories of the Great West Road were capable of inspiring awe and surprise. David Nye has explored this type of sublimity in the public view of American technology.[34] Nye tracks the development of the sublime through its origins in the American landscape through mechanisation and electrification into the atomic age. He pays particular attention to expositions and their use of electric lighting and floodlighting to dazzle and inspire their audience remarking that 'no one could visit a world's fair between 1883 and 1915 without seeing spectacular lighting displays'.[35] After the First World War, attention moved in the USA from the simple light bulb to the neon advertising sign, and this combination of white buildings, floodlighting and neon signage was found on the Great West Road.

The Great West Road in the 1930s provided an example of the American technological sublime in Britain that was not dependent on the artificiality of an exposition. Even when not floodlit, these new buildings produced a thrilled response.[36] For example, the Hoover Building on Western Avenue attracted the following observation:

> Along Western Avenue the traveller will see, a few miles only from the heart of the empire's capital, a gleaming palace in dazzling white and red, with

soaring white towers, the walls are almost all glass, set like a glittering gem in the midst of green lawns and gay flower beds. With its flat roof and general design, it might almost be the palace of some oriental potentate.[37]

With floodlighting, as Priestley noted, the effect was unusual and spectacular. The Firestone building was a popular site, and was recorded as such in the novel *Christopher Strong*, which reported that 'at night the electric signs on the new American tyre building blazed afar'.[38] Many of these new buildings used neon lighting to advertise their owners and their products. Hudson Motor Cars went one better by combining floodlighting and neon to produce an exciting and modern display.[39]

British companies imitated their American neighbours and thus produced a consistent floodlit avenue of factories and offices. The Currys house magazine gushed at the prospect: 'Have you seen this building by night? It's worth motoring many miles to see. Currys on the front; Currys on the tower; Cycles and Radio on the tower, too – all ablaze with vivid neon lighting; and the whole front flood-lit with glorious intensity – a really marvellous spectacle!'[40]

The Great West Road had an important difference from an exposition; the journey was most often seen from a car. This sublime view of the road was observed by London's motorists, at speed, through the narrow confines of a closed car's windscreen and side windows. Sara Danius describes this restricted view as generating a new modern aesthetic: 'Windshields delimit the view of the landscape, converting it into an object of visual pleasure – a mobile panorama. In other words, the car has become a vehicle of perception, paving the way for new forms of aesthetic gratification'.[41] This roadscape, seen from the car, is a vanishing point approached at speed, with the white buildings at the edge of the driver's view being set back and raised up to make them more visible.[42] As Tim Dant and Peter Martin have described it:

> The world becomes framed and flattened by the shape of the car window, presaging the view of the world through a television screen and related to that other tourist gaze through a camera lens, in the early years of the automobile, this was clearly a great attraction to users who experienced unusual places as images at the windows of cars.[43]

In the overwhelmingly pre-television days of the 1930s, the car window would mimic the experience of a visit to the cinema, source of much American cultural information. The combination of modern architecture, fast speeds and new ways of seeing a moving landscape produced, on the Great West Road, an unusual example of the American technological sublime transplanted to Britain.

This feeling was not restricted to motorists. As we have seen in Chapter 3, John Sowerby was a keen observer and enthusiastic user of the new suburban arterial road network. He liked their smooth surfaces and he was also happy to be surrounded by the heavy traffic of cars and lorries. He lived nearest to the Kingston Bypass and described his local arterial road in affectionate terms: 'And to my Kingston By-pass in the growing dusk'.[44] Although he was appreciative of the beauty of the Sussex and Surrey countryside, Sowerby was very modern in his approach to the new opportunities presented by the arterial road.

He recorded his feelings of cycling down the Great West Road:

> Then the Great West – a really glorious road by night – all colours of lights. All the wonder-factories floodlit, some in varying colours. Some have grand fountains playing, each jet turning different colours as the revolving light reaches it.[45]

> This modern architecture 'grows on one' and at night when floodlit it seems one long avenue of palaces and rather fairy palaces at that.[46]

Anti-sublimity

The 'Golden Mile' when coupled with Britain's sometimes rainy and misty climate could, alternatively, provoke artistic representations of a particularly damp kind. The excellently named Montague Tombs recorded his impressions of the Great West Road:

> When I arrive on a slightly misty evening and have to feel a way for the entrance to the Great West Road or some spot like that, amid the moving lights and the myriad signs and the petrol pump globes and the occasional street lights, I am lost as I should be if I were trying to pilot a boat into a strange crowded harbour on a wet night.[47]

F. Gordon-Crosby, renowned illustrator of lively motoring scenes for *The Autocar*, pictured a damp and rainy Great West Road at night in a manner that showed a sports car at speed heading towards a vanishing point in a tunnel of impressionistic illuminated factories, conveying an exciting modernity.[48] Later in the interwar period, as the innocence of the early 1930s evaporated, the writer and artist John Piper and the poet Louis MacNeice took a different view of the Great West Road.

Piper was an artist and architectural commentator who collaborated with John Betjeman on the well-known Shell guides to the English counties.[49] He considered, reporting on a long drive down the Great West Road, that 'none of the factories on the Great West Road are worth noting individually' and that 'they form the best existing studies of architectural horrors in a small space … and that they were pleasing if only in [their] strength and conviction'.[50]

MacNeice, who 'chartered the public landscape of 1938 from the perspective of a privately troubled observer', professed a more acerbic and far from sublime view of the developed and ribboned road.[51]

The next day I drove by night
Among red and amber and green, spears and candles,
Corkscrews and slivers of reflected light
In the mirror of the rainy asphalt
Along the North Circular and the Great West roads
Running the gauntlet of impoverished fancy
Where housewives bolster up their jerry-built abodes
With amour propre and the habit of Hire Purchase.
The wheels whished in the wet, the flashy strings
Of neon lights unravelled, the windscreen-wiper
Kept at its job like a tiger in a cage or a cricket that sings
All night through for nothing.
Factory, a site for a factory, rubbish dumps,
Bungalows in lath and plaster, in brick, in concrete,
And shining semi-circles of petrol pumps
Like intransigent gangs of idols.[52]

MacNeice was reflecting on a well-worn theme of 1930s intellectual discourse that ribbon development of cheaply built houses had eliminated any claims for modernity in these roads. The flashy strings of neon lights had unravelled.

Conclusion

The interwar period was a transformative time for motoring in Britain. London's suburbs led the way in the development of a recognisably modern form of driving. In twenty years, car driving changed from an elite masculine pursuit of speed and endurance in open cars on the open road, to a suburbanised and domesticated encounter on managed and constrained new roads.

In this way, motoring in London's suburbs closely reflected wider changes in interwar British society. Suburbanisation and domestication were two of the period's key themes, and to these one could add Americanisation and the culture of planning and control. The impact of each theme is seen in the contrast in how motoring was practised in 1919 and 1939.

The modernity of the initial excitement of driving on the unconstrained roads at speed in open cars developed in the 1920s and then diminished as its cycle unwound by 1929 or so. This period can be characterised as wealthy, male motorists driving in open cars on poorly made roads largely devoid of traffic. This produced a highly kinaesthetic and embodied experience that was characterised in literature and journalism as masculine and exploratory. This manner of driving was then added to and eventually replaced by a new cycle of modernity in the form of the technology of the closed car, which because of its low price was adopted by greater numbers of middle-class drivers.

The suburban residents of Greater London in the 1930s were one of the most likely sections of the public to become car-owners. At this time, the closed car had started to dominate the British car market and was particularly attractive to suburbanites. It was, in effect, a suburban semi on wheels, with, at the more luxurious end of the market, its leather armchairs, heater and radio. In it, men and, increasingly, women drivers could drive up and down the arterial road in a way that replicated their own new home lives. The roads they drove on were increasingly controlled by the end of the interwar period. As interventionist planning gained favour in fixing Britain's economy in the early 1930s and in preparation for a future war, its influence could also be felt on London's arterial roads, where speed limits and traffic signals and obstacles regulated the motorist. Motorists were doubly constrained by government and by the narrow windscreen of their cars. On the Great West Road, they could sit in splendid comfort and, moving in an ordered fashion, admire the new white factories. The result was, for some, a technological sublimity; for other more critical observers it produced a sense of the second rate, the superficial and the vulgar, but all would have appreciated the Americanised and cinematic impression produced by this road.

As ownership rates increased, the MoT's road safety constraints reduced both the excitement and level of danger of this practice, thus reducing this cycle of modernity to a new, slower, controlled way of driving that became the norm. Hence in 1939, a recognisably modern motoring was encountered on London's suburban arterial roads, and was then interrupted by war and austerity and not recovered until the late 1950s.

Notes

1 Part of the material for this chapter is reproduced from an article to be published in *The London Journal* as part of a special issue on Suburban Leisure (Volume 39 No. 3, November 2014), which will be published by Maney Publishing on behalf of The London Journal Trust.

2 T. Cresswell, *Place: A Short Introduction*, Oxford 2004, p. 34.

3 J. Urry, *Automobility, Car Culture and Weightless Travel: A Discussion Paper*, Lancaster 1999.

4 'On the Road' *The Autocar*, 3 July 1925.

5 A. Light, *Forever England: Femininity, Literature and Conservatism Between the Wars*, London 1991.

6 See R. Koshar, 'Driving Cultures and the Meaning of Roads' in C. Mauch and T. Zeller (eds), *The World Beyond the Windshield: Roads and Landscapes in the United States and Europe*, London 2008, p. 25.

7 J. J. Flink, 'The Ultimate Status Symbol, The Custom Coachbuilt Car in the Interwar Period', in M. Wachs and M. Crawford, *The Car and the City*, Ann Arbor 1992.

8 G. Robson, *Motoring in the 30s*, Cambridge 1979; L. J. K. Setright, *Drive On!: A Social History of the Car*, London 2003; M. Sedgwick, *Passenger Cars, 1924–1942*, London 1975.

9 O. Sitwell, *Left Hand, Right Hand!: An Autobiography, Volume 3: Great Morning*, London 1957, p. 234.

10 A. Huxley, excerpt from *Those Barren Leaves* (1928) quoted in D. Jewell (ed.), *Man & Motor: The 20th Century Love Affair*, London 1966.

11 I have relied on L. J. K. Setright, *Drive On!: A Social History of the Car*, M. Sedgwick, *Passenger Cars, 1924–1942*, and, in particular, P. Nieuwenhuis and P. Wells, 'The All-steel Body as a Cornerstone to the Foundations of the Mass Production Car Industry', *Industrial and Corporate Change*, 16:2, 2007, pp. 183–211, for the technical aspects of the closed car.

12 M. Sedgwick, *Passenger Cars, 1924–1942*, p. 9.

13 Letter from F. Fowell, *The Autocar*, 6 February 1925.

14 F. Gordon-Crosby, 'Comfort and Convenience in Bodywork', *The Autocar*, 6 February 1925.

15 *The Times*, 17 March 1926.

16 letter from H. Cox, *The Autocar*, 23 January 1925.

17 S. O'Connell, *The Car and British society: Class, Gender and Motoring 1896–1939*, Manchester 1998.

18 Letter from E. J. Burrow, *The Autocar*, 3 July 1925.

19 Letter from Tropwen, *The Autocar*, 10 April 1925.

20 Reply to above letter from B. G. Bouwens, *The Autocar*, 24 April 1925.

21 J. Betjeman, *Letters*, London 1994, p. 124.

22 See W. E. Bijker, T. P. Hughes T. J. Pinch (eds), *The Social Construction of Technological Systems: New Directions in the Sociology and History of Technology*, Cambridge, Mass. 1987.

23 B. H. Davies, 'Wireless and the Car', *The Autocar*, 13 March 1925.

24 G. Robson, *Motoring in the 30s*, p. 22.

25 C. Seiler, *Republic of Drivers: A Cultural History of Automobility in America*, London 2008, p. 60.

26 P. Ling, 'Sex and the Automobile in the Jazz Age', *History Today*, November 1989.

27 For a discussion on speed see J. Moran, *On Roads*, London, 2009.

28 A. Arculus, Correspondence with author, 11 June 2005.

29 E. D. C. Bowen, *To the North*, London 1932, p. 96.

30 P. Hamilton, *The Siege of Pleasure*, London 1932, p. 297.

31 T. Dant, 'The Driver-car', *Theory, Culture & Society*, 21:4/5, 2004, pp 61–79.

32 J. B. Priestley, *English Journey*, London 1934, p. 4, referring to Blackpool's illuminations.

33 D. E. Nye, *American Technological Sublime*, London 1994 and P. Blom, *The Vertigo Years: Change and Culture in the West, 1900–1914*, London 2008.

34 D. E. Nye, *American Technological Sublime*.

35 D. E. Nye, *American Technological Sublime*, p. 151.

36 See D. Linehan, 'A New England: Landscape, Exhibition and Remaking Industrial Space in the late 1930s' in D. Gilbert, D. Matless and B. Short (eds), *Geographies of British Modernity: Space and Society in the Twentieth Century*, Oxford 2003.

37 *Illustrated London News*, 20 May, 1933, quoted in W. Hitchmough, *Hoover Factory: Wallis, Gilbert and Partners*, London 1992.

38 G. Frankau, *Christopher Strong*, London 1932, p. 148.

39 From Charles K. Bowers archive.

40 *Currys Magazine*, Volume 1, August 1936.

41 S. Danius, 'The Aesthetics of the Windshield: Proust and the Modernist Rhetoric of Speed', *Modernism/Modernity*, 8:1, 2001, pp 99–126.

42 See the description for the Pyrene building in *The Autocar*, 28, June 1929.

43 T. Dant and P. Martin, 'By Car: Carrying Modern Society' in J. Gronow and A. Warde (eds), *Ordinary Consumption*, New York 2001; M. Schwarzer, *Zoomscape: Architecture in Motion and Media*, London 2004, p. 153.

44 J. Sowerby, *I Got on My Bicycle*, London 1939, p. 192.

45 J. Sowerby, *I Got on My Bicycle*, p. 277.

46 J. Sowerby, *I Got on My Bicycle*, p. 156.

47 M. Tombs, *The Autocar*, 21 February 1930.

48 *The Autocar*, 30 October, 1936.

49 David Fraser Jenkins, 'Piper, John Egerton Christmas (1903–1992)', *Oxford*

Dictionary of National Biography, Oxford 2004; online edn, May 2009 [www.oxforddnb.com.ezproxy.londonlibrary.co.uk/view/article/51284, accessed 8 May 2013].

50 J. Piper, 'London to Bath', *Architectural Review*, May 1939, p. 230.

51 P. McDonald, 'Believing in the Thirties' in W. Matthews and S. Williams (eds), *Rewriting the Thirties: Modernism and After*, London 1997, p. 71.

52 L. MacNeice, *Autumn Journal*, London 1939, p. 54.

Accidents and suburban modernity

Access to the new suburban arterial roads changed individual mobilities, firstly for the wealthy and then for a much wider group. The interwar suburban road was a site of accidents and danger, a location that privileged the rich and penalised the poor and the old. Accidents reflect the twin face of modernity that couples the order of the network of new well-engineered roads with simultaneously chaotic high-speed car crashes. Car drivers and motorcyclists put themselves at risk, but high-speed motoring was even more dangerous for the cyclists and pedestrians whom they came into contact with.[1]

In a similar manner, but on a smaller scale in human terms, London's airport was positioned to the public as a centre of a modern network of communications that spread out from Croydon to the major capitals of Europe and further afield to important outposts of the British Empire. Death was an expected consequence for the pioneers of this newish technology, but by the end of the interwar period this risk was shared more widely as the airport became surrounded by suburban housing with unforeseen consequences for pilots, passengers and suburban residents.

Roger Cooter and Bill Luckin, writing in *Accidents in History*, conclude that defining an accident is highly problematic, such that 'the accident seems ever destined to slide in to ambiguity, defying any fixity of meaning'.[2] Robert Campbell, more helpfully, writes that 'an accident is not something which cannot be foreseen, but something which was not foreseen', adding 'accidents are not uncaused events, an uncaused event is a miracle'.[3] Paul Virilio invokes Aristotle to explore the nature of the accident. Aristotle considered that the *accidens* revealed substance through time and Virilio uses this idea to suggest that the accident reveals the uncontrollable reality of modernity that hides in a positivist world.[4] He pointedly cites the invention of the car as an example of an artificial as opposed to a natural accident and suggests that each invention automatically generates its consequent accidents, with the human agency associated with the use of the invention relegated to passive inevitability.[5]

The histories of modernity and the accident are entwined. The technological developments and modernisations of the industrial revolution produced standardised objects such as machines, tools and vehicles that were repeatable in large quantities. What also became repetitive was the production of industrial accidents from unguarded, rapid and dangerous machines. Cooter and Luckin argue that, in the nineteenth century, accidents became 'normalized and legitimated' by capitalism in synchronisation with the introduction of automatically driven machinery.[6] Factory owners would neutralise the accident by placing the blame on the machine operator and leaving them without any redress. This process of neutralisation was repeated in motoring through the role of the pedestrian and is discussed later in this chapter.

Virilio redefines the accident not as the consequence of modernity but as its equal, formed at the same time as each invention and as strong a symbol for our changing world as each new technology. In his words, 'to invent the train is to invent derailment'.[7] As each new wave of technology follows another, a new type of accident forms simultaneously. Virilio's thesis seems highly plausible when one considers that the very first passenger railway journey resulted in the death of one of its leading sponsors; the introduction of the car and aeroplane immediately provoked violent death and injury. In a reflection of the way that modernity creates both order and chaos, it is a belief of the project of technological modernisation, focusing on only one of these two dimensions, that it can eliminate accidents. The French sociologist Robert Castel describes this as where 'The modern ideologies of prevention are overarched by a grandiose technocratic rationalising dream of absolute control over the accidental'.[8] This idea is borne out in governmental attempts to control motoring deaths and injuries, and is discussed later in this chapter.

This chapter considers the culture of speed that could be found in flying and motoring in interwar Britain and then builds the connections between modern transport and accidents first by considering the nature of accidents on London's suburban arterial roads and then by looking at how flying at Croydon Airport fatally impacted on its neighbouring semi-detached house owners.

The culture of speed in interwar Britain

Recent interpretations of the first three decades of new transport technologies have considered the relationship between the individual and speed. Jeffrey Schnapp identifies a 'thrill based culture of velocity' around 1900 as one of the key aspects of automobility and as one of the basic precepts of Futurism.[9] Kurt Möser has argued that the obsession with speed was formed in the period from 1905 to 1914 when 'automobilism and aeronautics provided a system of cultural references that could later be used to understand, shape and express wartime experience'.[10] The developments in technology and societal changes of the First World War had an impact on speed and the popular imagination in the interwar period. This urge was displayed in forms of popular music, in dance and in a restlessness and agitation for excitement and speed. One interwar commentator reflected on this idea:

> This cult of violence and speed, dating from the Great War and fostered by mechanical inventions-by the movies, by air travel, by-passes, roadhouses— has now become so universal that it is in danger of swallowing up all quiet, reflective influences.[11].

The recent death of so many young men had also contributed to the need for some to prove themselves and their masculinity in a world without soldiering. The death and destruction of the war led to a succeeding generation that was famously disrespectful of Edwardian and Victorian traditions and out, above all else, to enjoy itself. John Urry argues, for example, that, in this period, 'Many motorists described their experience of speed in mystical terms as though this was an experience not so much opposed to the natural worlds but one which expressed the inner forces of the universe'.[12]

This was also reflected in an obsession with speed records. In Britain this was seen in the national following for the exploits of Flight-Lieutenant Webster, a winner of the Schneider Trophy for the fastest seaplane.[13] For ordinary aeroplanes, the King's Cup, sponsored by George V, was the premier event, requiring competitors to fly round England, hitting specific way-points. In the 1930 race, for example, there were ninety-six entrants including one sponsored by the Prince of Wales, and another by his brother, Prince George. Six of the pilots were women.[14] One of these, Winifred Brown, was the eventual winner, beating the nearest male competitor into second place by twelve minutes.[15]

On land, Malcolm Campbell's 'Bluebird' epitomised both speed and the design obsession with streamlining that dominated this period.[16] Streamlining had a functional use in the reduction of wind resistance in making record-breaking attempts but it also crossed over as design short-hand for the modern in more everyday vehicles. Paul Atterbury considers that 'streamlining and speed became synonymous in the public mind, and so streamline forms were widely applied to domestic motor-vehicles despite having little or no impact on their actual performance'.[17]

Motor racing was a passion for many wealthy, young men and women, and frequent meetings were held at Aintree and Donnington and, most importantly of all, Brooklands. Brooklands had a concrete-banked oval track that allowed high-speed racing at over 100 mph, but with little in the way of safety features for either drivers or spectators. For thirty years, Brooklands was a focal point for British motor racing and private flying and was the site for a new form of social occasion. At the start of this period, motoring, of any sort, was the preserve of the wealthy and daring. A competitive spirit among young, elite drivers soon matched the earlier excitement of driving at speed on country roads.

Accidents at Brooklands were frequent and were often fatal. Drivers had only leather helmets to protect them if they flew out of their crashed cars at high speed. Local grandees and officials regarded this with horror; as early as 1908 the local coroner referred to the passion for high-speed driving as a 'degenerate taste'.[18] Watching the races at Brooklands and admiring the glamorous drivers soon became a popular activity; after a halt due to the First World War, attendances grew to as much as twenty thousand for one event in 1925.[19]

Motoring accidents in interwar Britain

The acceptance of frequent accidents, injuries and deaths at Brooklands was not found to be the case for the public road. The number of deaths and injuries to motorists and pedestrians was an item of great debate, setting motoring organisations against pedestrians' associations, with the government of the day sitting precariously on the fence between the two interest groups.

In the interwar period, motoring was an extremely dangerous activity, not only for drivers and passengers but also for cyclists and pedestrians and particularly the young and the elderly. One observer of the suburban

10   Crashed cars on the Kingston Bypass, 1939
                    J. A. Hampton/Topical Press Agency/Getty Images

arterial road recalled how 'accidents would regularly occur'.[20] The normality of accidents is also apparent in the literature of the period. In one example, the hero of a 1930s detective story is interesting in his acceptance of accidents as part of modern life and the road as being constantly dangerous.[21] A number of factors made motoring deaths likely at this time, and from a long list one can pick out: bad roads, failure to separate cars from pedestrians, little or no street lighting, inefficient drum brakes, lack of seat-belts, unforgiving car interiors and poor standards of driving. The experience of the accident would be not only more frequent but would be more unexceptionally primitive and bloody than we are used to.

The new arterial roads prompted a large number of fatal crashes. One can construct a typical fatal interwar road accident. The driver, although experienced in handling the car, had not taken formal instruction or a driving test.[22] The light sports car, although slow to accelerate by present-day standards, was easily capable of 70 miles per hour. Driving on to an arterial road at night, the car's dim headlights presented the driver with a poor view of the road. No road lighting was available; no reflective white lines or cat's-eyes guided the journey. If the road was wet, the new concrete surface of the road was shiny and slippery. Every few seconds, the car was

Table 8   UK Motoring accidents

	Total motor vehicles (000s)	Killed	Injured	Killed per 1000 vehicles	Injured per 1000 vehicles
1928	2038	6138	164,838	3.0	80.9
1930	2273	7305	177,895	3.2	78.3
1932	2227	6667	206,450	3.0	92.7
1934	2405	7343	231,603	3.1	96.3
1935	2570	6502	221,726	2.5	86.3
1936	2758	6561	227,813	2.4	82.6
1937	2928	6633	226,402	2.3	77.3
1938	3084	6648	226,711	2.2	73.5

Adapted from W. Plowden, *The Car and Politics, 1896–1970*, London 1971, Appendices.

jolted as it hit a bitumen joint in the concrete blocks that formed the road. An error of judgement preceded the seemingly inevitable accident. Hitting another car or a roadside tree, the driver and the passengers sitting uncon-strained in their open-top car were thrown on to the road into the line of approaching traffic or were thrown against the steering wheel, windscreen or windscreen support. The windscreen was toughened but not laminated and laceration or a fractured skull were likely outcomes. Paul Vaughan remembered 'the screaming of brakes, a sharp bang, a reverberating skitter of metal fragments, followed by even more sinister noises: the moans of the victims, the screams of women bystanders'.[23] Help would not come quickly; other drivers might, after driving some distance, find a house with a telephone that could call for an ambulance. The raw statistics show that, in the 1930s, motoring accidents killed approximately 75,000 people and injured approximately 2 million in the UK as a whole (see Table 8).[24] More specifically, an analysis of deaths on Greater London roads shows a clear distinction between the ages of motorised and unmotorised users of the road and their likelihood of dying (see Table 9).

This reveals an aggressive and privileged mobility where wealthy young drivers killed and injured older, poorer pedestrians and cyclists. This historical analysis reinforces James Kunstler's conclusion that driving 'disables those who are not car drivers by making their everyday habitats non-navigable'.[25] Peter Freund concurs: 'The young and the elderly, people with disabilities, women and poor people are disproportionately excluded'.[26]

Table 9 Road deaths in Greater London January to June 1933 and average age at death

	No. of deaths	Percentage of total	Average age at death (restricted sample)
Car drivers & passengers	45	7.2	31
Pedal cyclists	100	16.2	37
Motorcyclists	62	10.0	27
Pedestrians	411	66.6	46
Total	618	100.0	

Ministry of Transport, *Preliminary Report on Fatal Road Accidents*, Tables VI(a), London 1933; M. J. Law, unpublished MA dissertation, Birkbeck College, University of London, 2006, Analysis of road deaths on Kingston Bypass and Great West Road, from *The Times*, 1925 to 1939.

In considering the nature and causes of accidents at this time, arguments took one of two forms. Either accidents were considered inevitable or conversely they formed a motoring pathology that could be treatable. The inevitability argument sits well with the later cultural investigations into the relationship between accidents and modernity. The American inventor and travel writer Seth K. Humphrey put this case clearly: 'The trouble lies deeper than in bad driving. It lies in the fundamental incompatibility of machines and man, steel and flesh, in a running mix-up on the highways. Nothing on earth can make their intimacy safe.'[27]

The pathological approach fitted well into the interwar obsession with planning, which was a reflection of its wider influence in attempting to restart a failed economy. This approach considered that bad driving was based around the character of individual drivers and that observing, licensing, controlling and influencing bad driving could reduce the number of accidents.

As one might expect from this period, the government and driving organisations often used the class codes of 'gentlemanly' driving as the basis for their exhortations for safer motoring. Early explanations for bad driving often identified the source as non-gentlemen. This criticism was sometimes directed at chauffeurs, who were often foreigners, thus being seen as doubly non-gentlemen. In this way, the chauffeur could become a 'figure of power and menace'.[28] In the interwar period, bad driving was also associated with the widening ownership of cars, with lower-middle-class and working-class drivers taking the brunt of criticism.[29] In America, blame was laid at the door of 'loosened sexual norms ... [and] the popularity of degenerate mass culture and the cult of consumerism that all ate away at the consensual visions of public duty and civic responsibility'.[30]

Women drivers also received an unfair share of criticism for their driving and resultant accidents. Sean O'Connell has shown that, despite the reality that women drivers were good insurance risks, they were subject to a campaign of derision from male drivers.[31] This is seen in a 'humorous' scene in the documentary film *Roadways*, which shows a woman driver studying her recent shopping purchases and failing to notice the traffic lights change. When she finally pays attention to the hooting car horns of the drivers behind her, she sets off in a juddering crash of gears.[32]

In Britain, those who saw accidents as a controllable disease eventually won the debate over those who saw them as inevitable. The act of driving a car became inspected and controlled through the introduction of driving tests, traffic lights and speed limits. For the pedestrian, road safety education was an important aspect of the campaign to reduce accidents. Children were taught about the dangers of crossing the road and the introduction of pedestrian crossings and 'Belisha' beacons made this action safer.[33]

Motoring accidents in interwar literature

As has been shown, the modernity of motoring produces two coupled responses. Each act of liberation and individuality powered by the car matches with a potential or actual car crash crushing the all too vulnerable human form. The car has provided novelists and poets with a potent symbol of the modern world from its inception. The idea of driving as liberation was used by a number of leading authors, where they described the liberating effect of the open road and the freedom of the car. Malcolm Muggeridge, in his early incarnation as a sybarite, recalled: 'Movement exhilarated more than direction – just to keep moving, to move faster, air whistling by, and a foot languidly, effortlessly governing the acceleration'.[34]

Novelists also reflected on the accident as the consequence of this liberation. Car crashes were a day-to-day reality, so writers did not need to exaggerate for effect. The car accident also served as an effective literary device to conclude a build-up of suspense or to change direction for a story. *The Wind in the Willows* (1910) provided one of the earliest uses of the car both as a projection of modernity and as a moral device for punishing transgression against society's norms.[35] Toad famously speeds and crashes his car, satirising the new scorching, elite Edwardian motorist and positioning the mechanical modern against the traditional deep Englishness of the riverbank. Allen Samuels identifies, perhaps reading backwards from Ballard's *Crash*, a conjunction between the crash and the sexual in Toad's encounters with the car: 'he would lie prostrate amidst the ruins of the chairs apparently completely satisfied for the moment'.[36] The theme of modernity, repressed sexuality and the car is taken up, in more serious vein, in Forster's *Howards End (1910)*, which uses the car as a symbol for the transition of English sensibilities from the Victorian to those of the new twentieth century with its accompanying suburbanisation and social changes.[37] Andrew Thacker identifies two significant car crashes in *Howards End*, which are 'both used to symbolise forthcoming human tragedies'.[38] In each of these two texts, the driver is an overbearing and arrogant male.

In contrast, after the First World War, writers made a strong connection between the modernity of independent women driving cars and consequent car crashes.[39] Several novels from the interwar period exemplify this trope, some of them using the setting of the new suburban arterial road to emphasise how modern and metropolitan their characters were. For example, Virginia Woolf described the impressionistic effect that came from travelling by car at speed in suburban London: 'The process of motoring fast out of London so much resembles the chopping up small of identity which precedes unconsciousness and perhaps death'.[40]

Elizabeth Bowen's *To the North* (1932) is a novel of modernity where its characters are in constant motion and where driving and flying form a normalised but anxiety-provoking part of their lives.[41] The restlessness of travel agent Emmeline (an appropriately mobile occupation) concludes a nervy journey along suburban arterial roads and the Barnet Bypass with a crash on the Great North Road. The title of the book has a dual meaning. For one leading character, it represents a return to a cold, conventional Britain. For Emmeline, it comes from an AA signpost to her final journey through suburbia on to the unconstrained arterial road. Despair, female glamour and motoring sit together throughout: 'I'm sorry, Emmeline said: at a pressure from her silver slipper the speedometer needle went creeping up'.[42] Bowen may not have been aware of Fitzgerald's *The Great Gatsby* (1925), which was not fully successful until after the Second World War, but she repeats many of its themes of motoring, modernity and death. Once again, a car accident on new highways is the punishment for transgression powered by new mobilities. Male drivers are not exempt from literary punishment in this period but as they represent the orthodox and everyday their car crashes are the result of arrogance and unthinking speeding rather than the impact of modernity and sexual liberation.

Gilbert Frankau's popular 1932 novel *Christopher Strong* is the story of the doomed romance between the novel's eponymous hero and Felicity Darrington.[43] The couple meet for the first time in a motoring accident, and motorisation and mobility are key themes in this book. Christopher Strong pursues Felicity both romantically and physically in an extended high-speed car chase along the Great West Road, occasioning a number of near misses. Frankau describes Strong trying to catch up with his lover's car, Bingie Boy:

> Where Bingie Boy went, he would go. Even if this rotten second car of his blew up. Bingie Boy went to the right, avoiding the by-pass. A car was coming along the by-pass. He cut in front of it; hooting again; missed a cyclist, another cyclist, by three inches; didn't care-because the scarlet wheels were coming back to him.[44]

Lord de Clifford and Douglas Hopkins on the Kingston Bypass

Three years after the publication of *Christopher Strong*, life imitated art in an infamous arterial road crash that juxtaposed the privileged world of fast driving with the static, domestic world of the semi-detached suburban house.

At three o'clock in the morning on 15 August 1935, Harry and Ethel Ebdon, the occupiers of 6 Malden Way, a new house on the Kingston Bypass, were woken by an almighty crash followed, a few minutes later, by a thump on their front door. On their opening the door, in staggered Edward Russell, twenty-sixth Baron de Clifford, carrying Douglas Hopkins who had been seriously injured in a car crash outside their home.[45]

The participants in the car crash were representatives from at least three of the highly nuanced strata of metropolitan classes from the interwar period. Lord de Clifford was a member of the House of Lords and undisputedly upper-class. The unfortunate Douglas Hopkins was from a solid middle-class background in Finchley. The Ebdons are not so easily recoverable but the basis of on their geographical positioning in the new suburbia were likely to be representatives of the emerging new lower middle classes. It required a car crash to bring them together in such an unlikely way.

Lord de Clifford, an Irish peer of diminished fortune, was twenty eight years old at the time of the accident and had been married at nineteen to a 'dance hostess daughter of the shady nightclub hostess Kate Meyrick'.[46] He narrowly escaped jail for falsifying details on his marriage licence. Recovering from this early disgrace, Lord de Clifford, despite his father's death in an early motoring accident, became a successful racing driver and also, ironically, a progressive legislator on motoring topics in the House of Lords. His racing was undertaken at Brooklands and as a regular participant in Monte Carlo rallies. Here then was an unusual example of the interwar man-about-town, aristocratic, daring and with associations with London's underworld of illegal nightclubs.

De Clifford dined with friends in Windsor, and then drove them back to town and stayed for drinks and conversation. At half past two in the morning, de Clifford then drove his Lancia Augusta Lusso back to a roadhouse on the Kingston Bypass. The Augusta was the favoured road car of many leading Brooklands drivers and was a sophisticated and expensive car.[47]

Coming in the opposite direction was twenty-six-year-old Douglas Hopkins accompanied by his sister and his girlfriend. Hopkins was, coincidentally, also a driver at Brooklands although not as well known as Lord de Clifford. His father described him as a 'motor expert but not a racer'.[48] He was an engineer by profession and he had modified the car he was driving, a Frazer Nash.

The three friends were driving back to suburban North London from a party held at Banstead in Surrey. At 3.30 am on the unlit road they saw the headlights of a car coming towards them, at speed, on the wrong side of the road. They crashed into de Clifford's car, the impact throwing Douglas Hopkins on to the upright of his windscreen, fracturing his skull. His fellow passengers were shocked but unhurt. Lord de Clifford carried Hopkins in to 6 Malden Way where they awaited the arrival of the police and the ambulance. Hopkins died shortly after arriving at Kingston Hospital.

Number 6 Malden Way was one of a group of six houses built on the Kingston Bypass. The house typified a standard-plan 1930s small detached home with Tudor referencing in the tile roof and the weather-boarded elevation. At the trial, the house was described by the defence barrister as being 'of the character of a villa and of no great size'.[49] This could have been the home of a senior clerk, a teacher or perhaps a successful artisan.

With the evidence of the crash pointed against him, the police arrested

Lord de Clifford and charged him with manslaughter. After a hearing at a magistrate's court, it was realised that, as a peer, only the House of Lords could try him. His peers eventually acquitted him despite damning evidence and his refusal to make any statement in his defence. He gradually withdrew from public life and became increasingly impoverished, ending his working life owning a kennels and selling dog food door-to-door.

Douglas Hopkins's and Lord de Clifford's journeys show two examples of changed suburban mobility that would not have been possible a decade earlier. Even taking in to account that both protagonists were experienced drivers, it is remarkable to consider how easily they undertook journeys of thirty miles or more in the early hours of the morning.

These journeys present a casual culture of suburban mobility. Young wealthy men in their twenties purchased and drove powerful sports cars at speed and at night, transforming the traditional geographies of London. As motoring compressed space, The West End was no longer the centripetal locus of entertainment but became one of several potential destinations that now might lie in the suburbs or in small towns like Maidenhead.

Douglas Hopkins and Lord de Clifford became the unexpected house guests of, those members of that much-maligned group, the occupants of a house on the arterial road. These new houses provided a specific enjoyment of modern life. By purchasing a house on the arterial road it was possible to have a new home that had, perhaps temporarily, a rural outlook over fields coupled with the sight of fast cars streaming past and, occasionally, colliding outside its Crittall windows. For some, a small garage would house an Austin Seven or similar newly available cheap light car, providing them with their own independent mobility and direct access to the fast road.

Motorcycling on the Bath Road

As the statistics show, it was not only car drivers who were at risk on suburban arterial roads. On 14 May 1929, Arthur Graham borrowed his friend's motorcycle for the day. He rode it to Maidenhead and on the way home was killed in an accident with a car driven by Richard Reynolds, the heir to a vast American tobacco fortune. Graham, who was twenty-one years old and was married, was not racing his friend's motorcycle for fun. He was, in fact, using it to attend the inquest for his stepfather who had been killed the previous week in an accident on the Great West Road when he hitched a lift on a lorry that then had a collision. Graham's journey back was a straight run along the Bath Road from Maidenhead to Slough, and he was almost home when he was hit by a green Buick car.

Richard Reynolds was twenty-three years old at the time of the accident and a very wealthy young man living a life of leisure in London. Reynolds was an aviator and had held a pilot's licence since he was eighteen years old and was the owner of Roosevelt Field, where Lindbergh took off for his transatlantic flight.[50] He was in receipt of a vast trust income of $100,000 per year that he partly used to finance a hedonistic lifestyle.[51] On this particular Tuesday morning, his friend, twenty-two-year-old Ronald Bargate, joined Reynolds at his flat in St John's Wood. Reynolds hired a six-cylinder green Buick car for the day from Godfrey Davis, a West End rental company.[52] Their plan was to drive down to Hurley, a small village between Henley and Maidenhead, to play golf for the day. It started raining, so they decided to spend the day at a hotel rather than get wet at the golf club. While they were there, Reynolds admitted to drinking five Pimms No. 1 during the afternoon and evening without having anything to eat.[53] His friend Bargate had, for his part, drunk himself senseless, and was put in the back of the car for the journey home.

Reynolds drove as far as Burnham, it was dark now and, as has been seen, illumination was always a problem on the interwar road. Here Reynolds crashed into the back of Graham's motorcycle, fatally injuring him. Reynolds drove on, later saying that he thought that he had hit the kerb. Another driver spotted Reynolds driving badly on the Great West Road and eventually the police pulled him up in Chiswick where they arrested him. On being pulled out of the car, covered in his own vomit, Reynolds protested, 'Do you think I am drunk? You have made a big mistake.'[54] After two trials where Reynolds employed Sir Norman Birkett, Britain's most famous barrister, in his defence, and after compensating Graham's widow with an income for life, Reynolds was convicted of manslaughter and given five months in jail. He was sent, wearing a convict's outfit covered in the traditional arrows, in a Black Maria to Brixton Jail.[55]

As was seen in Chapter 3, the motorcycle was, throughout the interwar period, the primary means of motorised transport for the working-class male. A visiting American automotive engineer observed that 'the class of people who possess Fords in America have motorcycles in England'.[56] Arthur Graham, who was a driver for the local gas company, was such a working-class motorcyclist.[57]

Reynolds was an example of the many wealthy Americans who made London their home in the 1920s. Reynolds's day could have not been dreamt up better to typify the lifestyle of a wealthy and idle socialite. Get up late, meet a friend, take a taxi to Albemarle Street and hire a powerful six-cylinder Buick for the day. Drive to a golf course in the Home Counties, get put off by the rain, drink yourself insensible on cocktails in a country pub, then drive home.

The accident between Reynolds and Graham presents a further illustration of the link between mobility and leisure in this period and also shows the continuing association between drinking and driving. Graham's ride demonstrates the importance of the motorcycle to interwar motoring for the working-class male and also, in a week in which his stepfather also died on the London to Bath Road, how extremely dangerous it was to travel on the arterial road.

Resistance to the domination of the car

The number of accidents provoked the introduction of legislation to control the speed of vehicles and to improve the behaviour of drivers and standards of driving. In 1930, the government abolished its poorly enforced speed limit of 20 mph. Clive Emsley has shown how this reflected the political power of the driving lobby, which resented the taint of criminalisation for speeding offences.[58] The abolition of the speed limit prompted an immediate rise in injuries and deaths. The public clamour for change eventually led, in 1934, to the introduction of a well-enforced 30 mph speed limit in built-up areas, driving tests and the introduction of a highway code. This reduced deaths from 3.1 per thousand vehicles to a low of 2.2 per thousand in 1938.

Newspapers made motoring accidents a kind of spectator sport and reported them on a daily basis. *The Times* titled its accident statistics 'Road Deaths of the Week'.[59] Powerful interests ranged themselves on either side of the debate over road accidents. On the deregulation side were the AA and the RAC. The AA was founded as a pressure group against the imposition of speed limits and to help warn against and defend members against speed checks. Also on the side of the speeding motorist were SMMT, the motoring industry trade body, and the National Safety First Association, which Sean O'Connell has shown, despite its name, to be a motoring industry lobby group.[60] On the side of increased regulation were intellectual commentators, such as C. E. M. Joad, who saw motoring as vulgar, degrading and a despoiler of the countryside, and the most vociferous anti-motoring lobby group, the Pedestrians' Association. This organisation was founded in 1929, just as road deaths were reaching their peak. Its chairman, Lord Cecil of Chelwood, was a long-standing anti-motoring protester. Cecil was a well-known politician, a progressive Conservative and peace campaigner through the League of Nations. In his opening address, Cecil set the strident tone that characterised the Association's protests against motorists and the motoring lobby. He claimed the Association was needed 'to deal with a very serious and crying evil' which was 'comparable with any of the most serious evils against which human society had struggled'.[61] Cecil's reputation as a peace campaigner allowed him to hyperbolically conflate motoring deaths with the evils of warfare.

It became commonplace for pro-motoring campaigners, who generally took a libertarian and somewhat elitist view of driving, to place the blame for motor accidents involving pedestrians on the stupidity of the pedestrian rather than the speed of the driver. Newspapers and chapters in motoring journals positioned pedestrian deaths as suicides rather than accidents. One writer to *The Listener* complained of 'pedestrians hurling themselves in to traffic and bumpkins in the country veering off the road at the last minute'.[62] In a similar vein, the aviator and future Minister of Transport John Moore-Brabazon complained that 'over 6,000 people commit suicide every year and no-one makes a fuss about that'.[63] A writer to *The Manchester Guardian* agreed: 'Cars are bound to kill if people deliberately run in front of them and the motorist, whatever his speed, is no more to blame than the tide [for drowning a man]'.[64] Earlier in the debate, Lord Baden-Powell had encouraged eccentric behaviour from pedestrians as a patriotic cause. He denounced 'safety-first as a mollycoddling American slogan'. It was 'British to step off the kerb without looking and die asserting that the road belongs to foot-sloggers'.[65] Baden-Powell evoked an Englishness in which outdoor pursuits were considered masculine and healthy. Having healthy Englishmen driven off the road by a leisure pursuit such as popular motoring was, to him, a degradation of traditional freedoms.

After the introduction of the 30 mph speed limit, local residents lobbied for its imposition on stretches of arterial road that were adjacent to suburban housing. One notable example of this was at Western Avenue in 1937. Local mothers took action to protect their children against fast traffic, by staging a crossing and recrossing of the road with their prams. This proposed constraint on drivers provoked much resentment in motoring quarters. For example *The Motor* described these events as follows:

> The first section, at Shepherd's Bush opened fifteen years ago. Converted into a danger spot by the London County Council who put a housing estate on it. Hysterics and hooliganism by local inhabitants obtained a temporary speed limit here.[66]

This was not the action of teenage vandals; it was an early example of British civil disobedience. In 1938, the protestors were featured in a newsreel that showed them demanding more pedestrian bridges. Movietone insultingly titled its film '*Pons Ansinorum*' i.e. Bridge of Asses, a gesture that very few of its audience would have understood.[67]

The dangerous consequences of suburban air-mindedness

During the interwar period, flying was closely associated in the public's mind with death; it was, despite the technological advances of the First World War, a highly contingent activity. As Martin Pugh records, 'Aviation enthusiasts made no attempt to play down the dangers. *The Aeroplane*, a weekly journal, meticulously recorded every crash.'[68] Before the development of passenger planes, these deaths were in the ones and twos, but, when they arrived, the death toll for each crash rose accordingly. The worst and most important air calamity of the period was the destruction of the R101 airship in Beauvais, France, in October 1930. Graves and Hodge, writing at the end of the interwar period described it as 'the greatest disaster'.[69] This event signalled a permanent change in direction from dirigibles to fixed-wing aircraft and, for the first time, brought the idea of large-scale mass death in an aircraft to the public consciousness. Amongst the forty-seven dead were the Air Minister and most of the country's experts in dirigible aircraft. This event sat in marked contrast to the normal presentation of air-mindedness as a source of national prestige and an industry that was at the very heart of modern Britain.

Air-mindedness was one of the most important tropes in interwar fiction. Flying and air travel were used as a literary short cut to imply sophistication, wealth and excitement.[70] The most prominent example of flying as modern heroism was found in the Biggles books written for teenage boys by Captain W. E. Johns. Flying by commercial airline from to Paris from Croydon was an important element in many books, two well-known examples being *Death in the Air* by Agatha Christie and Bowen's *To the North*.

As was the case with novels about independent women drivers, women fliers in interwar novels were often punished for their independent modern attitudes by being killed in an air crash. In *Christopher Strong*, Felicity epitomised the way modern women were sometimes portrayed in interwar novels. She was, as we have seen, a fast driver, but she was fast in other ways. Secretly pregnant with her lover's child she attempted a high-flying record attempt in her plane that ended with her death. In John Rhys's *The Flying Shadow*, written in 1938, the hero, an ex-RAF flying instructor, meets prospective women pilots at the snobbish, suburban flying club where he works. One sexually experienced young woman is rejected by him and leaves to become a lady airline pilot. His true love, liberated from an awful marriage by her husband's death is, inevitably, killed in a flying accident just before they can marry:

> His voice was lost in the engine's roar, his words swept away in the slipstream. The impact being noiseless to him, was quite unreal. He saw part of the Tiger Moth break away and flutter downwards, he saw the plane itself spinning earthwards.[71]

In an earlier accident, the flying instructor has to crash-land his plane on to a new housing estate, built alongside his flying field. Rhys may have had some similar real-life examples at Croydon Airport in mind when writing about the consequences of suburban housing encroaching on the airfield.[72]

Imperial Airways and KLM at Croydon Airport

Croydon Airport was presented by its owners, airlines, commentators and the national press as the epitome of modern travel. This can be seen in many advertisements for Imperial Airways. One such was a 1934 poster advertising the GPO's airmail service to the empire. This presented *Scylla*, a four-engined giant biplane dwarfing surrounding workers and plane spotters. It was a large plane for the time, but here it is shown at an exaggerated scale, the new technology of the long distance aeroplane dominating ordinary people and life.[73] As airmail planes often left late at night to catch all the day's mail, many photographs of them showed them in *chiaroscuro*

Horatius at Croydon Airport, 1935   11
Photo by SSPL/Getty Images

style under the airport's floodlighting. Here the presentation of modern technology is enhanced by electrification and, standing alone, devoid of spectators or engineers, the aeroplane appears autonomous, silent and strong (see Figure 11).

These planes connected passengers and airmail with other European capitals and further afield to places as far flung as India. They were imperial in the way they supported communication networks within the Empire and how they supported the nation's prestige in competition with Luft Hansa and KLM in Europe. In its early years, the competition to get mail to European cities led pilots to race each other to their destination, but by the mid-1930s this had become rather frowned on as unprofessional. Airmail had become a normalised part of modern life. Airmail volumes peaked in December, and if you posted your airmail letter by mid-December you could be sure of it reaching its destination by Christmas. In 1935, for example the last aircraft to South Africa carried 2½ tons of mail, some 300,000 letters.[74] Today, we expect instantaneous, free, worldwide connections, but in the mid-1930s this represented an enormous contribution to imperial inter-connectivity.

Sunday flying and late-night airmail flying prompted a series of complaints from local residents, many of whom had arrived well after the construction of the airport. By 1935, Croydon Airport had become surrounded by new suburban development; some houses were built as close as 50 metres to the perimeter of the airfield. Virilio may well suggest that each new technology is accompanied simultaneously by its accident, but here the local council stacked the dice in favour of awkward collisions between suburbia and modernity.

The year 1936 saw two air crashes that brought new suburbia and flight together in a horrific way. At two o'clock in the morning on 10 August 1936, an Imperial Airways Vickers Vellox airmail plane set off to Paris from Croydon on a testing flight to check the performance of a new engine. Shortly after take off, the twin-engined mail plane with two pilots and two engineers on board suffered a problem with the fuel line in one of its engines. The pilot attempted to return to Croydon but didn't make it, crashing the plane into a house in Hillside Gardens.[75]. All four men were killed in the crash; their bodies were then incinerated along with two houses in the street. Both houses were unoccupied, which saved further loss of life.[76]

Later that year, a KLM passenger airliner crash killed fourteen people in Hillcrest Road, a street very close to the southern perimeter of the airport. The KLM DC2, bound for Germany and Holland, took off in very foggy conditions. The aids for taking off in fog were limited to a painted white line on the grass. After two unsuccessful attempts, the pilot got airborne, but much nearer to the perimeter than he thought, hit a tennis court fence and the conical cupola on an Edwardian house and then cartwheeled over the road, demolishing an empty house. Of the fourteen on board, twelve were killed. In a Virilion irony, one of the dead was the inventor of the autogiro, a precursor to the helicopter and an epitome of interwar innovation in flight.[77]

This latter crash was a minor, local sensation attracting pressmen and ghoulish visitors to the site. Figure 12 shows a devastated scene, the typical suburban house destroyed by new technology. The two locations for this crash, Hillcrest Road and Hillside Gardens, were aptly named to represent new suburbia of the 1930s. Their names conjured up an age where suburban life was marketed by the fresh air of an elevated situation and by the connection with the rural through the idea of life in the garden. The reality of their position in the real world was revealed by these accidents. The superficialities of suburban living were stripped away, to reveal not only the reality of their present but also their future. Figure 12 shows the shock of

The wreckage of a KLM DC-2, 1936   12
J. A. Hampton/Topical Press Agency/Hulton Archive/Getty Images

the arrival of a modern large, for the period, American plane on this suburban domesticity. The contradictions of modernity are well illustrated by the
juxtaposition of this wrecked metal machine and this arts-and-crafts-styled
home. This image prefigures the impact of the Blitz on suburban homes in
the widespread devastation of just four years later. In this way, the collision
between the modern aeroplane and an imagined bucolic life in the suburbs
showed how warfare, the ultimate product of modernity, would uproot all
that suburbanites held dear.

Conclusion

Speed and excitement on their own do not constitute modernity. Berman
identified the twin face of modernity that simultaneously required the
presence of excitement and danger and order and chaos. This fits well
with Virilio's thesis of the invention simultaneously creating the accident.
Modernity is, therefore, most clearly revealed through its accidents that
take the deployment of technology beyond mere modernisation. My analysis has positioned this modernity into the 1930s, but, in reality, modernity
works in cycles of initial exploration, dissemination, control and absorp-
tion that run over this period and in parallel with each other for different

technologies. It is in this way a far more complex periodisation than saying it was the creature of a particular decade.

For cars, the cycle played out in the following manner. In the late 1920s, the establishment of new arterial roads allowed wealthy Londoners, not necessarily suburban themselves, to enjoy high-speed motoring on fast roads that were clear of traffic. Their resultant accidents attracted much public concern that was resisted by various motoring lobbyists. By the early 1930s, they had been joined by an increasing number of middle-class motorists who enjoyed the novelty of driving. The increasing domination of the car in suburbia led to an unforgiving environment for those living in nearby housing estates. Pedestrians, cyclists, the poor and the old were punished for their lack of engagement with powerful technologies. At this point the excitement and pain associated with modernity are both very prominent. By the late 1930s, the motorist had become far more con-trolled and directed on the road with roundabouts, traffic lights and speed limits correcting his or her behaviour. By this time, driving had become normalised for middle-class audiences and distinction could be achieved not by owning a car but by having a particular type of car, just as it is today. So this form of suburban modernity, in the sense of it involving suburban agency rather than just occurring in suburbia, was in effect from roughly 1931 to about 1936.

Aeroplanes showed a similar cycle. This began as an individual explora-tory pastime for the wealthy that had concurrent and well-understood risks. This was certainly modernity, but not in a very suburban form even though the location for this flying was generally on London's outskirts. As flying became more widely available, the risk of death was transferred from the pilot to the passenger. As suburbia encroached on the airfields, the excitement of airships and passenger planes passing overhead on the way to Paris was matched by the possibility of one of the planes landing on your new suburban semi-detached house. The dangers of modernity were in this way transferred from passengers in suburbia to suburban resi-dents. This cycle of modernity began in the late 1920s and was becoming controlled and normalised by 1939. Croydon was, for example, no longer fit for purpose as a major airport, and interest transferred to Gatwick, which had a modern terminal building and clear lines of sight for its planes.

Motorcycling and cycling have been addressed in this chapter to note how dangerous these activities were. Cycling's wider adoption in the

1930s provided for new mobilities, particularly for women and children, but their dangerous interaction with cars made them victims of others' privileged modernity. Motorcyclists can be thought of as occupying an intermediate position. For working-class men, the motorcycle provided fast independent mobility that came with excitement and danger. Coupled with fast new suburban roads they were agents of their own modernity, but also, as seen in the Reynolds case, simultaneously the victims of interactions with cars.

Notes

1 Part of this chapter was first published as M. J. Law, 'Speed and Blood on the Bypass: the New Automobilities of Inter-war London', *Urban History*, 39:3, 2012, pp. 490–509, Cambridge University Press.

2 R. Cooter and B. Luckin (eds), *Accidents in History: Injuries, Fatalities and Social Relations*, Amsterdam 1997, p. 2.

3 R. Campbell, 'Philosophy and the Accident' in R. Cooter and B. Luckin, *Accidents in History*, p. 23.

4 P. Virilio, *The Original Accident*, Cambridge 2007, p. 1.

5 P. Virilio, *The Original Accident*, p. 9.

6 R. Cooter and B. Luckin (eds), *Accidents in History*, p. 5.

7 P. Virilio. *The Virilio Reader*, Oxford, 1998, p. 20.

8 R. Castel, 'From Dangerousness to Risk' in G. Burchell, C. Gordon, P. Miller (eds), *The Foucault Effect: Studies in Governmental Rationality*, Hemel Hempstead 1991, p. 289.

9 See J. T. Schnapp, 'Crash (Speed as Engine of Individuation)', *Modernism/Modernity*, 6:1, 1999, pp. 1–49.

10 K. Möser, 'The Dark Side of Automobilism, 1900–1930' *The Journal of Transport History*, 24:2, 2003, pp. 238–258.

11 S. Stevenson, 'Bourgeois Bodyguard', *The Spectator*, 12 March 1937, p. 12.

12 J. Urry, *Automobility, Car Culture and Weightless Travel: A Discussion paper*, Lancaster 1999.

13 R. Graves and A. Hodge, *The Long Week-end: A Social History of Great Britain 1918–1939*, London 1941, p. 229.

14 *Flight*, 13 June 1930.

15 *The Manchester Guardian*, 7 July 1930.

16 R. Graves and A. Hodge, *The Long Week-end*, p. 228.

17 Victoria and Albert Museum, *Art Deco 1910–1939*, London 2003, p. 316.

18 C. J. T. Gardner (ed.), *Fifty Years of Brooklands*, London 1956, p. 20.

19 C. J. T. Gardner (ed.), *Fifty Years of Brooklands*, p. 37.

20 P. Vaughan, *Something in Linoleum*, London 1994, p. 58.

21 E. C. R. Lorac, *Death on the Oxford Road*, London 1933, p. 44.

22 This is a composite example based on accounts from newspapers and coroners' reports.

23 P. Vaughan, *Something in Linoleum*, p. 58.

24 The present-day figure for killed per 1,000 motor vehicles is 0.06 and injured per 1,000 motor vehicles is 6.4 www.bbc.co.uk/news/10408417 and www.dft. gov.uk/pgr/statistics [accessed 10 September 2010].

25 J. Kunstler, *The Geography of Nowhere*, New York 1994, quoted in J. Urry, 'Inhabiting the Car', *The Sociological Review*, 54:1, 2006, pp. 17–31.

26 P. E. S. Freund, *The Ecology of the Automobile*, New York 1993, p. 45.

27 Seth K. Humphrey, 'Our Delightful Man Killer', *Atlantic*, 148, December, 1931 quoted in D. Blanke, *Hell on Wheels*.

28 A. Samuels, 'Accidents: the Car and Literature' in P. Wollen and Joe Kerr (eds), *Autopia: Cars and Culture*, London 2002, p. 56.

29 See S. O'Connell, *The Car and British Society: Class, Gender and Motoring 1896–1939*, Manchester 1998.

30 D. Blanke, *Hell on Wheels*, p. 104.

31 S. O'Connell, *The Car and British Society*, Chapter 2.

32 *Roadways*, Directors, A. Cavalcanti, S. Legg and W. Coldstream, GPO Film Unit, 1937, 2' 55".

33 J. Moran, 'Crossing the Road in Britain 1931–1976', *The Historical Journal*, 42:2, 2006, p. 477–496.

34 M. Muggeridge, *The Thirties: 1930–1940 in Great Britain*, London 1940, p. 197.

35 K. Grahame, *The Wind in the Willows*, London 1910.

36 A. Samuels, 'Accidents: the Car and Literature' in P. Wollen and Joe Kerr (eds), *Autopia: Cars and Culture*, p. 55.

37 E. M. Forster, *Howards End*, London 1910.

38 A. Thacker, 'E. M. Forster and the Motor Car', *Literature & History*, 9:2, 2000, pp. 37–52.

39 Michael Arlen's *The Green Hat* (1924) portrays its heroine, Iris Storm, as an example of the new woman whose motorisation provides access to new, independent mobilities, followed by a fatal accident. Evelyn Waugh's *Vile Bodies* (1930) parodies many of the themes of *The Green Hat* with Agatha Runcible crashing her sports car at a fashionable Brooklands-style meeting.

40 V. Woolf, quoted in A. Thacker, 'Traffic, Gender, Modernism', *The Sociological Review*, 54:s1, 2006 pp. 175–189.

41 E. D. C. Bowen, *To the North*, London, 1932.

42 E. D. C. Bowen, *To the North*, p. 306.

43 G. Frankau, *Christopher Strong. A Romance*, London 1932.

44 G. Frankau, *Christopher Strong*, p. 275.

45 This account is based on the trial of Lord de Clifford in the House of Lords and the previously held inquest to into the crash from papers held at the Parliamentary Archive HL/PO/DC/CP/33/7.

46 F. M. L. Thompson, 'Russell, Edward Southwell, twenty-sixth Baron de Clifford (1907–1982)', *Oxford Dictionary of National Biography*, Oxford University Press, 2004 [www.oxforddnb.com/view/chapter/56670, accessed 17 April 2008].

47 Correspondence between Don Williamson, Lancia Motor Club archivist, and the author, March 2008.

48 Coroner's Report, Parliamentary Archive HL/PO/DC/CP/33/7.

49 Parliamentary Archives, HL/PO/DC/CP/33/7, *Trial of Lord de Clifford*, p. 12.

50 'Richard Joshua Reynolds, Jr.' *Encyclopedia of World Biography* http://findchapters.com/p/chapters/mi_gx5229/is_2003/ai_n19151730.

51 Roughly equivalent to $1.2 million at today's values, www.measuringworth.com.

52 Metropolitan Police Reports, The National Archives, TNA MEPO 3/330, 1929.

53 *The Times*, 23 July 1929.

54 Statement of Constable Medley, Metropolitan Police Reports, TNA MEPO 3/330, 15 May 1929.

55 *The New York Times*, 1 August 1929.

56 S. Koerner, 'Four Wheels Good, Two Wheels Bad' in D. Thoms, L. Holden, T. Claydon (eds), *The Car and Popular Culture in the 20th Century*, Aldershot 1998, p. 155.

57 *The Slough, Eton and Windsor Observer*, 17 May 1929.

58 C. Emsley. '"Mother, What Did Policemen Do When There Weren't Any Motors?" The Law, the Police and the Regulation of Motor Traffic in England, 1900–1939', *The Historical Journal*, 36:2, 1993, pp. 357–381.

59 *The Times*, 12 June 1936.

60 S. O'Connell, *The Car and British Society.*

61 *The Times*, 5 November 1929.

62 Quoted in P. Thorold, *The Motoring Age: The Automobile and Britain 1896–1939*, London 2003, p. 204.

63 Quoted in P. Thorold, *The Motoring Age*, p. 205.

64 Letter from 'Realist', *The Manchester Guardian*, 3 January 1935.

65 Lord Baden-Powell quoted in P. Brendon, *The Motoring Century: The Story of the Royal Automobile Club*, London 1997, p. 198.

66 *The Motor*, 30 March 1937.

67 British Movietone, *Pons Ansinorum*, Story: 34291, 12 September 1938.

68 Pugh, M., *'We Danced All Night': A Social History of Britain Between the Wars*, London 2008, p. 307.

69 R. Graves and A. Hodge, *The Long Week-end: A Social History of Great Britain 1918–1939*, p. 288.

70 V. Cunningham, *British Writers of the Thirties*, Oxford 1988, p. 167.

71 J. L. Rhys, *The Flying Shadow*, London 1942, p. 185.

72 J. L. Rhys, *The Flying Shadow*, p. 146.

73 www.postalheritage.org.uk/page/designsondelivery-overseas.

74 *Flight*, 19 December 1935.

75 TNA AVIA 5/18, C350.

76 D. Cluett, J. Nash, R. Learmonth, *Croydon Airport: The Great Days, 1928–1939*, p. 115.

77 D. Cluett, J. Nash, R. Learmonth, *Croydon Airport: The Great Days, 1928–1939*, p. 116.

10

Everyday driving –
Mobile consumerism and commuting

As we have seen, buying a car was a key element in wealthier middle-class suburban life of the 1930s and it was, at first, mostly used for special journeys. For example, for the family weekend trip to the seaside and the countryside, and for driving at high speed, for the fun of driving in itself.[1] These are the journeys that are recorded with great frequency in memoirs and in contemporary accounts because they were great fun and exciting. Photograph albums made in the 1930s often turn up at auctions, and it is interesting to note that they often feature photos of the family's new car taken on such special outings; people did not usually take a photo when they drove to the tobacconist. This common distortion in how we remember the past has obscured the far more frequent everyday car journey. In suburban London, these everyday journeys were to a wide variety of nearby places where the car was 'indispensable' such as going to the shops, the golf club, the cinema, driving to the station and commuting to work.[2]

In order to demonstrate the significance of everyday journeys in suburbia, this chapter will concentrate on three areas. First, it will examine the role of the car in suburban shopping; second, it will re-examine the arterial road to look at the businesses established there to attract the motorised consumer, such as car showrooms, pubs and cinemas. These ideas take the car beyond being the subject of consumption itself to being an active agent in new mobilities of consumption. Third, it will examine the overlooked subject of the daily drive to work from the suburbs into central London.

Suburban shopping by car

The interwar years were the first time that middle-class households had sufficient surplus income or ready credit to be able to buy consumer goods and leisure activities in large quantities. This 'new consumerism' was mostly suburban in origin and at first focused on products for the home such as electric and gas cookers, radiograms and vacuum cleaners.[3] When these purchases had been made, suburban attention turned towards the car and, when that was acquired, to mobile leisure and consumption.

As the car infiltrated itself into suburban life in the 1930s, one of its more popular everyday uses was for shopping. In 1937, for example, *The Motor* carried a front-page advertisement for the Ford Ten, proposing to an imagined suburban family that it was the ideal vehicle for shopping.[4] The 1930s was a decade when the great department stores of the West End were at their peak.[5] Both metropolitan and suburban customers would have driven there to shop. Kathryn Morrison and John Minnis have, for example, shown that the West End garages offered a range of quite sophisticated car parks by the end of the 1930s.[6]

In order to identify shopping by car that was specifically suburban in origin and destination it is interesting to consider how department stores in outer London approached their motorised customers. One such store was Bentalls of Kingston, which was, in the interwar period, one of suburban London's most prestigious department stores, the local paper describing it as 'Greater London's greatest store'.[7] Kingston is located in one of the areas of outer London that led the way in the adoption of the car, and attracted wealthy customers living in areas such as Esher and Weybridge. This clientele was, because of their wealth, far more likely to visit Kingston by car rather than using the bus, tram or train.

In the 1920s, car parking in a suburban centre like Kingston was a haphazard affair. As early as 1930, Bentalls saw that it needed to provide secure car parking for its customers adjacent to the store. Rowan Bentall recalled that 'his [father's] constant intention throughout the 1920s was to attract car owners … It was for the benefit of these car owners that he planned his superb new covered-in car park.'[8] An accompanying photograph shows a very modern structure packed with cars neatly parked in their bays. Bentall claimed that on Saturdays it accommodated over a thousands cars and spaces became very prized.[9]

By the late 1930s, this structure was too small to cope with the demand and Bentalls planned and gained approval for a multi-storey car park with curving entrance and exit ramps that is reminiscent of many car parks built thirty years later. This innovation, despite its modification to include a bomb shelter, was not built because of the war, and the original car park was not replaced until 1969.

More unusual was the building, in Weybridge in 1936, of a new shopping centre with its own outdoor car park to service a very upmarket housing estate where houses were priced from £1500 to £1700. Although not, strictly, a part of suburban London, this development in one of the wealthiest areas of the South East, a dormitory town for London by the 1930s, led the way. The Temple Market shopping centre provided one hour's free parking for up to a hundred cars. It is interesting to see that even in 1936 parking had to be rationed by the hour.[10] This example prefigured the pedestrian shopping precincts envisaged by Abercrombie in his Greater London Plan, but, because it was the product of a speculative builder rather than from the mind of a progressive town planner, it encouraged the car and car parking.

Rowan Bentall was a very foresighted entrepreneur, who saw, as early as the 1920s, that in suburban south-west London his upmarket clientele would want to use their cars for shopping; it was more convenient than the bus or tram and allowed a customer to carry home much more from the store. It also indicated a certain status in suburban society that you had enough money to combine two forms of conspicuous consumption in driving a car to an upmarket department store. This arrangement can be thought of as a forerunner to the car-based shopping developments of the 1970s and onwards.

Mobile consumption on the arterial road

While using a car facilitated shopping at traditional locations such as the West End and in upmarket suburbs such as Kingston, modernity is demonstrated more strongly in the establishment of new forms of consumption triggered by increasing middle-class mobility. This is seen in motorists' consumption of goods and leisure services at businesses established on the arterial roads.

In its simplest form, this could be seen in motorists using shopping parades built on the arterial road. The shopping parade was a common feature of interwar suburbia, providing services to new housing estates, but those built on the arterial road attracted a different type of customer that mostly arrived by car. Jim Richards, in his early reassessment of interwar suburbia, recognised the arterial road shops' distinctive clientele:

It was also, of course, before the days when shops sprang up along the new by-pass ... Old residents, in fact, still do not acknowledge these shops as part of the suburb; they really belong to the world of by-pass roads where motorists only halt for petrol as they chase each other to the sea.[11]

In his autobiography, John Osborne remembered them with disdain:

This particular parade was just a curved corner consisting of a dozen small shops overlooking the busy roundabout. Was it a Borough Architect's joke to call these shop blocks parades? Or did some councillor think that the word itself would invest their dismal rows of newsagents and hairdressers with gaudy pomp.[12]

The newsagents and hairdressers of the shopping parades of London's arterial roads are still present, but to fully recover their interwar appearance today's pizza takeaways, minicab offices and sun-bed parlours have to be replaced in the imagination with butchers, grocers and bicycle dealers.[13] In the 1930s, parking was not regulated on arterial roads and their shopping parades would have been a convenient place for motorists to pick up a newspaper or something to eat for tea.

Brewers were also quick to see the opportunities presented by the arterial road. Their new 'improved' pubs aimed to attract the motorised consumer with a more sophisticated proposition than the traditional public house, which would have been more squarely aimed at working-class customers. The improved pub distinguished itself from its humble progenitors by proposing that drinking in a public house could be fashionable and socially acceptable for both men and women. As a consequence, they featured large saloon and cocktail bars that were designed specifically for middle-class customers, restaurants and dancing. They were larger and grander than town pubs and employed fashionable architectural styling.[14] They were sometimes called roadhouses, but this term will not be used here so as to differentiate them from their larger, Americanised brethren that were the subject of Chapter 7 of this book. Drinking and driving was a normalised behaviour in 1930s Britain as long as it wasn't taken to extremes. A motor-trip to the coast would be accompanied by a drink at an arterial road pub, or an evening drink would be enlivened by taking the car out for a spin. These pubs were the first to have specially designed car parks and would initially have received little in the way of passing trade from pedestrians.

One example that reveals much of its original design can still be seen at the Osterley Park Hotel on the Great West Road. The brickwork is painted and the windows have ugly blinds, the olde-worlde inn sign is absent, but much of the Tudorbethan original remains. Tudor was the norm, as Peter Haydon reports: 'The suburban pub was meant to have a distinctly suburban air... mock Tudor being very much their fashion'.[15] Many of these large interwar pubs are still in service today.

One notable alternative to Tudor design was found in pubs that aimed further up-market by adopting classical architectural features, known as 'Brewer's Georgian'. On Western Avenue, the architect E. B. Musman was responsible for a high-water mark in neo-Georgian pub design in the form of the Mylett Arms. This enormous public house, built in 1935, featured three public bars, a saloon bar, a saloon lounge and a music lounge with a small bandstand. An architectural writer of the period described how the Mylett Arms provided 'meals (cooked by a French chef) for a rather special clientele'.[16] Musman rejected the more commonplace Tudorbethan designs to produce a large improved public house that could attract a wide range of customers from the motorised to local residents from the new estates springing up along Western Avenue.

Musman was also responsible, one year later, in 1936, for the modernist pub the Comet in Hatfield on the Great North Road. In a spirited combination of transport modernities, the Comet references the De Havilland plane manufactured in a nearby factory and positioned itself for the passing trade of cars heading up the A1 to the North. The layout of the Comet makes it clear that it was aimed at wealthier drivers as it provided a chauffeur's rest room at the back of the property. Owner-driving was very much to the fore in 1936, so it was only the wealthiest who would have employed a chauffeur.

The suburban arterial road was, unsurprisingly, a favoured location for garages, filling stations and motor showrooms. For intellectuals, the filling station became one of the most despised elements of the interwar roadscape as its proprietors tried to accommodate a building for modern needs in rural or suburban settings.[17] Put bluntly, by the philanthropist Sir Arthur Stanley, 'Almost all existing petrol stations are ugly'.[18] Filling stations were built in an extremely wide variety of styles that included thatched, mock-Tudor and, on one occasion, Chinese.[19]

Various attempts were made to improve the presentation of roadside garages. The trade magazine *Motor Commerce* held a competition in 1927 to promote good design; the winners used a Spanish revival style, popular in America at the time, with much beautifying planting in evidence.[20] In 1930, the Design and Industries Association published *The Village Pump*, which promoted modern, appropriate design. Significantly, the winning garages were found on bypasses and arterial roads; a reflection of the need to provide services to new customers in these new locations.

Filling stations were to become increasingly influenced by examples taken from the USA; for example; *The Village Pump* features American gas stations as exemplars of attractive, functional design. *The Motor Trader*, a magazine for owners of British filling stations, often referred to proprietors visiting the USA to find out for themselves the best in design. A 1931 competition for filling station design found Tudor, Egyptian and modern designs competing for first prize.[21] By 1933, *The Motor Trader* had published a design for a modern service station and had described mock-Tudor and thatch as a charade.[22]

In contrast, its proposed design was for a combined garage, filling station and sales showroom in modernist style, flat roofed, in white render and using reinforced steel joists to support long window openings. It proposed a hybrid business model: 'Being flat, the roofs of the two blocks can be used for many purposes, according to the policy of the proprietor; sunbathing or a swimming pool, a tea garden or a badminton court can be arranged at little extra cost'.[23] This proposal recognised the arterial road as a new location for both material consumption and enjoyment of leisure, the latter idea fully realised in the roadhouse. Within a year, similar modernist designs, without the badminton courts, were erected on London's arterial roads.

The building of arterial roads prompted leading car dealers to move away from the West End to locations in suburbia with plenty of free space, new suburban customers and lots of passing motorists. Before the interwar suburbanisation project, car showrooms, aiming for a wealthy clientele, were based in Mayfair and around Great Portland Street, Euston Road and Tottenham Court Road.[24] In 1933, *The Autocar* declared that 'Great Portland Street, famous street celebrates its 40th anniversary as the centre of motordom'.[25] The year 1935 saw a turning point: garages started to sell cars from showrooms on the arterial road turning what had once been a functional stop for petrol and repairs into a drive out to the bypass for the purposes of consumption. Here, the potential customer could see new cars located in the most modern of premises and take a test drive on the nearby fast new motor road. The two companies most associated with this highly distinctive type of garage and showroom were Stewart and Ardern, and Henly's.

Stewart and Ardern was the exclusive dealer for Morris cars in the London area, with the rights to sell Britain's most popular cars at a time of rapid expansion of car sales; its head office was located in fashionable Berkeley Square in the West End. In the mid-1930s, it moved into the suburbs in an aggressive expansion programme and placed garages around the clock face of London's arterial roads. Most of these garages were conventional in appearance but the architectural press picked out three for attention at Catford, Ilford and Staines. Located on busy roads, these were specifically designed to project a modern image. *The Architect's Journal* described the garages as follows:

> The features, which enable the public to pick out at a glance the Car Service Stations as being those of Messrs. Stewart and Ardern's are two: the Tower, which can be seen from a great distance both by day and, when illuminated, by night; and the wide span shop front … which is fitted with a special kind of sliding-folding door supposed to be the largest of its kind in Europe.[26]

Inside the garage, customers were welcomed into a gleaming showroom featuring white-tiled floors and chrome and glass fittings. Figure 13 shows their showroom in Staines where the Bauhaus furniture proposes an ultra-modern, prestigious, Californian shopping experience.

Henly's was an equally big name in motoring in the 1930s, and it built two, striking arterial road showrooms in this period. The first of these opened in August 1935 on the North Circular Road, very near to the *La Delivrance* statue noted in Chapter 6.[27] The site became, and still is, known as Henly's Corner even though the garage has long since disappeared. This garage was promoted as a 'motordrome', making a claim to modernity through association with air-mindedness. The petrol and servicing parts of the garage were at street level with a terrace-loggia and tearoom on the first floor to give access to the car showroom.[28] The top floor of the garage provided a testing area for customers to try the car, although this must have been somewhat limited by the space available. The marketing of motor sales, in this example, was a very sophisticated proposition. Customers sat in the tearoom, took the sun on the terrace and then walked across to look at the latest offerings from Studebaker.

In 1937, Henly's opened a garage on the Great West Road that exceeded all the above examples in both scale and outrageousness of design. It was a mammoth construction, approximately 100 m long with a 40 m high tower. It cost £75,000 to construct and housed 175 employees.[29] The filling station part of the garage sheltered under a massive cantilevered roof

13   Stewart and Ardern car showroom and service station, Staines, 1934
Architectural Press Archive / RIBA Library Photographs Collection

that protected twenty-two petrol pumps grouped into five islands. The car showrooms, hidden behind folding doors, had a bay for each marque, and Henly's sold cars from Vauxhall, Ford, Humber, Hillman, Lanchester and Studebaker amongst others.[30] The 'advertising' tower was completely covered in sheet copper and it was positioned so that the word HENLYS was visible from both directions on the arterial road.[31] At the top of the tower was a massive neon clock, which must have made a striking impression at night.

By the end of the 1930s, the arterial roads of greater London were a popular location for many different types of garages and filling stations. It has been calculated that, in this period, 20 per cent of all Middlesex's garages were located on the Great West Road alone.[32] Clearly, not all garages on arterial roads were remarkable to look at, – some were scruffy and old-fashioned – but those that shone a beacon for modern consumption created a dramatic roadscape at this time.

The American corporations with the most profound impact on British society after the First World War were the Hollywood movie studios. Their impact was twofold. First, the presentation of consumer products in their native setting increased demand for American goods and, second, the consistent presentation of an idealised America on the screen influenced the way British filmgoers thought about themselves and their lives. Between the wars, the great Hollywood studios dominated the presentation of movies in Britain, forcing out the amateurish and stilted home-grown product.

The cinemas that showed this American content were British-owned, but their efforts to attract motorised customers by building on the arterial road mimicked the American experience. Jeffrey Richards has demonstrated that cinema was the preferred form of interwar entertainment for working- and lower-middle-class audiences, particularly for women and for children.[33] Richards reported a study that showed that, overall, '32% of the population went to the cinema once a week or more'.[34] Other writers, of whom the best known is Alan Eyles, have researched the development of British cinemas and have shown how the chains of cinemas such as Odeon and ABC came to dominate the market by providing a highly glamorous and luxurious offering in large and architecturally eye-catching cinemas.[35] The cinema chains responded to the suburbanisation of London by building large numbers of small cinemas in the new high streets. Richards reports that the arrival of talking pictures in 1928 increased demand for films just at the point when London's suburbia was developing.[36] A cinema in a shopping parade became a common sight and formed a key part of this new townscape. Alan Jackson described them as 'part of the very fabric of the new suburbia'.[37] Cinemas were, therefore, initially located near to the centres of population that they supported. Patrons would walk, cycle or catch a bus or tram to the local picture house just as they would to Sainsbury's or Timothy White's, shops that shared the same shopping parade. As late as 1927 cinemas expected their patrons to arrive by public transport: one architect commented that 'provided there is a good bus or tram service a super-cinema theatre will draw patrons from an extensive area'.[38]

As the 1930s progressed, and London's car ownership increased and spread towards the lower middle classes who were the cinema's key audience, cinema location and design began to change. A key figure in these changes was Oscar Deutsch, the founder of the Odeon chain of cinemas. Odeon cinemas became a leading example of interwar suburban style in their adoption of moderne architecture employing huge towers, neon lighting and cream tiling. They were responsible for many British super-cinemas that were larger and more luxurious than the humble picture-houses that preceded them.[39]

The development of London's road network provided an opportunity to build a new kind of cinema that was larger in scale and positioned on the arterial road and aimed directly at motorised cinemagoers. Oscar Deutsch recognised this and, in 1934, Odeon opened a cinema in Tolworth, which was, at the time, a crossing point on the Kingston Bypass still surrounded by fields.[40] Alan Eyles recorded that this greenfield site 'attracted much ridicule' from the trade press.[41] This demonstrated that in contrast to Bentalls' car-centric stance in the established suburbs, the bypass was not yet thought of as a location for motorised consumption. Deutsch's insight proved accurate and, by September 1936, the *Motion Picture Herald* noted that 'he can draw paying audiences from adjacent heavily populated areas linked by road or rail to his sites'.[42]

Odeon, in the period from 1936 to the start of the Second World War, would increasingly position its cinemas on main roads to gain access to motorised customers. One such, the Odeon at Colindale on the Edgware Road, combined an, at the time, isolated suburban shopping parade location with accommodation for motorists, Eyles noting that 'it seemed to have a rather remote location but with the busy flow of drivers, there was a substantial car park'.[43] The car park was an important change in the design of the suburban cinema and began to be used as a selling point to attract the motorised customer. By 1937, the trade paper *Cinema and Theatre Construction* was reminding its readers to 'study your car patrons by lighting your car park efficiently; promote a "quick getaway"'.[44]

An example of a fully developed arterial road cinema was the Odeon,

Odeon, Shannon's Corner, New Malden, 1938   14
Photo by Salisbury Photo Press, courtesy of Cinema Theatre Association Archive

Shannon's Corner on the Kingston Bypass (see Figure 14).[45] This was a super-cinema seating 1600 people, and was designed by George Coles, a leading cinema architect who drew from both American and European sources for his designs.[46] This site was distanced from both the new and Victorian suburbia of the area, but was easily accessible to those driving a car.

This cinema, which boldly featured its free car park in the advertisements for its opening in November 1938, was deliberately positioned to attract motorists; its main entrance at right angles to the old suburban road next to it rather than facing it in the old style.[47] The front and the tower, with its Odeon signage, was pointed at the arterial road and would have been a highly visible sight when driving from town to the countryside or the suburbs, particularly at night with the use of flood and neon lighting. This cinema had a very large car park that dwarfed the footprint of the cinema itself, and was in marked contrast to designs from earlier in the decade when cinemas made little allowance for motorists. Here was a cinema explicitly designed for motorists, positioned for rapid access by car, high visibility from the road and plenty of free parking for its patrons. This new trend in cinema location and design was cut short by the outbreak of war a year later, and was not revived until the out-of-town developments of cinemas in the late 1970s.

Driving to work

As proposed in the introduction to this book, historians have often ignored the use of the car for commuting to work before the Second World War.[48] I will reiterate, here, Paul Oliver's definitive statement that 'The car was not used for going to work'.[49] It is worth mentioning this again, because *Dunroamin* is such an important and influential work on London's suburbia. This is further evidence of a historiographical flattening of the interwar years, where key developments of the late 1930s are ignored in favour of a more general impression of this period. As we have seen, by the late 1930s drivers were beginning to use their cars for short casual local journeys, but they were also commuting to central London, thus developing new quotidian practices in their driving, and changing the nature of motoring.[50]

In 1939, Robinson and Browne in their satirical look at the parvenu driver, *How to Be a Motorist*, suggested that commuting by car was already producing problems for London's roads. They observed that: 'Things are different now, as will be apparent to anyone who cares to loiter in the middle of Hammersmith Broadway during the evening rush hour'.[51] Commuting by car is backed by evidence from two key sources: Colin Pooley's detailed study on journeys to work in the twentieth century and statistical surveys of the major roads leading in to London that reveal tidal flows of cars in the early morning and again in the opposite direction in the evening.

Pooley has undertaken a longditudinal survey of the patterns and means of commuting in the twentieth century and collated information from over twelve thousand journeys to work taken from 1,800 individual life histories. He calculates that, in London, the overall percentage of journeys to work by car, for the period 1920 to 1939, was 6 per cent.[52] By 1938, given the rise in the number of cars in London, one could guess that this percentage could have been as high as 10 per cent. Certainly, there is evidence to support Robinson and Browne's observation that enough drivers were commuting by car to London to produce a rush hour at Hammersmith. This location at the western gateway to London is suggestive that much of this commuting would have come from the suburbs.

The MoT undertook detailed road traffic censuses on London's major roads in August 1935 and again in August 1938. These show, in summary for each major road, the average number of passenger motor vehicles passing each census point for each hour of the day for both centripetal and centrifugal traffic. These censuses have a number of limitations. First, they do not distinguish between cars and motor cycles, second they include weekend traffic, which, as Sunday was the most popular day for motoring, dampens data on Monday to Friday commuting, as drivers would be likely to be heading in the opposite direction than on a weekday, i.e. to the seaside rather than to the office. Finally, the choice of August also distorts the data by emphasising traffic on holiday journeys and reducing the impact of commuting.

Despite all these limitations, my analysis of these road surveys indicates that approximately one half of them show a commuting pattern with most of these showing distinct morning and evening peaks. A small number also show an additional lower peak in driving towards London in the evening, which might be explained by people driving towards the West End for a night out.

This can be best illustrated with a specific example. At the A106 in Leyton, a passenger vehicle passed the census point heading towards the centre of London every 7 seconds between eight and nine in the morning.[53] This peak was 2.7 times greater than the daily average for this census point. A similar peak of 2.2 times the average was seen between five and six in the evening coming in the opposite direction.[54] This and similar charts suggest that in the latter part of the 1930s there were rush hours of passenger motor traffic in London's suburbs heading to and from town, similar to the tidal pattern we are familiar with today.

A map accompanying the MoT survey shows the overall traffic patterns in south-east England in 1938, where the relative volume of traffic is indicated by the width of each road.[55] The map shows some interesting details. First, the levels of traffic in the eastern section are as high as those in the west, which comes as a surprise in relation to the under-representation of east London motoring in historical sources. Second, the arteries arriving in western London tend to thicken in the outer suburban ring, whereas those on the eastern side tend not to. This suggests that western suburbs were more likely to add to the traffic than those in the east, which supports the data shown earlier in this book. The map also shows that non-radial journeys between suburbs were more likely to occur in western London. It is possible that the limitations of public transport's radial network and the western location of London's new industrial estates would make a car attractive for this type of journey.[56]

The census records also show a culture of casual motoring, with cars used for journeys in the middle of the day. The census does not record the purposes of the journeys, but the timings are indicative of car driving for convenience.

Conclusion

Everyday journeys in suburbia reveal much of importance in an examination of the condition of interwar modernity. These journeys demonstrate ideas that are often found in thinking about modernity, such as time-space compression, the increased distancing of home from work and leisure activity and in the middle-class obsession with consumption and display.

The widespread adoption of the car and the development of new, faster roads provided a more radical and less radial version of suburbia. Consumption and display were, as ever, at the heart of this extension to the many ways that the suburban middle classes hoped to find distinction from their neighbours.

The way that established suburban centres such as Kingston attracted motorised consumers to shop in department stores like Bentalls was in effect a transitional arrangement that reinforced Edwardian practices. The location for shopping hadn't changed, just the way of getting there. As well as providing an easier, more efficient journey for the new car-owner, shopping by car showed to the world that you were a wealthy, modern and sophisticated person.

The building of arterial roads and bypasses around these ancient suburban towns was the prompt for something genuinely new to arrive. Businesses that wished to attract wealthy customers could now establish themselves in suburbia in new arterial road locations that were not dependent on being in the vicinity of local railway stations, and that could appeal to a modern clientele. As Colin Campbell observed in his study of modern consumer behaviour, 'consumption habits may alter as a consequence of either an innovation in the use of resources or a modification to the pattern of gratification ... and the latter has a more intimate connection with the insatiability of wants than the former'.[57] In this case, arterial road development and wider car access fit the idea of an innovative use of resource, and the way that cars were used to distinguish their owners and to provide pleasure in themselves and as a means to enjoy new ways of buying things can be definitely thought of as a modification to the pattern of gratification. The association of consumption with personal mobility is an idea more associated with the demise of the high street and the rise of out-of-town shopping in the 1970s, but its antecedents were on display in the late 1930s.

Filling stations were the first businesses to arrive, fulfilling the car drivers' most immediate need. As has been shown, these were followed by 'improved' pubs, then car showrooms and finally cinemas. Driving to the pub for a drink with your friends signalled a strong sense of modernity, even though the buildings that provided this new location for pleasure were mostly in nostalgic architectural styles, which were both forward- and backward-looking at the same time. The middle-class driver could pop in for a drink with his wife in tow and they could both enjoy a stylish and convivial evening surrounded by other motorised suburbanites. Drinking cocktails would demonstrate an element of Americanised sophistication; knowledge of wine would show you were urbane and cultured.

Car showrooms on the arterial road combined the thrill and glamour of motoring with the opportunity to buy an American or continental car from Henly's or a British equivalent from Stewart and Ardern. Here, the showrooms were as modern as the consumerism they promoted. The spotless, white floored showrooms promoted the cars as an attainable glimpse of the future, where driving provided freedom from suburban constraints. The modern new roads and the stylish smart cars combined to produce a strikingly Americanised, Californian consumption on London's outskirts.

The arterial road cinema, driven to on the fast new road, was the apogee of this experience; it was a very short-lived phenomenon, lasting from about 1937 until 1939. In this way, middle-class suburbanites could emulate the version of Los Angeles life that was presented to them on the cinema screen. Streamlined cars and white roads combined with the moderne styling of the super-cinema to present a British version of Wilshire Boulevard. Motorised cinema patrons could drive home understanding that their journey had conferred on them a sense of being modern, American and successful.

On Monday morning, the same suburban drivers could drive on to the arterial road and commute to their offices in the West End and the City of London. Ten years earlier they would have waited on a suburban railway platform with their neighbours waiting for the train to take them to work.

Entering their first-class compartment, they would share curt conversations about the weather, before retiring behind their newspapers for the duration. Now, they were the pilots of their own vehicles, determining their own routes, leaving when they wanted to. On the arterial roads they experienced the modernity of autonomous travel.

Notes

1 See S. O' Connell, 'Motoring and Modernity: 1900–1950' in J. Strange, F. Carnevali, P. Johnson (eds), *Twentieth-century Britain: Economic, Cultural and Social Change*, Harlow 2007, p. 121.

2 *The Autocar*, 4 March 1938.

3 S. Bowden, 'The New Consumerism' in P. Johnson (ed.), *Twentieth-century Britain: Economic, Social and Cultural, Change*, London 1994.

4 *The Motor*, 14 December 1937.

5 S. Ashmore, B. Edwards, D. Gilbert, '"Mr Bourne's dilemma": Consumer Culture, Property Speculation and Department Store Demise: the Rise and Fall of Bourne and Hollingsworth on London's Oxford Street', *Journal of Historical Geography*, 38:4, 2012, pp. 434–446.

6 K. A. Morrison and J. Minnis, *Carscapes*, London 2012.

7 R. Bentall, *My Store of Memories*, London 1974, p. 73.

8 R. Bentall, *My Store of Memories*, p. 82.

9 R. Bentall, *My Store of Memories*, p. 85.

10 T. F. Nash Brochure, October 1936, London Metropolitan Archives, LMA/4430/04/02/022.

11 J. M. Richards, *The Castles on the Ground*, London 1946, p. 45.

12 J. Osborne, *A Better Class of Person: An Autobiography 1929–1956*, Harmondsworth 1982, p. 58.

13 *Kelly's Directory of Chiswick, Brentford and Gunnersbury*, London 1936.

14 D. Gutzke, *Pubs and Progressives: Reinventing the Public House in England, 1896–1960*, DeKalb, Ill. 2006.

15 P. Haydon, *The English Pub: A History*, London 1994, p. 287.

16 B. Oliver, *The Renaissance of the English Public House*, London 1947.

17 For example in C. Williams-Ellis, *England and the Octopus*, London 1928.

18 Open letter from Sir A. Stanley in Design and Industries Association, *The Village Pump*, London 1930.

19 D. Jeremiah, 'Filling Up: the British Experience, 1896–1940', *Journal of Design History*, 8:2, 1995, pp 97–116.

20 'Design for Filling', *Motor Commerce*, May 1934.

21 *The Autocar*, 20 March 1931.

22 G. A. Fortesque, quoted in *The Motor Trader*, 13 December 1933.

23 *The Motor Trader*, 11 October 1933.

24 K. A. Morrison and J. Minnis, *Carscapes*, London 2012, p. 59.

25 *The Autocar*, 24 February 1933.

26 *The Architects' Journal*, 8 August 1935, p. 201.

27 *The Motor Trader*, August 1935.

28 *The Architects' Journal*, 14 March 1935.

29 *The Autocar*, 19 February 1937.

30 *The Architects' Journal*, 11 March 1937.

31 www.ribapix.com, ref. RIBA24218.

32 J. P. Whitehouse, The *UK Petrol Filling Station to 1990, with Particular Reference to London and Middlesex*, unpublished thesis, University of London, 2002.

33 J. Richards, *The Age of the Dream Palace: Cinema and Society in Britain, 1930– 1939*, London 1989.

34 J. Richards, *The Age of the Dream Palace*, pp. 14 and 15.

35 For example, A. Eyles, Cinema Theatre Association and British Film Institute, *Oscar Deutsch Entertains Our Nation*, London 2002, and R. Gray and Cinema Theatre Association, *Cinemas in Britain: One Hundred Years of Cinema Architecture*, London 1996.

36 J. Richards, *The Age of the Dream Palace*, p. 16.

37 A. A. Jackson, *Semi-detached London: Suburban Development, Life and Transport, 1900–39*, London 1973, p. 176.

38 G. Coles, quoted in D. Atwell, *Cathedrals of the Movies: A History of British Cinemas and Their Audiences*, London 1980.

39 A. Eyles, *Oscar Deutsch Entertains Our Nation*.

40 M. Webb, *The Amber Valley Gazetteer of Greater London's Suburban Cinemas, 1946–86*, Erdington 1986.

41 A. Eyles, *Oscar Deutsch Entertains Our Nation*, p. 31.

42 B. Allen, quoted in A. Eyles, *Oscar Deutsch Entertains Our Nation*, p. 31.

43 A. Eyles, *Oscar Deutsch Entertains Our Nation*, p. 62.

44 *Cinema and Theatre Construction*, January 1937.

45 From the collection of the Cinema Theatre Association.

46 D. Dean and Royal Institute of British Architects, Drawings Collection, *The Thirties: Recalling the English Architectural Scene*, London 1983, p. 102.

47 *The Surrey Comet*, 5 November 1938.

48 The section on commuting to work is largely taken from M. J. Law, '"The Car Indispensable": the Hidden Influence of the Car in Inter-war Suburban London', *Journal of Historical Geography*, 38:4, 2012, pp. 424–433, published by Elsevier.

49 P. Oliver, 'Great Expectations – Suburban Values and the Role of the Media' in P. Oliver, I. Davis and I. Bentley, *Dunroamin: The Suburban Semi and Its Enemies*, London 1981, p. 123.

50 See S. O'Connell, *The Car and British Society: Class, Gender and Motoring 1896–1939*, Manchester 1998.

51 W. H. Robinson and K. R. G. Browne, *How to Be a Motorist*, London 1939, p. 7.

52 Data provided by Colin Pooley and derived from a national sample of 12,439

journeys to work taken from 1,834 individual life histories. For more details of the source see C. Pooley and J. Turnbull, 'The Journey to Work: a Century of Change', *Area*, 31, 1999, pp. 282–292; C. Pooley and J. Turnbull, 'Modal Choice and Modal Change: the Journey to Work in Britain Since 1890', *Journal of Transport Geography*, 8:1, 2000, pp. 11–24.

53 As has been shown, this is an area that was not in the vanguard of new car adoption, but the survey is silent on where each vehicle originated.

54 TNA MT/44/16, A106 at Leyton, August 1938, Census point 1224.

55 MoT, Road Traffic Census 1938 Report, London 1939.

56 For a discussion of British commuting choices over a wider period, see C. Pooley and J. Turnbull, 'Coping with Congestion: Responses to Urban Traffic Problems in British cities c1920–1960', *Journal of Historical Geography*, 31:1, 2005, pp. 78–93.

57 C. Campbell, *The Romantic Ethic and the Spirit of Modern Consumerism*, Oxford 1987.

Part V

Conclusion

11

Modern marvels

New suburban mobilities

In the second half of the nineteenth century, Britain was transformed by a revolution in its public transport. In an exemplification of modernity, this was associated with dramatic time-space compression, a new order in the timetable and a sense of chaos, as urban and rural space were uprooted for the arrival of the train. From the 1880s, new inventions led to the introduction of the modern bicycle, motorcycle, car and finally the aeroplane. Between the wars, these technologies were further developed through the use of Fordist mass-production systems that improved their efficiency and reduced their price.

The increasing domination of the city over the countryside and the rise in consumer industries and offices then led, in London and other large British cities, to the formation of new suburbia fuelled by a recursive cycle of self-interested capitalism controlled by public transport providers and speculative builders. The result was that London spread outwards and, when combined with previously independent towns, formed a new outer suburban ring of contiguous housing.

This book has proposed that rising real incomes and changing patterns of consumption powered the wider adoption and deployment of independent transport technologies that remade this suburban life. A suburbia that was previously in thrall to the radial journey to the city centre, prisoner to its timetables, found new mobilities that transformed the lives of those who could afford them and adversely affected the lives of those who could not.

Working-class suburbanites got the worst deal from both public and private transport. New suburban council estates were often, in their early days, remote from tramlines and railway stations, leaving a long walk before a commute to work. Despite the prominence of the garden city model at this time, little provision was made for work within easy access of home. The technology that provided independence and faster travel for workers was the humble bicycle. The reduction in new prices and a wide second-hand market meant that cycling was a possibility for those in regular work. Bicycles were used for commuting to work over long distances and for more local use. For some better-off working men, who might have first learned how to ride in the Great War, the motorcycle provided speed from a dirty and noisy machine that attracted disdain from the more respectable classes.

Moving to the top of the suburban social pyramid, the wealthy would be highly likely to have access to a car if they wanted one. In prosperous old suburbs and some aspirational newer ones, the middle layer of the middle classes was also buying cars in large numbers. These lucky car owners could spontaneously drive to the seaside, to the countryside, to the shops, and could drive to work. The very wealthiest and forward-looking could take advantage of short flights to nearby European capitals, or even learn to fly. All these services were available to them at nearby suburban airports and airfields. Most of the middle-class houses would also have access to bicycles, a means of transport that was particularly useful for women and children who relied on the man of the house to drive the car. Motorcycling was a hobby for a small number in this group, part of a masculine enthusiasm for speed that typified this period.

In between these first two groups were the lower middle classes and prosperous working classes, the archetypical residents of semi-detached suburban London. Some of this group had access to cars, bought cheaply second hand or, as they became cheaper, on instalment credit, or both. These families were certainly well off enough to own a motorcycle or sidecar combination if they wanted to, swapping it for a car as soon as they could afford to. They took trips to London's airfields, enjoyed five-bob joyrides and plane and celebrity spotting. They were habitual users of motorcycles and bicycles for everyday transport, and were also keen joiners of clubs. This most uncertain group within suburban society, with the wish to move upwards but without, for the time being, the means, were the heart and soul of cycle and motorcycle club membership. With their desire for fellowship and fun, the less wealthy London suburbs were busy with club members enjoying ride outs every weekend.

By adopting newly affordable private transport in this way, London's lower middle classes were able to experience an exciting and enjoyable way of life that was based around independent mobility. Unexpectedly, the new suburbs of outer London were the location for this great change that foreshadowed a mobile, consumerist way of life that became widespread in Britain in the second half of the twentieth century.

New patterns of consumption

We had push bikes first, then we had a tandem – we had three tandems, had it made to measure and we thought it was lovely. And then when the children came, we got a motor-bike and sidecar. And when the girl came, well we thought we'd get a car.[1]

This memory from the Burton family epitomises the aspirational and changing materialities of independent mobility in London's interwar suburbs, but it conceals as much as it reveals in proposing that their change in mobilities was determined by the increasing size of their family.

In reality, this young family was typical of many in suburban London in the years between the wars. Not only was the family growing, but so was their real disposable income which allowed them greater choice about how they spent it. In a 1930s boom period in the South East, aided by easy credit for consumer goods, families like the Burtons began to form part of the new consumerism. They would have already obtained its touchstones, a gramophone, a wireless and perhaps a gas cooker. Owning a car was not just determined by the needs of a growing family, it designated that they were a success, provided distinction from their neighbours and, in one generation, had distanced them from the tram and train that provided the mobility for their parents.

For their wealthier neighbours in the smarter houses a few miles down the arterial road, owning a car was no longer enough for suburban distinction. By the late 1930s, the choice of car was very important. Foreign marques could be thought vulgar, baby cars were too closely associated with the semi-detached house. These smarter drivers could afford to use their status symbol for everyday use and to engage in mobile consumption, where the car provided the means for display and acquisition simultaneously. The roadhouse epitomises this type of mobile destination. Roadhouse car parks were full of expensive cars, where their drivers could then enjoy dining and dancing till the early hours, or during the day sunbathe by the pool in a convincing impersonation of an American country club. In the evening they could drive to a cinema and see this American lifestyle played out in

Hollywood films, and when it was time to return home they could drive home on the arterial road, just like in the movies.

The world of suburban modernity

It has been the intention of this book to demonstrate that a condition of modernity was in operation in suburban London in the 1930s. For this to be the case there had to be something happening that amounted to more than modernisation or behaving in a modern way. These last two ideas can be clearly seen in a simple form in many interwar books aimed at younger audiences. My father's childhood book from the 1930s, *The Modern Marvels Encyclopaedia*, sits on my bookshelf a few feet from where I am writing this. It contains detailed explanations of the latest, fastest cars and aeroplanes and other technical wonders. It would have seemed obvious to the suburban readers of books like this that they lived in a transformed, modern world.

To experience a condition of modernity requires the presence of a number of important elements. The first is usually typified by the idea of time-space compression. Suburban life is of course entirely determined by the time-space compression brought about by new technologies. Without it suburbia is impossible, the journey to work needs to be less than an hour, whether that is by foot, horse bus, tram or train. Effectively pre-car suburbia was an extension of urban modernity with its purpose being the support of an ever-increasing urbanisation of work. For suburban modernity to be evident, time-space compression needs to be evidenced within the suburb. This certainly was the case, in the form of increased speed on non-radial journeys that was enabled by the much wider adoption of the bicycle, motorcycle and car. In particular, the closed car, with its replication of a domestic suburban interior, normalised fast speeds and comfort. Attending air displays was modern but, strictly, only joyriders had a direct encounter with speed and a totalising view of the suburban landscape, thus providing experience of this element of modernity.

A second related element of modernity can be thought of as a remaking of space. This constant cycle of remaking is generally thought to have an urban quality; it is very evident in city centres, but suburbia was remade in the 1930s. In the cliché of intellectual disdain, suburbia is unchanging. By providing the possibility of autonomous, spontaneous movements, new technologies allowed for the creation of a different suburbia that was not necessarily linked to the railway station and the high street. The practices of the independently mobile changed suburbia from its dependence on the city to something that provided new possibilities in the way that suburban life could be led.

A third element is found in the idea of a simultaneous occurrence of order and chaos. In suburbia, the establishment of new arterial roads and airports provided a network of connections and possibilities. Under the control of central and local government politicians and engineers, these constructions regulated the experimental and exploratory practices of the early motorist and aviator. As Virilio suggests, these inventions were simultaneously vested with their own accidents to provide chaos. This chaos was vested in those living near suburban airports in a series of crashes and much more regularly in the large number of deaths of motorists, pedestrians and cyclists in road accidents. Much of the debate on the location of airports and road speeds was, in this way, a negotiation between the forces of order and chaos, with order just about coming out ahead in the contest.

So, in suburban London in the 1930s, a condition of modernity was demonstrated in the adoption and experience of new technologies by increasing numbers of its residents. This was not a permanent condition, as these new practices became increasingly regulated they became the new norm and a blueprint for later British suburban life.

Resistance to modernity

Although much of this book has been devoted to understanding how the technologies of transport were enjoyed in suburbia, it has also recorded a wide variety of resistance to these forces. This resistance was powered by the highly uneven way in which modernity provided its exciting benefits. For every young man driving a two-seater sports car, there were many poorer suburbanites who crossed the road in fear of being knocked down.

Resistance to the increasing domination of the car in suburban London was diffuse and disorganised. The Pedestrians' Association held meetings and mounted a letter-writing campaign but was unable to convince a government that was ideologically committed to laissez-faire that intervention was necessary. Its campaign was, initially, overpowered by the lobbying from the car industry and from influential car drivers. By the 1930s, the mood of the country swung towards regulation, not for ideological reasons, but because the number of motoring deaths and injuries had become unacceptable. By the end of the 1930s, regulation was considered normal, but, where it was inconsistently applied, as at Shepherd's Bush, direct action by women was needed to win the argument. It is interesting that, even this late in the decade, this protest could be described as hooliganism by a motoring magazine.

Resistance to the arterial roads came in a number of forms; it was not always just a predictable response to the consequence of accidents. We have seen, for example, how teenage vandals responded to the idea of creating an arterial road memorial to the recently fallen in the Great War. Tearing up these heartfelt, personal plaques was an unwelcome resistance to the order of the new road. Bored and alienated teenagers did not see a sacred road but a place to waste time and kick things around. The well-intentioned Roads Beautifying Association's resistance was a more complex aesthetic proposition. It accepted that modern roads were necessary, welcome even, but it found their plain and repetitious roadscapes ugly. The RBA's planting schemes attempted to disguise the modern roads, but their use of both foreign and native plants suggests a more sophisticated proposition than a simple return to old England. Organised cyclists were a surprisingly radical feature of interwar life. They welcomed the well-made new roads in London's suburbia, but were not prepared to accept that driving a car had now superseded their right to use the road. They were right to criticise the cycle paths that had been built for their use; they were poorly made and were dangerous when they met with side roads. They protested by riding many abreast, blocking the cars trying to pass them, in an early incidence of an argument that is still unresolved in Britain.

Suburban airfields were also a locus of contention. This first arose as a result of the competition for space between airfields and suburban housing. The forces of speculative building eventually pushed airfields further away from the outer housing ring, but in the 1930s this juxtaposition was a problem for residents and airports. Local suburban residents were probably the least likely group of people to be radicalised in protest; their angry letters to the paper about low flying and noise got them nowhere.

The nationalistic fervour for aviation distance records and air displays that saw tens of thousands attending London's airports in the early part of the 1930s unravelled later in the decade when it became clearer what the implications of nationalistic air competition would be. Radical protests at air displays were followed by a wider public unease and a desire for peace;

Chamberlain's return to Heston airport in 1938 provided a symbolic, but short-lived return to suburban normality.

Forward to the 1950s

The arrival of the Second World War has occluded the developments in private transport in London's suburbia in the latter part of the 1930s. The introduction of petrol rationing halted this new middle-class way of life, where autonomous and instantaneous mobility was increasingly the norm. Even after the war had finished, rationing continued; it was not until 1950 that petrol became freely available.[2] Furthermore, new cars were very difficult to obtain as motor industry production was directed at export markets. It was not until 1954 that Austin was able to claim that, once again, the car was indispensable to suburban life.

These missing fifteen years have hidden the developments in the late 1930s, aided and abetted by historians who have portrayed the interwar period in a flattened way. In reality, the late 1930s was a very different world from the late 1920s. A counter-factual consideration of a Britain without a second war suggests that unbroken development could have produced, by the 1950s, a largely consumerist, mobile, Americanised suburban world, perhaps twenty years early than its eventual realisation.

Notes

1 Muriel Burton, born 1909, Royal Borough of Kingston, Local History Room, OH47.
2 W. Plowden, *The Car and Politics, 1896–1970*, London 1971, p. 301.

Appendix

Car adoption rate and number of cars in Greater London for 1938

	All outer London suburbs	Hendon	Kingston
Average number of new cars per 1,000 population 1934[1]	3.94	12.40	5.10
Overall growth factor in cars 1934 to 1938[2]	1.57	1.59	1.56
therefore			
Estimated number of new cars per 1,000 population 1938	6.19	19.72	7.96
Ratio of new cars to total cars in 1938[3]	6.00	6.00	6.00
therefore			
Total number of cars per 1,000 population 1938	37.14	118.30	47.74
Population 1938[4]	5,500,000		
therefore			
Estimated total number of cars in Suburban London 1938[5]	204,000		
Actual number of cars in inner (County of) London 1938[6]	144,000		
Estimated total number of cars in Greater London 1938	348,000		
Number of people in each household[7]		4.0	3.8
therefore			
Overall car adoption rate per household		47.3%	18.1%

Notes

1 Society of Motor Manufacturers and Traders, *Home Counties Registrations*, London 1934. Population interpolated on a straight line basis from data in L. P. Abercrombie, *Greater London Plan 1944*, London 1945, p. 188. As discussed in the chapter, this base data is understated by as much as 20 per cent providing some contingency in these estimates.

2 Based on data in Society of Motor Manufacturers and Traders, *The Motor Industry of Great Britain 1939*, London 1939, using county level data.

3 Based on data for Middlesex in Society of Motor Manufacturers and Traders, *The Motor Industry of Great Britain 1937*, London 1937, and estimates in Associated Newspapers Ltd, *Sell to Britain Through the Daily Mail*, London 1935.

4 1931 Census, visionofbritain.org.uk [accessed 25 January 2010], and L. P. Abercrombie, *Greater London Plan 1944*, London 1945, p. 188.

5 Actual number of cars in Home Counties including outer suburban London was 381,000: Society of Motor Manufacturers and Traders, *The Motor Industry of Great Britain 1939*, London 1939.

6 Society of Motor Manufacturers and Traders, *The Motor Industry of Great Britain 1939*.

7 Data from 1931 census.

Bibliography

Primary sources (including secondary sources before 1950)

Archives

Borehamwood Museum
British Film Institute
Cinema Theatre Association, London
City of London, London Metropolitan Archives
Hampshire County Council, Hampshire Record Office
London Borough of Hounslow Library, Local History Archive
London School of Economics
Maidenhead Heritage Centre
Modern Records Centre, University of Warwick
The National Archives
The Parliamentary Archives
The RIBA archive at the Victoria and Albert Museum
Royal Borough of Kingston upon Thames, Local History Service
Surrey County Council, Surrey History Centre
Sutton Local History Service
University of Reading, The Museum of Rural Life

Newspapers and magazines

The Aeroplane
Air Pictorial
The Architects' Journal
The Architectural Review
The Autocar
Cinema and Theatre Construction
Currys Magazine
Cycling
The Cyclist

The Daily Mirror
Flight
The Geographical Magazine
The Homefinder Small Property Guide
The Illustrated London News
Jewish Telegraphic Agency
The London Mercury
The Maidenhead Advertiser
The Manchester Guardian
The Middlesex Chronicle
The Motion Picture Herald
Motor Commerce
The Motor Cycle
The Motor Cycle and Cycle Trader
Motor-Cycling
The Motor Trader
The New Statesman and Nation
The New York Times
The News of the World
The Observer
Popular Flying
Punch
The Slough, Eton and Windsor Observer
The Spectator
The Surrey Comet
Time
The Times
Wallington and Carshalton Advertiser

Films

Britain Today, Director, unknown, 1936
Roads Across Britain, Director, S. Cole, Realist Film Unit, 1939
Roadwards, Director, P. Rotha, British Independent, 1933
Roadways, Director, A. Cavalcanti, S. Legg and W. Coldstream, GPO Film Unit, 1937
The Face of Britain, Director, P. Rotha, Gaumont-British Instructional, 1935
The Open Road, Director, C. Friese-Green, 1925
Things to Come, Director, W. Menzies, 1936

Newsreels

37th Annual Hill Climb Championship 1931, Pathé reel: 871.30, 1931
Air Port of London, Amy's Wonderful Welcome Home, Pathé reel: 721.16, 1930
Amy Johnson's Arrival at Croydon, British Movietone, Story: 801, 1930

Get Airminded Cheaply!, Pathé reel: 877.28, 1931

Graf Zeppelin, Pathé reel: 683.05, 1932

I Am a Car, Pathé reel: 2721.02, 1954

London's Famous Clubs and Cabarets – 'The Ace of Spades Club', Pathé reel: 1072.14 24 April 1933

Lord de Clifford Stands Trial by His Peers, Pathé reel: 4132.16, December 1935

Modern Circus Drops into Town, British Movietone, Story: 1761, 1932

Outer London Clubs and Cabarets – 'The Ace of Spades', Pathé reel: 1086.02, 7 August 1933

Outer London Clubs and Cabarets 'The Bell', Pathé reel 1076.07, 17 July 1933

Outer London Clubs and Cabarets 'The Showboat', Pathé reel 1088.18, 18 September 1933

Pons Ansinorum, British Movietone, Story: 34291, 12 September 1938

Roadhouse Nights, Pathé reel 1058.14, 18 July 1932

The Order of the Bath, Pathé reel 1174.06, 8 August 1938

The Water Cabaret, Pathé reel 1100.12, 16 July 1934

Books and journals

Anonymous, *Chums Annual 1934–35*, London 1934

Anonymous, *Cycling Manual*, London 1937

Anonymous, *The New Motoring Encyclopedia*, London 1936

Anonymous, *Roadhouses and Clubs of the Home Counties, 1934*, London 1934

Anonymous, *Roads and Road Construction Year Book and Directory*, London 1931

Anonymous, *Royal Commission on London Traffic (Report, Minutes of Evidence, &c)*, London 1905

Anonymous, *Kelly's Directory of Chiswick, Brentford and Gunnersbury*, London 1936

Abercrombie, L. P., 'New Arterial Roads in Course of Construction', *The Town Planning Review*, 9:2, 1921, pp. 67–72

Abercrombie, L. P., 'The Preservation of Rural England', *Town Planning Review*, 12:1, 1926, pp. 5–56

Abercrombie, L. P., *Town & Country Planning*, London 1933

Abercrombie, L. P., *Greater London Plan 1944*, London 1945

Addenbrooke, V., *Motor-Cycling*, 1928

Air Ministry, *Guide to Croydon Aerodrome (the Air Port of London)*, London 1929

Anderson, R. M. C., *The Roads of England*, London 1932

Architecture Club, *Recent English Architecture 1920–1940*, London 1947

Associated Newspapers Ltd, *Sell to Britain Through the Daily Mail*, London 1935

Attaboy, pseud. [John R. Hetherington], *Cycling for Fun. With a dash of cricket for make-weight and a preface for motorists, etc*, Birmingham 1936

Bell, A., *The Legacy of England: An Illustrated Survey of the Works of Man in the English Country*, London 1935

Belloc, H., *The Road*, London 1924

Board of Trade, *London Traffic Branch Reports*, London 1910

Boff, C., *Boys' Book of Flying. The Latest in the Air*, London 1937

Boumphrey, G. M., *British Roads*, London 1939

Bridge, T. C., *The Romance of Motoring*, London 1933

British Cycle and Motor Cycle Manufacturers' and Traders' Union, *Review of the British Cycle and Motor Cycle Industry*, Coventry 1927, 1929, 1937

Brown, I. J. C., *The Heart of England*, London 1935

Browne, K. R. G., *Suburban Days*, London 1928

Burke, T., *London in My Time*, London 1934

Burns, C. D., *Leisure in the Modern World*, London 1932

Carrington, N., *The Shape of Things, an Introduction to Design in Everyday Life*, London 1939

Clunn, H. P., *Face of the Home Counties*, London 1936

Clunn, H. P., *London Marches On*, London 1947

Collier, J., *Just the Other Day: An Informal History of Great Britain Since the War*, 1932

Commager, H. S., *America in Perspective: The United States Through Foreign Eyes*, New York 1948

Cooke, S., *This Motoring: Being the Romantic Story of the Automobile Association*, London [date unknown]

Cornish, V., *National Parks and the Heritage of Scenery*, London 1930

Design and Industries Association, *The Face of the Land*, London 1930

Design and Industries Association, *The Village Pump*, London 1930

Giles, C. W. S. (ed.) *The Road Goes On: a Literary and Historical Account of the Highways*, London 1946

Gloag, J. E., *Design in Modern Life*, London 1934

Graves, R. and Hodge, A., *The Long Week-end: A Social History of Great Britain 1918–1939*, London 1941

Greater London Regional Planning Committee, *First Report of the Greater London Regional Planning Committee*, London 1929

Greenwood, G. A., *England Today: A Social Study of Our Time*, London 1922

Grossmith, G. and Grossmith, W., *The Diary of a Nobody*, London 1892

Hamilton, C. M., *Modern England as Seen by an Englishwoman*, London 1938

Hawks, E., *The Marvels and Mysteries of Science*, London 1939

Hoare, R., *This Our Country: An Impression After Fourteen Years Abroad*, London 1935

Huxley, A., *Along the Road: Notes and Essays of a Tourist*, London 1925

Jeffreys, R., *The King's Highway*, London 1949

Joad, C. E. M., *The Horrors of the Countryside*, London 1931 reprinted in *The Book of Joad*, London 1939

Keun, O., *I Discover the English*, London 1934

Lancaster, O., *Progress at Pelvis Bay*, London 1936

Lancaster, O., *Pillar to Post: English Architecture Without Tears*, London 1938

Le Corbusier, *[Urbanism] The City of To-morrow and Its Planning*, London 1929

Le Corbusier, *[La Ville radieuse] The Radiant City*, London 1935

Leavis, Q. D., *Fiction and the Reading Public*, 1932

Lewis, R. and Maude, A., *The English Middle Classes*, 1949

Local Government Board, *Arterial Roads in Greater London, Report of Sectional Conferences*, London 1914

London County Council, *Statistical Abstract for London*, London 1936

London Society, *The Journal of the London Society*

London Society and Webb A., *London of the Future*, London 1921

Long, G., *English Inns and Road-houses*, London 1937

Macminnies, W. G., *Signpost to the Road Houses, Country Clubs and Better and Brighter Inns and Hotels of England*, London 1935

Mais, S. P. B, 'The English Highway', *The Geographical Magazine*, May 1937

Massingham, H. J., *London Scene*, London 1933

Maxwell, G., *Highwaymen's Heath*, Hounslow, 1935

Melville, L., *The London Scene*, London 1926

Ministry of Transport, *The Highway Code*, London 1930

Motor Cycle Association, *22nd International Bicycle and Motor-cycle Show, Earls Court, Catalogue*, London 1937

Morton, H. V., *In Search of England*, London 1927

Muggeridge, M., *The Thirties: 1930–1940 in Great Britain*, London 1940

New Education Fellowship, *The Challenge of Leisure*, London 1936

Oliver, B., *The Renaissance of the English Public House*, London 1947

Orwell, G., *The Lion and the Unicorn: Socialism and the English Genius*, London 1941

Pepys, M. E., *Motoring To-day and To-morrow*, London 1928

Priestley, J. B., *English Journey. Being a Rambling but Truthful Account of What One Man Saw and Heard and Felt and Thought During a Journey Through England During the Autumn of the Year 1933*, London 1934

Priestley, J. B., *Midnight on the Desert: A Chapter of Autobiography*, London 1937

Prioleau, J., *Motoring for Women*, London 1925

Richards, J. M., *An Introduction to Modern Architecture*, Harmondsworth 1940

Richards, J. M. and Piper, J., *The Castles on the Ground*, London 1946

Richardson, A. E., *The Old Inns of England*, London 1934

Roads Beautifying Association, *Roadside Planting*, London 1930

Roads Beautifying Association, *Annual Report of the RBA, 1931*, London 1932

Roads Beautifying Association, *The Roadside Halt, A Joint Plea by the Automobile Association and the Roads Beautifying Association*, London 1935

Robinson, W. H. and Browne, K. R. G., *How to Be a Motorist*, London 1939

Shand, P. M., *Modern Theatres and Cinemas*, London 1930

Sharp, T., *English Panorama*, London 1936

Sinclair, R., *Metropolitan Man: The Future of the English*, London 1937

Smith, D. H., *The Industries of Greater London: Being a Survey of the Recent Industrialisation of the Northern and Western Sectors of Greater London*, London 1933

Society of Motor Manufacturers and Traders, *Home Counties Registrations: Mechanically-propelled Road Vehicles Registered for the First Time Under the Roads Act 1920*, London 1934

Society of Motor Manufacturers and Traders, *The Motor Industry of Great Britain 1937*, London 1937

Society of Motor Manufacturers and Traders, *The Motor Industry of Great Britain 1939*, London 1939

Southcott, E. J. (ed.), *The History of the Catford Cycling Club*, London 1937

Sowerby, J., *I Got on My Bicycle*, London 1939

Stamp, L. D., *The Land of Britain: Its Use and Misuse*, London 1948

Thompson, W., 'The Arterial Roads of Greater London in Course of Construction', *The Town Planning Review*, 9:2, 1921, pp. 73–76

Unwin, R., *Greater London Planning Committee Report*, London 1929

Wilkinson, T. W., *From Track to By-pass: A History of the English Road*, London 1934

Williams-Ellis, C., *England and the Octopus*, London 1928

Williams-Ellis, C. and Keynes, J. M., *Britain and the Beast*, London 1937

Williams-Ellis, C. and Summerson, J. N., *Architecture Here and Now*, London 1934

Memoirs of the period

Age Exchange and Schweitzer, P. (eds.), *The Time of Our Lives: Memories of Leisure in the 1920s and 1930s*, London 1986

Annan, N., *Our Age: Portrait of a Generation*, London 1990

Bentall, R., *My Store of Memories*, London 1974

Betjeman, J., *Letters*, London 1994

Cutforth, R., *Later Than We Thought: A Portrait of the Thirties*, Newton Abbot 1976

Holloway, C. J., *A London Childhood*, London 1966

Hughes, M. V., *A London Family Between the Wars*, London 1940

Middlesex Federation of Women's Institutes, *Middlesex Within Living Memory*, Newbury 1996

Osborne, J., *A Better Class of Person: An Autobiography 1929–1956*, Harmondsworth 1982

Richards, J. M., *Memoirs of an Unjust Fella*, London 1980

Sitwell, O., *Left Hand Right Hand!: An Autobiography, Volume 3: Great Morning*, London 1957

Sitwell, O., *Left Hand Right Hand!: An Autobiography, Volume 4: Laughter in the Next Room*, London 1958

Tomlinson, A. W., *Tales from a Roadhouse*, London 1954

Vaughan, P., *Something in Linoleum*, London 1994

Novels

Arlen, M., *The Green Hat: A Romance for a Few People*, London 1924

Bowen, E. D. C., *To the North*, London 1932

Brown, Z. J., *The By-pass Murder*, London 1932

Du Maurier, D., *Rebecca*, London 1938

Duff, C. S. L., *Anthropological Report on a London Suburb*, London 1935

Ellis, G. U., *The Hungry Road*, London 1930

Ewer, M., *Roadhouse*, London 1935

Fitzgerald, F. S., *The Great Gatsby*, New York 1925

Forster, E. M., *Howards End*, London 1910

Frankau, G., *Christopher Strong. A Romance*, London 1932

Grahame, K., *The Wind in the Willows*, London 1910

Greene, G., *Brighton Rock*, London 1938

Greene, G., *The Confidential Agent*, London 1939

Hamilton, P., *The Siege of Pleasure*, London 1932

Hamilton, P., *Hangover Square; or, the Man with Two Minds. A Story of Darkest Earl's Court in the Year 1939*, London 1941

Hamilton, P., *Mr. Stimpson and Mr. Gorse*, London 1953

Holtby, W., *South Riding. An English Landscape*, London 1936

Lorac, E. C. R., *Death on the Oxford Road*, London 1933

Orwell, G., *Coming Up for Air*, London 1939

Owen, J., *The Road and the Wood*, London 1936

Peck, W. F., *They Come, They Go: The Story of an English Rectory*, London 1937

Priestley, J. B., *The Good Companions*, London 1929

Priestley, J. B., *Let the People Sing*, London 1939

Rhys, J. L., *The Flying Shadow*, London 1942

Sayers, D. L., *Lord Peter Views the Body*, London 1928

Sayers, D. L., *Busman's Honeymoon*, London 1937

Wallace, E., *The Coat of Arms*, London 1931

Waterhouse, R. D., *Butter Side Up*, London 1932

Waterhouse, R. D., *Week-end Ticket*, London 1934

Warner, R., *The Aerodrome: A Love Story*, London 1941

Waugh, E., *Vile Bodies*, London 1930

Poetry

Berry, F., 'A ride in a sports car', *The Snake in the Moon*, London 1936

Betjeman, J., *Continual Dew. A Little Book of Bourgeois Verse*, London 1937

Betjeman, J., *A Few Late Chrysanthemums*, London 1954

Betjeman, J., *The Best of Betjeman*, London 1978

Eliot, T. S., *Selected Poems*, London 1954

Mann, F. O., *London & Suburban. Poems*, London 1925

MacNeice, L., *Autumn Journal*, London 1939

Plays

Hackett, W., *Road House. A Play in Three Acts*, 1933

Secondary sources

Journal articles

Adey, P., 'Airports and Air-mindedness: Spacing, Timing and Using the Liverpool Airport, 1929–1939', *Social & Cultural Geography*, 7:3, 2006, pp. 343–363

Adey, P., 'Architectural Geographies of the Airport Balcony: Mobility, Sensation and the Theatre of Flight', *Geografiska Annaler: Series B, Human Geography*, 90:1, 2008, pp. 29–47

Alexander, S., 'A New Civilization? London Surveyed 1928 – 1940s', *History Workshop Journal*, 64:1, 2007, pp. 297–320

Ashmore, S., Edwards, B., Gilbert, D., '"Mr Bourne's dilemma": Consumer Culture, Property Speculation and Department Store Demise: the Rise and Fall of Bourne and Hollingsworth on London's Oxford Street', *Journal of Historical Geography*, 38:4, 2012, pp. 434–446

Atwell, D., 'The Rise and Fall of the London Picture Palace', *Journal of the Royal Institute of British Architects*, 80, 1973, pp. 8–10

Banham, R., 'New Way North', *New Society*, 20, 4 May 1972, pp. 241–243

Barker, P., 'Non-Plan Revisited: or the Real Way Cities Grow', *Journal of Design History*, 12:2, 1999, pp. 95–110

Bates, C., 'Hotel Histories: Modern Tourists, Modern Nomads and the Culture of Hotel-Consciousness', *Literature & History*, 12:2, 2003, pp. 62–75

Baxendale, J., '"I Had Seen a Lot of Englands": J. B. Priestley, Englishness and the People', *History Workshop Journal*, 51, 2001, pp. 87–111

Beckmann, J., 'Automobility – a Social Problem and Theoretical Concept', *Environment and Planning. D, Society and Space*, 19, 2001, pp. 593–607

Beckmann, J., 'Mobility and Safety', *Theory, Culture & Society*, 21:4/5, 2004, pp. 81–100

Benjamin, D. K. and Kochin, L. A., 'Searching for an Explanation of Unemployment in Inter-war Britain', *The Journal of Political Economy*, 87:3, 1979, pp. 441–478

Böhm, S., Jones, C., Land, C., Paterson, M., 'Introduction: Impossibilities of automobility', *The Sociological Review*, 54:s1, 2006, pp. 3–16

Bowden, S. M., 'Demand and Supply Constraints in the Inter-war UK Car Industry: Did the Manufacturers Get It Right?' *Business History*, 33:2, 1991, pp. 241–267

Cresswell, T., '"You Cannot Shake That Shimmie Here": Producing Mobility on the Dance Floor', *Cultural Geographies*, 13:1, 2006, pp. 55–77

Danius, S., 'The Aesthetics of the Windshield: Proust and the Modernist Rhetoric of Speed', *Modernism/Modernity*, 8:1, 2001, pp. 99–126

Dant, T., 'The Driver-car', *Theory, Culture & Society*, 21: 4/5, 2004, pp. 61–79

De Grazia, V., 'Mass-Culture and Sovereignty – the American Challenge to European Cinemas, 1920–1960', *The Journal of Modern History*, 61:1, 1989, pp. 53–87

Dimendberg, E., 'The Will to Motorization: Cinema, Highways and Modernity', *October*, 73:Summer, 1995, pp. 91–137

Divall, C. and Revill, G., 'Cultures of Transport Representation, Practice and Technology', *Journal of Transport History*, 26:1, 2005, pp. 99–112

Dwyer, C., Gilbert, D., Shah, B., 'Faith and Suburbia: Secularisation, Modernity and the Changing Geographies of Religion in London's Suburbs', *Transactions of the Institute of British Geographers*, 38: 3, 2013, pp. 403–419

Edensor, T., 'Automobility and National Identity: Representation, Geography and Driving Practice', *Theory, Culture & Society*, 21:4/5, 2004, pp. 101–120

Elliott, B., 'Historical Revivalism in the Twentieth Century: a Brief Introduction', *Garden History*, 28:1, 2000, pp. 17–31

Emsley, C., '"Mother, What Did Policemen Do When There Weren't Any Motors?" The Law, the Police and the Regulation of Motor Traffic in England, 1900–1939', *The Historical Journal*, 36:2, 1993, pp. 357–381

Fagge, R., 'J. B. Priestley, the "Modern" and America', *Cultural and Social History*, 4:4, 2007, pp. 481–494

Ford, E., 'Byways Revisited', *Landscape Design*, 234, 1994 pp. 34–38

Gartman, D., 'Three Ages of the Automobile: the Cultural Logics of the Car', *Theory, Culture & Society*, 21:4/5, 2004, pp. 169–195

Gilbert, D., 'London of the Future: the Metropolis Re-Imagined after the Great War', *Journal of British Studies*, 43:1, 2004, pp. 243–268

Guy, C., 'From Crinkly Sheds to Fashion Parks: the Role of Financial Investment in the Transformation of Retail Parks', *The International Review of Retail, Distribution and Consumer Research*, 10:4, 2000, pp. 389–400

Glancy, M., 'Temporary American citizens? British Audiences, Hollywood films and the Threat of Americanisation in the 1920s', *Historical Journal of Film, Radio and Television*, 26:4, 2006, pp. 461–484

Hornsey, R., '"Everything Is Made of Atoms": the Reprogramming of Space and Time in Post-war London', *Journal of Historical Geography*, 34, 2008, pp. 94–117

Jain, S., '"Dangerous Instrumentality?": the Bystander as Subject in Automobility', *Cultural Anthropology*, 19:1, 2004, pp. 61–94

Jain, S., 'Violent Submission: Gendered Automobility', *Cultural Critique*, 61, 2005, pp. 186–214

Jeremiah, D., 'Filling Up: the British Experience, 1896–1940', *Journal of Design History*, 8:2, 1995, pp. 97–116

Jones, M. E. F., 'The Economic History of the Regional Problem in Britain, 1920–1938', *Journal of Historical Geography*, 10:4, 1984, pp. 385–395

Koerner, S., 'Whatever Happened to the Girl on the Motorbike? British Women and Motorcycling, 1919 to 1939', *International Journal of Motorcycle Studies*, March 2007

Koshar, R., 'Cars and Nations', *Theory, Culture & Society*, 21:4/5, 2004, pp. 121–144

Kuisel, R., 'Americanization for Historians (Reply to Jessica Gienow-Hecht)', *Diplomatic History*, 24:3, 2000, pp. 509–515

Ling, P., 'Sex and the Automobile in the Jazz Age', *History Today*, November 1989, pp. 18–24

Luce, H., 'The "American Century" (Reprinted from "Life" magazine)', *Diplomatic History*, 23:2, 1999, pp. 159–171

Mandler, P., 'Against Englishness: English Culture and the Limits to Rural Nostalgia, 1850–1940', *Transactions of the Royal Historical Society*, 7, 1997, pp. 155–175

Merriman, P., 'Driving Places: Marc Augé, Non-places, and the Geographies of England's M1 Motorway', *Theory, Culture & Society*, 21:4/5, 2004, pp. 145–167

Merriman, P., '"A New Look at the English Landscape": Landscape Architecture, Movement and the Aesthetics of Motorways in Early Postwar Britain', *Cultural Geographies*, 13, 2006, pp. 78–105

Merriman, P., 'Mirror, Signal, Manoeuvre: Assembling and Governing the Motorway Driver in Late 1950s Britain', *The Sociological Review*, 54, 2006, pp. 75–92

Moran, J., 'Crossing the Road in Britain 1931–1976', *The Historical Journal*, 42:2, 2006, pp. 477–496

Möser, K., 'The Dark Side of "Automobilism", 1900–1930: Violence, War and the Car', *Journal of Transport History*, 24:2, 2003, pp. 238–258

Nieuwenhuis, P. and Wells, P., 'The All-steel Body as a Cornerstone to the Foundations of the Mass Production Car Industry', *Industrial and Corporate Change*, 16:2, 2007, pp. 183–211

Patton, D. L., 'Aspects of a Historical Geography of Technology: a Study of Cycling, 1919–1939', *Cycle History – Proceedings of the 5th International Cycle History Conference*, San Francisco, 1995

Pooley, C. and Turnbull, J., ' The Journey to Work: A Century of Change', *Area*, 31, 1999, pp. 282–292

Pooley, C. and Turnbull, J., 'Modal Choice and Modal Change: the Journey to Work in Britain Since 1890', *Journal of Transport Geography*, 8:1, 2000, pp. 11–24

Pooley, C. and Turnbull, J., 'Coping with Congestion: Responses to Urban Traffic Problems in British Cities c1920–1960', *Journal of Historical Geography*, 2005, 31:1, pp. 78–93

Potter, C., 'Motorcycle Clubs in Britain During the Inter-war Period, 1919–1939: Their Social and Cultural Importance', *International Journal of Motorcycle Studies*, March 2005

Rollins, W., 'Whose Landscape? Technology, Fascism and Environmentalism on the National Socialist Autobahn', *Annals of the Association of American Geographers*, 85:3, 1995, pp. 494–520

Samuel, R., 'Middle Class Between the Wars', *New Socialist*, January/February 1983, pp. 30–36, March/April 1983, pp. 28–32, May/June 1983, pp. 28–30

Schnapp, J. T., 'Crash (Speed as Engine of Individuation)', *Modernism/Modernity*, 6:1, 1999, pp. 1–49

Sheller, M., 'Automotive Emotions – Feeling the Car', *Theory, Culture & Society*, 21:4/5, 2004, pp. 221–242

Sheller, M. and Urry, J., 'The City and the Car', *International Journal of Urban and Regional Research*, 24:4, 2000, pp. 737–754

Sheller, M. and Urry, J., 'The New Mobilities Paradigm', *Environment and Planning A*, 38:2, 2006, pp. 207–226

Thacker, A., 'E. M. Forster and the Motor Car', *Literature & History*, 9:2, 2000, pp. 37–52

Thacker, A., 'Traffic, Gender, Modernism', *The Sociological Review*, 54:s1, 2006, pp. 175–189

Thrift, N. J., 'Driving in the City', *Theory, Culture & Society*, 21:4/5, 2004, pp. 41–59

Todd, S., 'Flappers and Factory Lads: Youth and Youth Culture in Inter-war Britain', *History Compass*, 4:4, 2006, pp. 715–730

Urry, J., *Automobility, Car Culture and Weightless Travel: A Discussion Paper*, Lancaster 1999

Urry, J., 'The "System" of Automobility', *Theory, Culture & Society*, 21:4/5, 2004, pp. 25–39

Urry, J., 'Inhabiting the Car', *The Sociological Review*, 54:s1, 2006, pp. 17–31

Waters, C., 'Beyond Americanization: Rethinking Anglo-American Cultural Exchange Between the Wars', *Cultural and Social History*, 4:4, 2007, pp. 451–453

Whitehand, J. and Carr, C., 'The Creators of England's Inter-war Suburbs', *Urban History*, 28:2, 2001, pp. 218–234

Whitehand, J. and Carr, C., 'England's Inter-war Suburban Landscapes: Myth and Reality', *Journal of Historical Geography*, 25:4, 1999, pp. 483–501

Monographs and edited collections

Adey, P., *Aerial Life: Spaces, Mobilities, Affects*, Oxford 2010

Allen, W. (ed.), *Looping the Loop: Posters of Flight*, Carlsbad, Calif. 2000

Appleyard, D. S., *View from the Road*, Cambridge, Mass. 1963

Archer, J., *Architecture and Suburbia: From English Villa to American Dream House, 1690–2000*, Bristol 2005

Arthurs, J. and Grant, I. (eds), *Crash Cultures: Modernity, Mediation and the Material*, Bristol 2002

Atwell, D., *Cathedrals of the Movies: A History of British Cinemas and Their Audiences*, London 1980

Augé, M., *Non-places: Introduction to an Anthropology of Supermodernity*, London 1995

Bailey, V., *Delinquency and Citizenship: Reclaiming the Young Offender, 1914–1948*, Oxford 1987

Ballard, J. G., *Crash*, London 1973

Banham, R., *Los Angeles: The Architecture of Four Ecologies*, London 1971

Banham, R., *A Critic Writes: Essays by Reyner Banham*, London 1996

Barker, T. C., Gerhold, D. and Economic History Society, *The Rise and Rise of Road Transport, 1700–1990*, London 1993

Bassett, P., *A List of the Historical Records of the Roads Beautifying Association*, Birmingham 1980

Belasco, W. J., *Americans on the Road: From Autocamp to Motel, 1910–1945*, Cambridge, Mass. 1979

Berman, M., *All That Is Solid Melts Into Air: The Experience of Modernity*, London 1983

Bijker, W. E., Hughes, T. P., Pinch, T. J. (eds), *The Social Construction of Technological Systems: New Directions in the Sociology and History of Technology*: Workshop: Papers, Cambridge, Mass. 1987

Blanke, D., *Hell on Wheels: The Promise and Peril of America's Car Culture, 1900–1940*, Lawrence, Kan. 2007

Blom, P., *The Vertigo Years: Change and Culture in the West, 1900–1914*, London 2008

Blythe, R., *The Age of Illusion: Glimpses of Britain Between the Wars, 1919–1940*, Oxford 1983

Borden, I., Hall, T., Miles, M., *The City Cultures Reader*, London 2000

Borden, I., *Drive: Journeys Through Film, Cities, and Landscapes*, London 2013

Boyce, F., *SOE: The Scientific Secrets*, Stroud 2003

Branson, N., *Britain in the 1930s*, London 1971

Brendon, P., *The Motoring Century: The Story of the Royal Automobile Club*, London 1997

Brewer, J. and Porter, R. (eds), *Consumption and the World of Goods*, London 1994

Brewer, J. and Trentmann, F. (eds), *Consuming Cultures: Global Perspectives, Historical Trajectories, Transnational Exchanges*, Oxford 2006

Brilliant, A., *The Great Car Craze: How Southern California Collided with the Automobile in the 1920's*, Santa Barbara 1989

British Road Federation, *Britain's Bypass Progress*, London 1995

Brottman, M. (ed.), *Car Crash Culture*, New York 2002

Bruegmann, R., *Sprawl: A Compact History*, Chicago 2005

Buchanan, C., *Mixed Blessing: The Motor in Britain*, London 1958

Buchanan, C., *London Road Plans, 1900–1970*, London 1970

Bunce, M., *The Countryside Ideal: Anglo-American Images of Landscape*, London 1994

Burchell, G., Gordon, C., Miller, P. (eds), *The Foucault Effect: Studies in Governmental Rationality*, Hemel Hempstead 1991

Burden, R. and Kohl, S. (eds), *Landscape and Englishness*, New York 2006

Burnett, J., *A Social History of Housing, 1815–1985*, London 1986

Caffrey, K., '*37–39': Last Look Round*, London 1978

Campbell, C., *The Romantic Ethic and the Spirit of Modern Consumerism*, Oxford 1987

Campbell, N., Davies, J., McKay, G., *Issues in Americanisation and Culture*, Edinburgh 2004

Carey, J., *The Intellectuals and the Masses: Pride and Prejudice Among the Literary Intelligentsia, 1880–1939*, London 1992

Carr, E. H., *What Is History?*, Basingstoke 2001

Chambers, I., *Popular Culture: The Metropolitan Experience*, London 1986

Chapman, T., *Cornwall Aviation Company*, Falmouth, 1979

Clapson, M., *Suburban Century: Social Change and Urban Growth in England and the United States*, Oxford 2003

Clapson, M. and BACTA, *Amusement Machines*, London 2000

Clarke, D., *Driving Women: Fiction and Automobile Culture in Twentieth-century America*, Baltimore 2007

Cleeve, B. T., *1938, a World Vanishing*, London 1982

Cluett, D., Nash, J., Learmonth, R., *Croydon Airport: The Great Days, 1928–1939*, Sutton 1980

Cockburn, C., *Bestseller: The Books that Everyone Read, 1900–1939*, Harmondsworth 1975

Cooter, R. and Luckin, B. (eds), *Accidents in History: Injuries, Fatalities and Social Relations*, Amsterdam 1997

Costigliola, F., *Awkward Dominion: American Political, Economic, and Cultural Relations with Europe, 1919–1933*, London 1984

Crang, M., *Cultural Geography*, London 1998

Cresswell, T., *In Place*, London 1996

Cresswell, T., *Place: A Short Introduction*, Oxford 2004

Cresswell, T., *On the Move: Mobility in the Modern Western World*, London 2006

Croft, A., *Red Letter Days: British Fiction in the 1930s*, London 1990

Crowe, S., *The Landscape of Roads*, London 1960

Cruddas, C., *Those Fabulous Flying Years: Joy-Riding and Flying Circuses Between the Wars*, Tunbridge Wells 2003

Cunningham, V., *British Writers of the Thirties*, Oxford 1988

Daunton, M. J. and Rieger, B., *Meanings of Modernity: Britain from the Late-Victorian Era to World War II*, Oxford 2001

Dean, D. and Royal Institute of British Architects, Drawings Collection, *The Thirties: Recalling the English Architectural Scene*, London 1983

De Certeau, M., *The Practice of Everyday Life*, London 1984

De Grazia, V., *Irresistible Empire: America's Advance Through Twentieth-century Europe*, London 2005

Delderfield, R. F., *The Dreaming Suburb*, London 1958

Delgado, A., *Have You Forgotten Yet? Between the Two World Wars*, Newton Abbot 1973

Delgado, A., *The Annual Outing and Other Excursions*, London 1977

Demaus, A. B., *Motoring in the 20's & 30's*, London 1979

Demaus, A. B., *The Halcyon Days of Motoring, 1900–1940*, Stroud 2006

Dennis, R., *Cities in Modernity: Representations and Productions of Metropolitan Space, 1840–1930*, Cambridge 2008

Dentith, S., *Thirties Poetry and the Landscape of Suburbia*, London 1997

Dettelbach, C. G., *In the Driver's Seat: The Automobile in American Literature and Popular Culture*, London 1976

Dodge, P., *The Bicycle*, London 1996

Dowsett, A., *Handley Page: A History*, Stroud 2003

Dyos, H. J., *Victorian Suburb: A Study of the Growth of Camberwell*, Leicester 1961

Edwards, A. M., *The Design Of Suburbia: A Critical Study in Environmental History*, London 1981

Ellwood, D. W., Kroes, R., Brunetta, G. P. (eds), *Hollywood in Europe: Experiences of a Cultural Hegemony*, Amsterdam 1994

Elwall, R. and British Architectural Library, *Bricks & Beer: English Pub Architecture, 1830–1939*, London 1983

Eyles, A., Cinema Theatre Association and British Film Institute, *Oscar Deutsch Entertains Our Nation*, London 2002

Featherstone, M., Thrift, N., Urry, J. (eds), *Automobilities*, London 2005

Fiske, J., *Reading the Popular*, London 1989

Fiske, J., *Understanding Popular Culture*, London 1989

Flink, J. J., *The Car Culture*, Cambridge, Mass. 1975

Floud, R. and Johnson, P., *The Cambridge Economic History of Modern Britain*, Cambridge 2004

Ford, B. (ed.), *The Cambridge Guide to the Arts in Britain*, Cambridge 1988

Freund, P. E. S., *The Ecology of the Automobile*, New York 1993

Gardiner, J., *The Thirties: An Intimate History of Britain*, London 2011

Gardner, C. J. T. (ed.), *Fifty Years of Brooklands*, London 1956

Garreau, J., *Edge City: Life on the New Frontier*, London 1991

Gartman, D., *Auto Opium: A Social History of American Automobile Design*, London 1994

Giedion, S., *Space, Time and Architecture: The Growth of a New Tradition*, Oxford 1962

Gilbert, D., Matless, D. and Short, B. (eds), *Geographies of British Modernity: Space and Society in the Twentieth Century*, Oxford 2003

Giles, J., *The Parlour and The Suburb: Domestic Identities, Class, Femininity and Modernity*, Oxford 2004

Giles, J. and Middleton, T. (eds), *Writing Englishness 1900–1950: An Introductory Sourcebook on National Identity*, London 1995

Gillies, M., *Amy Johnson*, London 2003

Gloversmith, F., *Class, Culture and Social Change: A New View of the 1930's*, Brighton 1980

Gray, R. and Cinema Theatre Association, *Cinemas in Britain: One Hundred Years of Cinema Architecture*, London 1996

Gronow, J. and Warde, A. (eds), *Ordinary Consumption*, London 2001

Gutzke, D., *Pubs and Progressives: Reinventing the Public House in England, 1896–1960*, DeKalb, Ill. 2006

Hamilton, R., *Accident: A Philosophical and Literary History*, Bristol 2007

Hapgood, L., *Margins of Desire: The Suburbs in Fiction and Culture, 1880–1925*, Manchester 2005

Harris, R. and Larkham, P. J. (eds), *Changing Suburbs: Foundation, Form, and Function*, London 1999

Harvey, D., *The Condition of Postmodernity: An Enquiry into the Origins of Cultural Change*, Oxford 1989

Haslam, R. and Williams-Ellis, C., *Clough Williams-Ellis*, London 1996

Haydon, P., *The English Pub: A History*, London 1994

Hebdige, D., *Subculture: The Meaning of Style*, London 1979

Hitchmough, W., *Hoover Factory: Wallis, Gilbert and Partners*, London 1992

Hoggart, R., *The Uses of Literacy: Aspects of Working-class Life, with Special Reference to Publications and Entertainments*, London 1957

Honer, J. and English Heritage (eds), *London Suburbs*, London 1999

Horwood, C., *Keeping Up Appearances: Fashion and Class Between the Wars*, Stroud 2005

Houlbrook, M., *Queer London: Perils and Pleasures in the Sexual Metropolis, 1918–1957*, Bristol 2005

Inwood, S., *A History of London*, London 1998

Jackson, A. A., *Semi-detached London: Suburban Development, Life and Transport, 1900–39*, London 1973

Jackson, A. A., *The Middle Classes, 1900–1950*, Nairn 1991

Jackson, K. T., *Crabgrass Frontier: The Suburbanization of the United States*, Oxford 1985

Jeffrey, I., *The British Landscape: 1920–1950*, London 1984

Jeremiah, D., *Architecture and Design for the Family in Britain, 1900–1970*, London 2000

Jeremiah, D., *Representations of British Motoring*, Manchester 2007

Jewell, D. (ed.), *Man & Motor: The 20th Century Love Affair*, London 1966

Johnson, P. (ed.), *Twentieth-century Britain: Economic, Social, and Cultural Change*, London 1994

Jones, S. G., *Workers at Play: A Social and Economic History of Leisure, 1918–1939*, London 1986

Kammen, M. G., *American Culture, American Tastes: Social Change and the 20th Century*, New York 1999

Karol, E. and Allibone, F., *Charles Holden: Architect 1875–1960*, London 1988

Kern, S., *The Culture of Time and Space 1880–1918*, London 1983

King, A., *Memorials of the Great War in Britain: The Symbolism and Politics of Remembrance*, Oxford 1998

King, A. D., *The Bungalow: The Production of a Global Culture*, 1984

Klapper, C. F., *Roads and Rails of London, 1900–1933*, London 1976

Knowles, R., *Two Superiors: The Motor-cycling Friendship of George Brough & T. E. Lawrence*, Upper Denby 2005

Kroes, R., Rydell, R. W., Bosscher, D. F. J. (eds), *Cultural Transmissions and Receptions: American Mass Culture in Europe*, Amsterdam 1993

Ladd, B., *Autophobia: Love and Hate in the Automotive Age*, London 2008

Lambert, J. A. and John Johnson Collection, *Motoring in Britain 1895–1940: From Contemporary Images Drawn Chiefly from the John Johnson Collection*, Oxford 1998

Laver, J., *Between the Wars*, Boston 1961

Lawrence, C. and Mayer, A. (eds), *Regenerating England: Science, Medicine and Culture in Inter-war Britain*, Amsterdam 2000

Learmonth, R., *First Croydon Airport, 1915–1928*, Sutton 1977

Lefebvre, H., *The Production of Space*, London 1991

LeMahieu, D. L., *A Culture for Democracy: Mass Communication and the Cultivated Mind in Britain Between the Wars*, Oxford 1988

Light, A., *Forever England: Femininity, Literature and Conservatism Between the Wars*, London 1991

McKay, G. (ed.), *Yankee Go Home: (and Take Me with U): Americanization and Popular Culture*, Sheffield 1997

McKernan, L. (ed.), *Yesterday's News: The British Cinema Newsreel Reader*, London 2002

McKibbin, R., *Classes and Cultures: England, 1918–1951*, Oxford 1998

Margolies, J., *Pump and Circumstance: Glory Days of the Gas Station*, London 1994

Marling, S., *American Affair: the Americanisation of Britain*, London 1993

Marshall, J., *The History of the Great West Road: Its Social and Economic Influence on the Surrounding Area*, Hounslow 1995

Marx, L., *The Machine in the Garden. Technology and the Pastoral Ideal in America*, Oxford 1964

Mason, F. K., *Hawker Aircraft Since 1920*, 2nd ed., London 1971

Matthews, W. and Williams, S. (eds), *Rewriting the Thirties: Modernism and After*, London 1997

Matless, D., *Landscape and Englishness*, London 1998

Mauch, C. and Zeller, T. (eds), *The World Beyond the Windshield: Roads and Landscapes in the United States and Europe*, London 2008

Merriman, P., *Driving Spaces: A Cultural-historical Geography of England's M1 Motorway*, Oxford 2007

Miller, D., *Car Cultures*, Oxford 2001

Miller, M., *Raymond Unwin: Garden Cities and Town Planning*, Leicester 1992

Moran, J., *On Roads*, London 2009

Morley, D., *Media, Modernity and Technology: The Geography of the New*, London 2006

Morrison, K. A. and Minnis, J., *Carscapes*, London 2012

Mort, F., *Capital affairs: London and the Making of the Permissive Society*, London 2010

Mowat, C. L., *Britain Between the Wars, 1918–1940*, London 1955

Naremore, J. and Brantlinger, P. (eds), *Modernity and Mass Culture*, Bloomington 1991

Nava, M. and O'Shea, A., *Modern Times: Reflections on a Century of English Modernity*, London 1996

Nobbs, D., *The Fall and Rise of Reginald Perrin*, Harmondsworth 1978

Nye, D. E., *American Technological Sublime*, London 1994

O'Connell, S., *The Car and British Society: Class, Gender and Motoring 1896–1939*, Manchester 1998

Ogborn, M., *Spaces of Modernity: London's Geographies, 1680–1780*, London 1998

Oliver, D., *Hendon Aerodrome – A History*, Shrewsbury 1994

Oliver, P., Davis, I., Bentley, I., *Dunroamin: The Suburban Semi and Its Enemies*, London 1981

Paul Mellon Centre for Studies in British Art, *The Architecture of British Transport in the Twentieth Century*, New Haven, Conn. and London 2004

Pells, R. H., *Not Like Us: How Europeans Loved, Hated, and Transformed American Culture Since World War II*, New York 1997

Peto, J. and Loveday, D. (eds), *Modern Britain 1929–1939*, London 1999

Pile, S. and Thrift, N. J. (eds), *City A–Z*, London 2000

Platt, E., *Leadville: A Biography of the A40*, London 2001

Plowden, W., *The Car and Politics, 1896–1970*, London 1971

Pugh, M., *'We Danced All Night': A Social History of Britain Between the Wars*, London 2008

Richards, J., *The Age of the Dream Palace: Cinema and Society in Britain, 1930–1939*, London 1989

Richards, J. and Aldgate, A., *Best of British: Cinema and Society, 1930–1970*, Oxford 1983

Riding, R. T. (ed.), *De Havilland: The Golden Years 1919–1939*, Sutton 1981

Rieger, B., *Technology and the Culture of Modernity in Britain and Germany, 1890–1945*, Cambridge 2005

Robbins, K. (ed.), *The British Isles 1901–1951*, Oxford 2002

Robson, G., *Motoring in the 30s*, Cambridge 1979

Ross, C. and Museum of London, *Twenties London: A City in the Jazz Age*, London 2003

Rydell, R. W., *Buffalo Bill in Bologna: The Americanization of the World, 1869–1922*, Bristol 2005

Sachs, W. and Reneau, D., *For Love of the Automobile: Looking Back into the History of Our Desires*, Oxford 1992

Savage, J., *Teenage: The Creation of Youth Culture*, London 2007

Schwarzer, M., *Zoomscape: Architecture in Motion and Media*, London 2004

Sedgwick, M., *Passenger Cars, 1924–1942*, London 1975

Sedgwick, M., *A–Z of Cars of the 1930s*, London 1989

Seiler, C., *Republic of Drivers: A Cultural History of Automobility in America*, London 2008

Setright, L. J. K., *Drive On!: A Social History of the Car*, London 2003

Sharp, D., *The Picture Palace, and Other Buildings for the Movies*, London 1969

Sheail, J., *Rural Conservation in Inter-war Britain*, Oxford 1981

Sinclair, I., *London Orbital: A Walk Around the M25*, London 2002

Silverstone, R. (ed.), *Visions of Suburbia*, London 1997

Skinner, J., *Form and Fancy: Factories and Factory Buildings by Wallis, Gilbert & Partners, 1916–1939*, Liverpool 1997

Slater, D. and Taylor, P. J. (eds), *The American Century: Consensus and Coercion in the Projection of American Power*, Oxford 1999

Stevenson, J., *The Slump*, London 1979

Stevenson, J., *British Society, 1914–45*, Harmondsworth 1984

Stilgoe, J. R., *Borderland: Origins of the American Suburb, 1820–1939*, New Haven 1988

Strange, J., Carnevali, F. and Johnson, P. (eds), *Twentieth-century Britain: Economic, Cultural and Social Change*, Harlow 2007

Sutton, J. R., *Motor Mania: Stories from a Motoring Century*, London 1996

Taylor, A. J. P., *English History 1914–1945*, London 1965

Taylor, J., *A Dream of England: Landscape, Photography and the Tourist's Imagination*, Manchester 1994

Taylor, J. W. R. (ed.), *Fairey Aviation*, Stroud 1997

Thompson, F. M. L., *The Rise of Suburbia*, Leicester 1982

Thoms, D., Holden, L., Claydon, T. (eds), *The Car and Popular Culture in the 20th Century*, Aldershot 1998

Thorold, P., *The Motoring Age: The Automobile and Britain 1896–1939*, London 2003

Thorpe, A., *Britain in the 1930s: The Deceptive Decade*, Oxford 1992

Thrift, N. J., *Spatial Formations*, London 1996

Tomlinson, J., *The Culture of Speed: The Coming of Immediacy*, London 2007

Tosh, J., *The Pursuit of History: Aims, Methods and New Directions in the Study of Modern History*, Harlow 2010

Tuan, Y., *Space and Place: The Perspective of Experience*, London 1977

Urry, J., *The Tourist Gaze: Leisure and Travel in Contemporary Societies*, London 1990

Urry, J., *Consuming Places*, London 1994

Veblen, T., *The Theory of the Leisure Class*, New York 1912

Venturi, R., *Learning from Las Vegas*, London 1972

Victoria and Albert Museum, *Art Deco 1910–1939*, London 2003

Virilio, P., *The Virilio Reader*, Oxford 1998

Virilio, P., *The Original Accident*, Cambridge 2007

Wachs, M. and Crawford, M. (eds), *The Car and the City*, Ann Arbor 1992

Walford, R., *The Growth of 'New London' in Suburban Middlesex (1918–1945) and the Response of the Church of England*, Lampeter 2007

Walkowitz, J. R., *Nights Out*, London 2012

Webb, M., *The Amber Valley Gazetteer of Greater London's Suburban Cinemas, 1946–86*, Erdington 1986

Webster, D., *Looka Yonder!: The Imaginary America of Populist Culture*, London 1988

Weightman, G. and Humphries, S., *The Making of Modern London 1914–1939*, London 1984

Weinreb, B. and Hibbert, C. (eds), *The London Encyclopaedia*, London 1987

West, W. T., *The Trial of Lord de Clifford, 1935: The Last Trial of a British Peer by His Fellow Peers*, York 1984

White, J., *London in the Twentieth Century: A City and Its People*, London 2001

Wilmott, P., *Growing Up in a London Village: Family Life Between the Wars*, London 1979

Witzel, M. K., *The American Gas Station*, Osceola 1992

Wollen, P. and Kerr, J. (eds), *Autopia: Cars and Culture*, London 2002

Worpole, K., *Dockers and Detectives: Popular Reading, Popular Writing*, London 1983

Wrigley, C. (ed.), *A Companion to Early Twentieth-century Britain*, Oxford 2002

Zeller, T., *Driving Germany: The Landscape of the German Autobahn, 1930–1970*, Oxford 2007

Films

The Lost World of Friese-Greene, Director, D. Cruikshank, BBC 2007

Reyner Banham Loves Los Angeles, Director, J. Cooper, 1972

Theses and dissertations

Miliward, A., *Factors Contributing to the Sustained Success of the UK Cycle Industry 1870–1939*, PhD University of Birmingham, 1999

North, D. L., *Middle-class Suburban Lifestyles and Culture in England 1919–1939*, D.Phil Oxford, 1989

Potter, C., *An Exploration of Social and Cultural Aspects of Motorcycling During the Inter-war period*, PhD University of Northumbria at Newcastle, 2007

Whitehouse, J. P., *The UK Petrol Filling Station to 1990, with Particular Reference to London and Middlesex*, PhD University of London, 2004

Vidal, R., *Death and Desire in Car Crash Culture: The Many Returns of Futurism*, PhD University of London, 2007

Conference proceedings

Bournemouth University, School of Conservation Sciences, *Explorations in Motoring History: The Proceedings of the First United Kingdom History of Motoring Conference*, 12 October 1996

Cycle History – Proceedings of the 5th International Cycle History Conference, San Francisco, 1995

Index